Friendly Business

Bernd Werse · Christiane Bernard
(Eds.)

Friendly Business

International Views on Social Supply, Self-Supply and Small-Scale Drug Dealing

Springer VS

Editors
Bernd Werse
Frankfurt/Main, Germany

Christiane Bernard
Essen, Germany

This publication was partially funded by the German Research Foundation (*Deutsche Forschungsgemeinschaft, DFG*), as part of the project "The Distribution of Illicit Drugs" (*"Die Distribution illegaler Drogen"*).

ISBN 978-3-658-10328-6 ISBN 978-3-658-10329-3 (eBook)
DOI 10.1007/978-3-658-10329-3

Library of Congress Control Number: 2016940350

Springer VS

Printed on acid-free paper

This Springer VS imprint is published by Springer Nature
The registered company is Springer Fachmedien Wiesbaden GmbH

Table of contents

Introduction

Christiane Bernard & Bernd Werse

Illicit drug trafficking is a worldwide phenomenon, and some trafficking routes cover significant parts of the globe. In many countries on every continent, cultivation and/or production of illicit substances takes place. Accordingly, virtually every nation, at least to some degree, has to handle the issue of drug dealing. In order to get the substance to the customer, there need to be retail suppliers who are the crucial interface between drug producers and/or traffickers and drug users. In recent years, this issue has increasingly become subject to international social research (e.g., Parker 2000, Hough et al. 2003, Coomber & Turnbull 2007, Werse 2008, Potter 2009, Moyle et al. 2013, Belackova & Vaccaro 2013, Coomber et al. 2014, Grigg et al. 2015)[1]. These publications made clear that drug distribution on the retail level not only consists of the profit-oriented exchange of money and drugs, but also includes sharing and gift giving (which already cover the needs of a large proportion of occasional users), as well as social supply; i.e. 'friendly', non-profit-oriented drug distribution among fellow users, which is a very common phenomenon among recreational drug users. The boundaries between these types of drug distribution and 'real' drug dealing are blurred, with some social suppliers proceeding to 'minimally commercial supply' (Coomber & Moyle 2013) or even to making considerable profits. Careers of recreational drug users may include several alternating phases of buying, receiving, selling and profit making. Therefore, the social reality of drug distribution on the users' level does not even come close to popular images of drug dealing as a network characterized by intrigues, violence and other criminal activities.

In addition, the relevance of self-supply, mostly in the form of cannabis cultivation, has grown in most developed countries in recent years, resulting in an increasing scientific interest in that issue (for an overview see Decorte et al. 2011). This phenomenon is not only relevant in terms of market structure (with many countries having turned from cannabis-importing to mainly cannabis-producing countries), but also with regard to the meanings associated with the cultivation and use of the drug.

These developments, along with the fact that research on retail drug distribution is still relatively rare, motivated the Centre for Drug Research at the Goethe University in Frankfurt to start a research project ("The Distribution of Illicit

1 For further references, see most of the chapters in this anthology.

Drugs", TDID), funded by the German Research Foundation (*Deutsche Forschungsgemeinschaft, DFG*), in late 2010. After the end of the project, we decided to publish the essential results as several chapters of an anthology, but also to include contributions from other countries, containing different theoretical and empirical views on the issue of small-scale drug distribution and home growing. The results of the TDID project can be found in three consecutive chapters (Werse & Bernard, Werse & Müller and Bernard in this volume). In addition, this anthology contains empirical studies and theoretical considerations from Austria, Belgium, the Czech Republic, Finland, UK and Australia, plus an international study on cannabis growing. A focus of this book lies on qualitative studies that are rich with drugs users' and suppliers' own accounts.

Since cannabis is by far the most prevalent recreational drug worldwide, most of the chapters refer to the provision and/or cultivation of marijuana or hashish. However, there are also a few chapters, which also broach the issue of other drugs such as cocaine, amphetamine or ecstasy. Interestingly, the modes and characteristics of small-scale distribution do not seem to differ significantly by substance, but rather by setting and/or scale. At least among socially integrated users, the fact that these drugs are illegal might have led to similar distribution practices, including various 'social' features.

Furthermore, the contributions to this book show many similarities in the characteristics of small-scale drug distribution in different countries, but also some noticeable differences. We hope that in this way, the book can add some valuable evidence to the research on this subject.

We lead off the book with a chapter by Ross Coomber, Leah Moyle and Nigel South who reflect on three decades of research on social supply in the UK. They start their chapter with the post-1960s sociological research literature and its social model of drug use and move on to consider how the idea of social supply as a significant aspect of the drug market came to be more thoroughly explored and conceptually formalised in the late 1990s/early to mid-2000s. They conclude with how the concept of social supply got expanded from cannabis markets to other illicit substances in recent years.

Based on earlier work of Coomber and colleagues, Simon Lenton, Jodie Grigg, John Scott and Monica Barratt draw on quantitative and qualitative data from an Australian study to explore the importance of friendship and profit motives in cannabis social supply transactions and what constitutes a 'real dealer'. They further consider implications for the definition of social supply and how low-level supply offences might be addressed in law.

By comparing two countries with different drug policies – i.e. the U.S. and the Czech Republic – Vendula Belackova and Tomas Zabransky assess to which extent social supply is policy-responsive as well as the risks related to it. Drawing on quantitative and qualitative datasets, their findings show that punitive drug policies (like in the U.S.) not only provide incentives to shrinking the market into friendly/social networks but also impose risks on users.

Bernd Werse & Christiane Bernard present quantitative results of the mixed-methods research project TDID (see above) conducted between 2010 and 2013 in Germany. Based on a sample of 214 socially integrated illicit drug users, most of them also experienced in supplying drugs, their findings show that dealing activities within networks of recreational drug users are usually not profit-driven and often carried out as a favour to friends. Further, gaining profit generally seems to be of low importance. A substantial part of supply activities is completely free of charge through shared drugs and gift giving.

Drawing on a subsample of the same research project (114 respondents who had ever sold drugs with profit) and referring to Murphy et al.'s concept of "drifting into dealing" (1990), Bernd Werse and Daniela Müller examine the ways in which people get into and out of profit-oriented dealing. While most respondents entered the market as social suppliers, there seem to be special conditions under which persons start dealing in order to make money. Smaller subsamples are analysed for the intensification, reduction and/or cessation of dealing activity, the latter mostly following a 'maturing-out' mode.

Based on qualitative interviews with the 51 female respondents of the TDID project, Christiane Bernard explores the phenomenon of social supply and retail dealing from a female perspective, studying women's strategies for acquiring and financing drugs, their involvement in drug distribution activities as well as the factors that encourage or hinder women's involvement in drug dealing activities. Her results show that drug dealing was rarely profit-driven and that most interviewees distanced themselves from the identity of a drug dealer and managed to maintain a non-deviant identity.

Marieke Vlaemynck employs a network perspective to analyse the phenomenon of social supply. She argues that social network analysis can provide a more profound insight and understanding of the nature of cannabis supply. By putting social supply in its relational context, she develops a view on supply as a tie in a wider social network in which cannabis is present. In this way, her chapter aims to unravel some of the complexity of different supply patterns.

Potter et al.'s chapter offers a global perspective on cannabis cultivation. Based on an international online survey from eleven different countries, the authors provide insights into the demographic characteristics of predominantly small-scale cannabis growers, their experiences with and their methods and scale of growing operations, their reasons for growing, their personal use of cannabis and other illicit drugs, as well as their participation in drug markets and their contacts with the criminal justice system. Furthermore, they discuss important similarities and differences between the national samples.

Bringing the phenomenon of small-scale cannabis growing to a national level, Pekka Hakkarainen and Jussi Perälä use three different datasets to trace the prevalence of home growing in Finland and to portray the growers: their practices and purposes of growing and their thinking. A special feature of cannabis growing in this Northern country seems to be the growers' motivation to compensate for the bad quality and limited availability of cannabis products from the Finnish black market.

We conclude our book with Meropi Tzanetakis' in-depth qualitative study on upper-level drug dealers in Austria. In contrast to the other chapters of this volume and their discussion of the concept of social supply, Tzanetakis offers insights into a world of professional drug dealers, characterised by gaining profit and striving for personal enrichment. Her analysis focuses on the mechanisms used for building trust and loyalty as well as the role of using violence within a context that is not only shaped by the constant threat of prosecution but also by conflicts and disputes among drug dealers and their networks. By showing that even on this level, threats seem to be rather the exception than the rule, let alone physical violence, Tzanetakis highlights some similarities between upper-level and small-scale dealing. By referring to the interrelations of wholesale and retail, this chapter is an important contribution to the discussion on social supply.

The chapters featured in this book show a strong relation between the economic and social aspects of illicit drug use. Users in different settings tend to compensate the disadvantages of prohibition by being, to some degree, part of a distribution network, often without any financial benefits. In this way, the illegality of psychoactive substances contributes to tightening social bonds between fellow users, which might, one the one hand, have positive individual outcomes such as reduced risk of being subject to law enforcement or some degree of informal social control on their patterns of use. On the other hand, these mechanisms may also increase the general frequency of use and/or associated risks. In any case, the analyses indicate that official efforts to reduce drug supply are systematically undermined by the complex network of (social) drug distribution.

As editors, we would like to thank all contributing authors for their work, cooperation and time. Without their commitment, this anthology would not have been possible. We also like to thank the German Research Foundation (DFG) for the financial support on the TDID project as well as this book. Moreover, thanks to the International Society for the Study of Drug Policy (ISSDP) and the European Society for Social Drug Research (ESSD), whose annual conferences and their side events contributed a lot to bringing the editors and authors together. Finally, thanks to the members of the Global Cannabis Cultivation Research Consortium (GCCRC) and to everyone else who contributed to the TDID project and all other research projects mentioned in this volume.

Given the growing scientific interest in the issue in recent years, we, as editors, think it was about time to release the first international anthology on retail-level drug dealing. We are happy to have put our efforts into publishing this book.

References

Belackova, V. & Vaccaro, C. A. (2013): A friend with weed is a friend indeed: Understanding the relationship between friendship identity and market relations among marijuana users. Journal of Drug Issues, 43(3): 289-313.

Coomber, R., & Turnbull, P. (2007): Arenas of drug transaction: adolescent cannabis transactions in England - social supply. Journal of Drug Issues 37 (4): 845.

Coomber, R. & L. Moyle (2013): Beyond drug dealing: developing and extending the concept of 'social supply' of illicit drugs to 'minimally commercial supply. Drugs: Education, Policy and Prevention 21 (2): 157-164.

Coomber, R., Moyle, L., Hatton, Z. & Gavin, J. (2014). A rapid appraisal of the illicit drug market in the City of Plymouth, Devon. Full report: Drug and Alcohol Research Unit: Plymouth University.

Decorte, T., Bouchard, M. & Potter, G. (eds.) (2011): World wide weed – Global trends in cannabis cultivation and its control. Farnham: Ashgate.

Grigg, J., Scott, J., Lenton, S. & Barratt, M. (2015): The social supply of cannabis in Australia (National Drug Law Enforcement Research Fund, Monograph Series No. 59). Canberra: Commonwealth of Australia.

Hough, M., Warburton, H., Few, B., May, T., Man, L.-H., Witton, J., et al. (2003): A Growing Market: The Domestic Cultivation of Marijuana. York: Joseph Rowntree Foundation.

Moyle, L., Coomber, R. & Lowther, J. (2013). Crushing a Walnut with a Sledge Hammer? Analysing the Penal Response to the Social Supply of Illicit Drugs. Social & Legal Studies, 22(4): 553-573. doi: 10.1177/0964663913487544 (Accessed 09.12.2015).

Murphy, S., Waldorf, D. & Reinarman, C. (1990): Drifting into Dealing: Becoming a Cocaine Seller. Qualitative Sociology, 13 (4): 321-343.

Parker, H. (2000): How young britons obtain their drugs: Drugs transactions at the point of consumption. M. Natarajan, & M. Hough (eds.), Illegal drug markets: From research to prevention policy (pp 59-81). Monsey, N.Y.: Criminal Justice Press.

Potter, G. R. (2009): Exploring retail-level drug distribution: Social supply, 'real' dealers and the user/dealer interface. Z. Demetrovics, J. Fountain, & L. Kraus (eds.), Old and new policies, theories, research methods and drug users across Europe (pp 50-74). Lengerich: Pabst Science Publishers.

Werse, B. (2008): Retail markets for cannabis - Users, sharers, go-betweens and stash dealers. D. J. Korf (ed.), Cannabis in Europe: Dynamics in perception, policy and markets (pp 106-123). Lengerich: Pabst Science Publishers.

Reflections on three decades of research on 'social supply' in the UK

Ross Coomber, Leah Moyle and Nigel South

Abstract

This chapter reviews how forms of friend and acquaintance supply that might be considered less than 'drug dealing proper' are not new and have existed over many years. It reflects on how, over time, views on these types of supply have developed and evolved in concert with changed and changing drug use and supply landscapes in the UK. In particular it considers the shift from some early forms of socially engaged recreational drug use and supply that were often bleeding, culturally, into myriad forms of counter culture and sat, to some degree at least, outside the everyday norm, to the sea change from the 1990s where a relatively normalised context around recreational drug use and some forms of friend/acquaintance supply moved more normatively towards the centre even for some parts of the criminal justice system. Following a consideration of how social supply has evolved over time the chapter culminates with an argument for a broadening of the concept to *minimally commercial supply* as a somewhat more refined position and that criminal justice approaches to non-commercially orientated supply need a more research evidence based framework for effective understanding and response.

1 Introduction

> "Dealing was different in those days: no violence, no rip-offs, people actually trusted each other. When you bought or sold, dealer and client invariably sat down and got stoned together – partly sampling the wares but partly social. Nowadays it all seems to be 'sell and run'." ('Harry', the Cannabis Dealer, circa 1990, in Dorn et al. 1992, 3).

This quote sums up Harry's disappointment at what he perceived to be the disappearance of a 'social age' of drug use and friendly supply as the 1980s turned into the 1990s. Yet in fact, the social supply of drugs through the channels of friendship networks (or 'friends of friends'), dependent upon individuals providing guarantees of trustworthiness and non- or minimally-profit orientated transactions, have all persisted and, in a broader societal context, evolved. This chapter draws upon interviews and impressions from research spanning over three decades. It initially situates the discussion in the post-1960s sociological research literature that presented a social model of drug use as opposed to the then dominant psychopathology approaches and moves on to consider the emergent 'normalisation' of both certain types of drug use and drug supply. These developments opened up and changed patterns, locations and styles of recreational drug use – from dance drugs to cocaine, to strong varieties of cannabis – and with them nuances in patterns of social supply, some of which have strong echoes of Harry's golden days. This early literature features various descriptions of users and dealers who 'drifted in and out' of their networks and of groups based on systems of trade, trust and minimal profit. Following this, we consider how the idea of social supply as a significant aspect of the wider drug market came to be more thoroughly explored and conceptually formalised in the late 1990s and early to mid-2000s to inform an analysis of social, and minimally commercial supply, in the more recent context, drawing on the authors' research into cannabis supply among young people, club drug supply among friend networks and even the supply of heroin among user-dealers.

2 Back to the '60s and '70s – drug use as psychopathy or social?

During the 1960s and 1970s the British drug policy landscape was slowly but surely re-shaped as a result of a modest (at least by later measures) rise in heroin use. Policy debate and direction largely applied to the treatment system and very much reflected a view of the world as seen from London (Ruggiero & South 1995; Mott 1991; Pearson 1991). However, more broadly speaking, liberal and conservative positions concerning drugs, morality, young people and the changing times generally revolved around 'soft' drugs (Ruggiero & South 1995; Measham & South 2012). Although fears of 'gateways' and 'escalators' were already expressed – cigarettes leading to marijuana, LSD leading to heroin, and so on – drug policy and legislation could find some comfort in a fairly simple dichotomisation of a world of hard drugs and soft drugs supplied by evil pushers to foolish and naive consumer users. Debates aired around these dichotomies were reflected in the core distinction made in the Misuse of Drugs Act 1971 between the offences of possession and supply.

The 1960s opened a window into a world of more colourful possibilities than the post-war period of rationing and reconstruction had offered. For some, full-blown politics of leisure and liberation were being explored with counter-culture guides like Richard Neville's *Playpower* (1970) featuring chapters with titles like "Johnny Pot wears gold sandals and a black derby hat" (Dorn & South 1989, 172-177). Sociological accounts of drug use and its meanings for participants still approached the subject via the category of 'deviance' but began to shift from positivist and functionalist accounts which relied on the language and diagnoses of 'normlessness', 'impulsivity' and psychopathy (Young 1971). The newly emerging sociology of deviance located drug use and users within a framework which tried to understand meanings and values from the point of view of the participants and the *social* character of drug culture(s). Earlier sociological perspectives had offered possible explanations for drug use in terms of retreat or withdrawal into personal and private spaces and experiences (Merton 1957, Cloward & Ohlin 1960) but the new labelling theories and related interpretative approaches placed users in the social contexts in which they lived, worked and had fun (Becker 1963, Finestone 1957) or else within an understanding of the alternative value systems that users felt they were developing and representing. Becker's important contributions in *Outsiders* (1963) were based on observation and interviews with jazz musicians and others who smoked marijuana. This was interpreted as an emphatically social experience, involving introduction into a social circle or network, learning about a drug, its use and how to enjoy its effects and, in the face of moral and legal disapproval and prohibitions, engage in rituals of secrecy to secure supply and continued use. In the UK, Young (1971; 1973a) applied this kind of perspective in his work on 'bohemian' middle-class subcultures of drug use in London in which he saw the 'use of drugs, sexual excess, lack of planning or deferment of impulse' as related to a 'general subterranean value' of short-term hedonism. This celebration of the social and playful dimension of drug use was an important counter-view to clinical and psychological determinism but could itself be hard to align with the real experience of ordinary users who were perhaps in some ways better described by Plant (1975, 258) in his study of non-metropolitan *Drugtakers in an English Town*:

> "The study group was so varied that no single theory adequately explains their behaviour. Most did not seem problematic in terms of the factors examined. *Often, drug taking was simply a leisure activity or a token of idealism.*" [emphasis added]

As Ruggiero and South (1995, 133-134) pointed out, regardless of the popular images of 'youth in revolt' right across Europe in the late 1960s and early 1970s:

> "...in reality, only a relatively small percentage of youth were aligned with political groups or fully fledged counter cultures. Similarly, the extent of drug use was quite modest when compared to the 1980s and 1990s. Furthermore, although frequently associated with oppositional groups and protest, drug use also had expressive and functional value for groups that in other respects were seriously conformist – for example, the Mods who worked by day and raved at weekends."

Questions of social choice vs determinism and pathology re-emerged in the 1980s in the context of increases in unemployment and a dramatic rise in heroin use, but the correlation between the two while clear in some cases was not a matter of simple, direct causality. Social and economic constraints apply to shape opportunities and culture, but actors exercising choice make of these conditions what they can. This is the case in social worlds of recreational drug use as much as anywhere else. South (2004, 529) reports on one group of low-paid and insecurely employed recreational users that:

> "...there is a question here about the nature of the choices being exercised i.e. what rewards and satisfactions are being sought and prioritised – those deriving from legal market-place success or those from the valuing of leisure/pleasure? One clear answer is that: 'most of the smokers [cannabis] and clubbers [users of ecstasy, amphetamines and cocaine] I know are doing naff jobs - labouring, office work, shop assistants... they're too busy having a good time to make the effort to achieve anything more' (female, 19yrs)."

This expression of 'choice' is at variance with Merton's (1957) category of market place 'failure' as an explanation of 'retreat' into pathological drug use and is closer to the pursuit of enjoyment and sensation described by more recent cultural interpretations offered by Katz (1988) or Collison (1996) but of course, 'choice' still has to be placed in the context of constraints and influences.

3 Low-profit dealing: trading charities and mutual societies

Studies of some forms and sources of drug supply from the late 1960s and 1970s onward remarked on the ways in which a counter cultural ethic was combined with a spirit of alternative entrepreneurship – as if a counter economy could be created and could now co-exist, even if uncomfortably and inefficiently so (see e.g. the discussion of 'hippy economics' in Young 1973b). Leigh (1985, 29) described Hashish, bought from Lebanon or Pakistan, in the following way: "It's the great liberating drug. Selling it isn't a business. It's more like a crusade!" Langer's (1977, 384) study of drug entrepreneurs and dealing in Melbourne in the mid-1970s found that dealers in psychotropic drugs "moved from a hang-loose ethic linked with the values of the counterculture to a specific attitude which sanctions the accumulation of profit for services rendered". However, the embrace of entrepreneurship did not always align with personal inclinations or the occupational problem of temptation:

> "Entrepreneurial practices related to marketing behaviour have not been entirely co-ordinated or systematised... For example, there is much waste of their product through constant personal use, gift-giving of entertaining." (ibid.)

Drug use and friendship-based dealing can be integrated into everyday life and routines, comfortably coexisting "with (…) conventional roles and activities" as Murphy et al. (1990, 321) report in their study of U.S. cocaine sellers, where the "use of illicit drugs had gone on for so long, was so common in their social worlds, and had not significantly affected their otherwise normal lives, [that] they hardly considered it deviant at all". In other U.S. case studies, Reuter et al. (1990) and Hagedorn (1994) provide examples of those working as dealers in the illegal market but who make irregular forays back into legal employment with varying degrees of success. In the UK, this phenomenon might be mirrored in varying ways by those in similar situations in the informal economies that bridge illegal and legal markets and include those involved in mutual assurance of supply and low- or non-profit trading of drugs – "mutual societies" and "trading charities" in the terms used by Dorn et al. (1992, 10-13). Pearson's (2001) in-depth ethnography of an "adult network of recreational drug users in inner-London" describes how users sociably managed the normative continuum of conventionality accepted within their network, as reflected for example in conversations about relationships and weddings, the use of cannabis to overcome boredom at work or cocaine to liven up a holiday, to stories about selling counterfeit goods. Importantly though, those involved "did not think of themselves as 'drug users' – it is merely something that they do, or do not do, as an ancillary to other aspects of their lives, whether work or leisure… these were people for whom drug use was a peripheral but 'normal' aspect of life" (ibid, 173).

By the early 1990s, Britain had developed what remains a pattern of predominantly 'polydrug' use. Mixing drugs, selection for different effects, and/or use of alternatives to the preferred 'drug of choice' in times of scarcity, were not in themselves new phenomena. What was new was the integration into young people's drug cultures of a pick 'n' mix approach to a growing repertoire of increasingly available legal and illegal drugs at reduced price across the 1990s (Parker et al. 1998; South 1999). The ecstasy dance culture involved 'ordinary' people whose 'deviance' lay in being weekend enthusiasts of dance music and dance drugs but without pre-existing offending careers or drug dependency (Shapiro 1999; Sanders 2005; Hunt et al. 2010). Parker et al. (1998) have suggested that a process of 'normalisation' of 'recreational' drug use was under way from the early 1990s within the lifestyles and attitudes of the adolescents that they surveyed. 'Normalisation' does not mean 'everyone' is now a drug user, nonetheless acquaintance with 'recreational' drugs and/or users is no longer unusual and drug users are as likely to come from a range of 'normal' backgrounds across the social spectrum as be linked to categories of the socially excluded. Debates about whether or not we have seen a widespread normalisation of use or process of 'cultural normalisation' (Pearson 2001) are important (South 1999; 2004) and have led to the further refining of the concept of normalisation (Aldridge et al. 2011; Measham & Shiner 2009). The idea has also been applied in other cultural contexts such as Denmark (Jarvinen & Demant 2011), Finland (Hakkarainen et al. 2007), Australia (Duff 2005; Pennay & Moore 2010; Wilson et al. 2010) and New Zealand (Hutton 2010).

Normalisation underpins contemporary forms of supply and use where these are not seen as 'abnormal' by those involved and/or where those involved have a clear personal (moral, political, social) standpoint that supports the idea that supply and use as behaviour should be permitted. In one set of interviews carried out in the early 2000s (South 2004) all respondents saw drug use as a 'normal' feature of their day-to-day approach to 'life management'. Importantly for them, the context of "cultural normalisation" (Pearson 2001; South 1999) is one in which regular drug use is seen as by no means incompatible with the normatively valued aims and aspirations of 'making it' in the legal marketplace and all these respondents had good jobs and managed their varied patterns of drug use in a successful balance with work demands and careers. Brian was part of a strong social circle in the gay scene, where trust, mutual support, sharing and the drugs-equivalent of 'round buying' were valued: "'I have a good circle of friends doing that... if somebody doesn't have money I buy, if I don't have money, it kind of swings around... It might be [me] one week, the next week it depends on who has got it.' For Adam with a menu of drug choices that included 'cannabis, ... cocaine, ecstasy', his preference was to buy from 'friends' but he would also obtain drugs 'just in night clubs... whatever is easiest – cheapest.' Chris described obtaining drugs 'always through black market connections... Pot, I know people who grow it, so I can get it cheap... cocaine – always through someone that you know, rather than off the street'" (South 2004, 531-533).

The normalisation of drug use also introduces an element of normalisation into small-scale dealing, justified simply as social transactions between friends.

Life on the 'continuum of conventionality' blurs distinctions and there is a fuzzy area of overlap between the licit and the illicit.

4 Legal policy and policing

Regardless of the evidently social basis of much drug use and related culture in the 1960s and 70s, the fear of pathology and loss of control remained a defining feature of official responses. In the U.K, although other significant legislation on social matters in these 'permissive' years could be characterised as moving in the direction of liberalisation (for example laws concerning decriminalisation of homosexuality, legalisation of abortion, easing of divorce laws and abolition of capital punishment), drugs received quite conservative treatment. This was notably exemplified in the dismissive rejection of a call from the respectable Advisory Council on Drug Dependence (the Wootton Committee 1968) for relaxation of the law on cannabis (Young 1971, 198–201). By and large, for succeeding decades, this is the direction in which drug policy, legal classification and the tariff of penalties has tended to continue to go (even when there have been one or two steps in a different direction these have been quickly reversed). Although police, customs and intelligence analysts appreciate there is diversity in the drug market this can, to be fair, be hard to translate into clear legal language. So the default positions have been either 'homogeneity', all drug dealing is the same, favoured by those supporting the logic of the 'drugs gateway' thesis and appealing to those like parents groups and popular media. The other default is the pyramidal hierarchy model with small scale, local dealers at the bottom and Mr Big at the top. One of the key points of the new wave of critical drug market research from the 1980s onward was that the pyramid model needed to be demolished as it was a poor reflection of reality (Reuter 1983; Dorn et al. 1992).

From the mid-1980s, the principles of a harm reduction approach began to be taken up across not only health and social care agencies but also (some) police forces (Fraser & George 1992). Harm reduction can be defined as the idea that policies, programmes, services and practices can be devised that can help to reduce health, social and economic harms to individuals, communities and society that are associated with the use of drugs (Newcombe 1992). The acceptance of (at least) some features of this approach by police forces led to cautions and to processes for the onward referral of drug users to helping agencies. On the one hand, where it was taken up, this was a very significant development, 'reaching out' rather than 'driving away'. On the other hand, this was simply an updated response to the bifurcation at the heart of the 1971 Misuse of Drugs Act, providing support for users, perhaps tolerating some minor possession, but remaining in pursuit of all sources of supply. Only in recent years have there been signs of more radical guidance being contemplated to guide enforcement and court proceedings as they affect users who may be engaged in social supply to other users – and this is discussed below.

5 The development of social supply practices and social supply as a concept

By the late 1990s, various studies of drug markets and suppliers (e.g. Blum et al. 1972; Dorn et al. 1992; Murphy et al. 1990; Parker et al. 1998) had shown that not all dealers were the same and that for many, rather than the motivation for supplying drugs being that of commercial gain, many were in fact simply 'sorting out' friends. Some had what might be termed an 'advocate' position whereby they perceived certain types of recreational drug use (e.g. hallucinogens but also cannabis) as having positive outcomes for general well-being and consciousness expansion. Others, such as some 'friend suppliers', simply sold for little or no gain to those they knew, or acted as 'go-betweens' (Murphy et al. 1990; Coomber & Turnbull 2007) so as to help them buy/access drugs and (for some) thus protect them from the perceived 'dangers' of contact with the 'drug dealer'. As we have already seen, research on large cohorts of adolescents in the north of England carried out by Parker and colleagues reported that the supply of drugs among young people was extensively supplied from, and between, friends and acquaintances (Parker et al. 1995 & 1998; Parker 2000). The young people described by this and other research since, as well as many of the suppliers previously described by Dorn et al. (1992), Murphy et al. (1990) and Blum et al. (1972), simply didn't fit the stereotype of the 'drug dealer' enshrined in the laws around supply and the 1971 Misuse of Drugs Act. In essence, and in contrast, these individuals were non-predatory, not 'commercially' motivated, and supply was inextricably related to the cultural mores of the groups they belonged, or connected, to (cf. Coomber & Turnbull 2007).

In 2000, as a response to this obvious disjunction, the Police Foundation published its report *Drugs and the Law: the Report of the Independent Inquiry into the Misuse of Drugs Act 1971* and in it put forward the opinion that too many of those prosecuted for supply offences differed in meaningful ways to the kind of supplier ('drug dealer') that the Act was designed to encapsulate and prosecute and recommended that:

> "There should be a separate offence of dealing, the main ingredient of which would be the pattern of activity of illicitly transacting business in drugs. The offence should be capable of being charged as a continuing offence so that the prosecution can show that the defendant has been dealing over a period of time by putting before the court evidence of the true scope and nature of his activities" (Police Foundation 2000, 63).

This unease, occurring in the late 1990s and early 2000s, around how well the laws on supply offences distinguished between suppliers also coincided and coalesced with a growing sense that the relative normalisation of drug use (among young people in particular) meant that recreational users were increasingly vulnerable to being caught up in legislation not designed for them in the first place and that, as a consequence, they could suffer long-term negative life-chances as a result. By May 2002, the term 'social supply' had begun to be used in official discourse on differentiated supply as discussed by the UK Parliamentary Select Committee on Home Affairs that year, and the following year, Hough et al (2003) contextualised the idea further in relation to the burgeoning practice of small scale home cultivation of cannabis.

Reporting on research that had looked closely at the small scale cultivation of cannabis for personal use 'and use with friends', Hough et al argued that there seemed to be a convincing argument for treating 'home-grown' cannabis cultivation of moderate amounts as possession rather than as dealing and that seeing cultivators/users of this kind as sellers was possibly problematic when their actual practice was looked at closely. After an examination of different forms of involvement in cannabis cultivation at modest levels (e.g. the sole grower cultivating for personal use; those growing to provide therapeutic cannabis; or more commercially motivated sellers), Hough et al. saw value in describing social supply in a way similar to that previously outlined by the Police Foundation (2000, 36) and specifically as: "...defined as the non-commercial (or non-profit-making) distribution of cannabis to non-strangers".

Further conceptual clarification emerged following research looking at the supply of cannabis among young people in three urban and three rural areas in England (Duffy et al. 2008). From this research, Coomber and Turnbull (2007) argued that almost all supply of cannabis among the young people in the sample was between friends and acquaintances and that the evidence strongly suggested that: young people using and supplying cannabis almost never came into contact with the 'drug market proper'; that social supply acted as a structural buffer in this regard; and that this 'market' – for all practical purposes – 'sits outside' the adult, 'sales for profit'-motivated drug market, as conventionally depicted and understood. It was further argued that, more than any other form of supply, young people's supply of cannabis typified the difference between social supply and drug dealing proper. In this kind of case, the potential application of the 'drug dealer' label to so many young people provided the clearest example of how the law could inappropriately capture too broad a segment of users as dealers, and left social suppliers open to the vagaries of politics and mood within the criminal justice system as to how severely a social supplier should or should not be punished. Although Potter (2009) has correctly pointed to some of the difficulties in distinguishing between 'friends' and acquaintances and the difficulties this can pose for the criminal justice system, it is the case that in recent years in the UK the sentencing guidelines have attempted to resolve this difficulty, having now accepted some of the key principles of social supply (Moyle et al. 2013).

Whilst some genuine progress has been made in the UK to accommodate social supply as a concept and apply this in relation to arrest, prosecution and sentencing practice, there are nonetheless a number of genuine problems with how this has been done. This has revealed some naivety and ignorance within the criminal justice system about the forms and practices that genuinely constitute social supply (cf. Moyle et al. 2013 for further explanation) resulting in continued disproportionate sentencing for some. One area where this is particularly true relates to those supplying non-recreational, addictive street drugs like heroin and crack cocaine.

6 Minimally Commercial Supply

For the most part, social supply has been associated with the supply of recreational substances such as cannabis, ecstasy, and other dance/club drugs, but the most recent conceptual shift (Coomber & Moyle 2013) has seen social supply developed into something more inclusive and broadened out to encompass the practice of supplying even highly addictive street drugs when that supply is, in essence, not motivated by profit as such and thus only *minimally commercial*. The extension of the concept into Minimally Commercial Supply (MCS) was considered necessary for two primary reasons: first, to address the ongoing tendency for the law to view social supply as fundamentally linked to an absence of profit and thus to prosecute those proven to have profited from supply, however moderately and, second, to bring into fuller consideration addicted drug users who supply drugs to other addicted drug users, *primarily to ensure they can reliably reproduce their own supply*. In Coomber and Moyle (2013) user-dealers as classified, commit fewer or no other types of crime, are non-predatory and sell only to a small(ish) group of other (known to them) addicted users and do so, once the costs of their own drug supply are taken into consideration, with only minimal personal gain. Compared to those commercially/profit motivated dealers who may be predatory or have no structurally defined upper-limit to their client base, their culpability is argued to be less (see Moyle & Coomber 2015).

7 The modern day manifestation of social supply[1]

Although much previous research on social supply in the UK has reported it as having a 'best fit' with cannabis users, social supply is now developing – or is established practice – in other recreational psychoactive drug markets, particularly in regard to club drugs such as MDMA, ecstasy and ketamine (Aldridge et al. 2011; Joe-Laidler & Hunt 2008) but also latterly, in relation to a range of New or Novel Psychoactive Substances (NPS) or so-called 'Legal Highs' (Coomber & Pyle 2015). Even so, while the substances exchanged – and the context in which a drug is supplied – may have changed over the years, in many instances the motivations and ways of 'doing' social supply in the UK appear to have much in common with that which has gone before.

In many instances a social supplier of recreational drugs is either a member of a group that has access to a supplier or may be a nominated person (sometimes 'turns' are taken) who will approach a known source. Notions of reciprocity and sharing still have a strong influence and if a member of a social group is already planning to obtain drugs through a source, particularly for an event in which numerous or all members of the group were attending, they would then be expected to provide for the rest of the group. Planning access to drugs for events is part of a user's routine, and as such, acquiring drugs just for oneself will not generally represent a normative option for social suppliers (as defined here).

8 Sharing, Sociability, Profit and 'Hassle'

Sharing recreational drugs is central to both use and supply activity. Explanations for drug sharing within social circles may revolve around notions of sociability and a desired shared experience including a more social way of *purchasing* drugs. However, while the principles of 'doing it for the group' are understood and the process of obtaining drugs might become routine, nonetheless the downside is also understood in the sense that social suppliers know that some risk is being

1 This section draws on findings reported in Moyle (2013), Coomber & Moyle (2013) and Coomber et al (2014).

taken and some extra effort on their part is required. For social suppliers the 'profit' to compensate for this extra effort can be conceptualised as minimal in two important ways: first, the proportionate amount of profit from a purchase is usually negligible compared to commercially orientated sales; second, in terms of the importance or motivation that 'gain' plays in the act of supply itself.

9 Conclusion: toward a research-based framework for understanding social supply

Social supply often involves strong social ties and social meanings that are, in essence, divorced from the actual exchange process but surround it with a social contextual framework. This is very different from the non-social exchange processes of commercial, profit-orientated suppliers and it is still in need of further examination and explanation – not least for legal and policy audiences.

In contrast to the recommendations of the Police Foundation Report (2000), but consistent with wider research (Nicholas 2008; Shearer 2005; Joe-Laidler & Hunt 2008), we argue that social supply is an activity that is not only present in cannabis networks but also highly prevalent in psychoactive Class A (and B) drug markets (particularly cocaine, ecstasy, MDMA and ketamine). Studies by Moyle (2013), Coomber and Moyle (2013), and Coomber et al. (2014), demonstrate that social suppliers will almost certainly have a core group of close friends that they will routinely distribute to and they may also supply to other acquaintances or 'known faces' who have been directed to the supplier by other contacts (this is similar to the findings of Hough et al. 2003). Consistent with Potter (2009), this creates a 'grey area' in the conceptualisation of drug supply behaviour and problematises traditional assumptions about the relationship between the supplier and the receiver of drugs, particularly in a legal context (Potter 2009). Another key implication is that it is *not* the quantity of substance that is of importance when defining social supply. For example, a large social group attending a festival or other events may make provision to obtain, hold and then distribute (i.e. supply) quite large amounts of drugs at one time. Given such scenarios, a threshold-based definition is probably not the most suitable basis for determining what is social supply rather than commercial supply. Instead, the intent or motivation should be considered as the primary indicator of the nature of the purchase (social supply or commercial supply).

The scope of the social supply act is perhaps wider than has been portrayed in the current research base (see Duffy et al. 2008; Coomber & Turnbull 2007; Hough et al. 2003). While it is undoubtedly the case that the roles undertaken by social suppliers are characterised by a certain level of diversity with regard to the quantities and nature of the drug purchased, the way the substances are distributed, and the relationship with the receiver of the drug – it also seems likely that certain characteristics can be found as common. A social supply transaction or 'offence' would be likely to entail: the social supplier using the drugs that were being supplied; some element of gain such as 'free drugs' or a small sum as means of recompense for the effort of the social supplier; the transaction *not being primarily* motivated by the aim to gain financial profit; and the social supplier distributing drugs to friends, acquaintances or 'known individuals' (non-strangers) (Moyle 2013).

There is much more that needs to be pursued in this area of research and in policy debate and discussion concerning the concept of social supply. However some recognition has already occurred in the UK with the Sentencing Council inserting the notion of 'absence of any financial gain' as a characteristic of a 'lesser role' in the culpability matrix of their new definitive sentencing guidelines. This is an important start.

References

Aldridge, J., F. Measham, H. Parker & L. Williams (2011): Illegal leisure revisited: changing patterns of alcohol and drug use in adolescents and young adults. London: Routledge.

Becker, H. (1963): Outsiders: studies in the sociology of deviance. New York: Free Press.

Blum, R. H., & Associates (1972): The Dream Sellers. San Francisco: Jossey-Bass.

Cloward, R. & L. Ohlin (1960): Delinquency and Opportunity: A Theory of Delinquent Gangs. Free Press, New York.

Collison, M. (1996): In search of the high life: drugs, crime, masculinity and consumption. British Journal of Criminology 36 (3): 428–44.

Commonwealth of Australia (2008): The Impact of Social Networks and Not-for-profit Illicit Drug Dealing on Illicit Drug Markets in Australia. Tasmania: National Drug Law Enforcement Research Fund.

Coomber, R. (2015): A tale of two cities: understanding differences in levels of heroin/crack market related violence - a two city comparison. Criminal Justice Review, 40(1): 7-31.

Coomber, R. & L. Moyle (2013): Beyond drug dealing: developing and extending the concept of 'social supply' of illicit drugs to 'minimally commercial supply. Drugs: Education, Policy and Prevention 21 (2): 157-164.

Coomber, R., Pyle, E. & Moyle, L. (2015) Legal-High/NPS use by persistent and prolific offenders engaged with IOMS/TurnAround Teams in Devon and Cornwall. Full Report. Drug and Alcohol Research Service (October). 38pp.

Coomber, R., L. Moyle, Z. Hatton, & J. Gavin (2014). A rapid appraisal of the illicit drug market in the City of Plymouth, Devon. Full report: Drug and Alcohol Research Unit: Plymouth University.

Coomber, R., & P. Turnbull (2007): Arenas of drug transaction: adolescent cannabis transactions in England - social supply. Journal of Drug Issues 37 (4): 845.

Dorn, N., & N. South (1989): Drugs and leisure, prohibition and pleasure: From subcultures to the 'drugalogue'. In: Leisure for leisure: critical essays, edited by C. Rojek. London: Macmillan.

Dorn, N., K. Murji, & N. South (1992): Traffickers: drug markets and law enforcement. London: Routledge.

Duff, C. (2005): Party drugs and party people: examining the 'normalization' of recreational drug use in Melbourne, Australia. International Journal of Drug Policy 16 (3): 161-170.

Duffy, M., N. Schafer, R. Coomber, L. O'Connell, & P. Turnbull (2008): Cannabis supply and young people: 'It's a social thing'. York: Joseph Rowntree Foundation.

Finestone, H. 1957. Cats, kicks and color. Social Problems 5 (1): 3-13.

Fraser, A., & M. George (1992): "The role of the police in harm reduction". In The reduction of drug related harm, edited by P. O'Hare, R. Newcombe, R. Matthews, E. Buning, & E. Drucker. London: Routledge.

Hagedorn, J. (1994): Homeboys, dope fiends, legits, and New Jacks. Criminology 32 (2): 197–219.

Hough, M., H. Warburton, B. Few, T. May, L-H Man, J. Witton, & P. Turnbull (2003): A growing market: the domestic cultivation of cannabis. York: Joseph Rowntree Foundation.

Hunt, G., M. Moloney, & K. Evans (2010): Youth, Drugs, and Night Life, Oxon: Routledge.

Hutton, F. (2010): Kiwis, clubs and drugs: club cultures in Wellington, New Zealand. Australian and New Zealand Journal of Criminology 43: 91-111.

Jarvinen, M., & J. Demant. (2011): The normalisation of cannabis use among young people: symbolic boundary work in focus groups. Health, Risk and Society 13 (2): 165-182.

Katz, J. (1988): Seductions of Crime: Moral and Sensual Attractions in Doing Evil. New York: Basic Books.

Langer, J. (1977): Drug Entrepreneurs and Dealing Culture. Social Problems 24 (3): 377-86.

Leigh, D., (1984): High Time: the life and times of Howard Marks. London: Unwin.

Measham, F., & M. Shiner (2009): The legacy of 'normalisation': the role of classical and contemporary criminological theory in understanding young people's drug use. International Journal of Drug Policy 20 (6): 502-508.

Measham, F., & N. South. (2012): Drugs, alcohol and crime. In: The Oxford Handbook of Criminology, edited by M. Maguire, R. Morgan, and R. Reiner. 5th ed. Oxford: Oxford University Press.

Merton, R. K. (1957): Social Theory and Social Structure. 2nd ed. New York: Free Press.

Mott, J. (1991): Crime and heroin use. In: Policing and prescribing: the British system of drug control, edited by D. Whynes, & P. Bean. London: Macmillan.

Moyle, L. (2013): An exploration of how the social supply and user-dealer supply of illicit drugs differs to conventional notions of drug dealing and consideration of the consequences of this for sentencing policy. PhD thesis, Plymouth University.
Moyle, L., & R. Coomber, (2015): Earning a score: an exploration of the nature and roles of heroin and crack cocaine user-dealers. British Journal of Criminology, 55, 534-555.
Moyle, L., R. Coomber, & J. Lowther (2013): Crushing a walnut with a sledge hammer? Analysing the penal response to the social supply of illicit drugs. Social and Legal Studies. 22 (4): 446-466.
Murphy, S., D. Waldorf, & C. Reinarman (1990): Drifting into dealing. Becoming a cocaine seller. Qualitative Sociology, 13 (4): 321–343.
Neville, R. (1970): Play Power. London: Jonathan Cape Ltd.
Newcombe, R. (1992): The reduction of drug-related harm: A conceptual framework for theory, practice and research. In: The reduction of drug related harm, edited by E. C. Buning, E. Drucker, A. Matthews, R. Newcombe & P. A. O'Hare. London: Routledge.
Parker, H. (2000): How young Britons obtain their drugs: drugs transactions at the point of consumption. Crime Prevention Studies 11: 59-82.
Parker, H., J. Aldridge & F. Measham (1995): Drugs Futures: Changing Patterns of Drug Use amongst English Youth. London: Institute for the Study of Drug Dependence.
Parker, H., J. Aldridge, & F. Measham (1998): Illegal Leisure: The Normalization of Adolescent Recreational Drug Use. London: Routledge.
Pearson, G. (1991): (Drug-control Policies in Britain. In Crime and Justice: A Review of Research, edited by M. Tonry. Chicago: University of Chicago Press.
Pearson, G. (2001): Normal Drug Use: Ethnographic Fieldwork among an Adult Network of Recreational Drug Users in Inner London. Substance Use and Misuse 36 (1-2): 167–200.
Pennay, A., & D. Moore (2010): Exploring the micro-politics of normalisation: narratives of pleasure, self-control and desire in a sample of young Australian 'party drug' users. Addiction Research and Theory. 18(5): 557-571.
Plant, M. A. (1975): Drugtakers in an English Town. London: Tavistock Publications.
Potter, G. (2009): Exploring retail level drug distribution: social supply, 'real' dealers and the user/dealer interface. In: Old and New Policies, Theories, Research Methods and Drug Users Across Europe, edited by T. Demetrovics, J. Fountain, & L. Kraus. Lengerich: Pabst Science Publishers.
Reuter, P. (1983): Disorganized Crime: Illegal Markets and the Mafia. Cambridge, Mass.: MIT Press.
Reuter, P., R. MacCoun, & P. Murphy (1990): Money from Crime: A Study of the Economics of Drug Dealing in Washington, D.C. Santa Monica: The RAND Corporation.
Ruggiero, V., & N. South (1995): Eurodrugs: Drug Use, Markets and Trafficking in Europe. London: UCL Press.
Sanders, B. (2005): In the Club: Ecstasy Use and Supply in a London Nightclub. Sociology 39 (2): 241–58.

Sentencing Council (2012): Drug Offences Definitive Guidelines. London: Sentencing Council.
Shapiro, H. (1999) Dances with Drugs: Pop Music, Drugs and Youth Culture. In: Drugs: Cultures, Controls & Everyday Life, edited by N. South. London: Sage Publications.
Shearer, J., J. Johnston, C. L. Fry, & L. Collins (2007): Contemporary cocaine use patterns and associated harms in Melbourne and Sydney, Australia. Drug and Alcohol Review 26 (5): 537-543.
South, N. (1999): Debating Drugs and Everyday Life: Normalisation, Prohibition and 'Otherness'. In: Drugs: Cultures, Controls & Everyday Life, edited by N. South. London: Sage Publications.
South, N. (2004): Managing work, hedonism and 'the borderline' between the legal and illegal markets: Two case studies of recreational heavy drug users. Addiction Research and Theory 12 (6): 525-538.
The Police Foundation (2000): Drugs and the Law: Report of the Independent Inquiry into the Misuse of Drugs Act 1971. London: The Police Foundation.
Wilson, H., J. Bryant, M. Holt, & C. Treloar (2010): Normalisation of recreational drug use among young people: evidence about accessibility, use and contact with other drug users. Health Sociology Review. 19 (2): 164–175.
Young, J. (1971): The Drugtakers: The social meaning of drug use. London: Paladin.
Young, J. (1973a): Student drug use and middle class delinquency. In: Contemporary Social Problems in Britain, edited by R. Bailey and J. Young. Farnborough: Saxon House.
Young, J. (1973b): The hippie solution: an essay in the politics of leisure. In: Politics and Deviance: Papers from the National Deviancy Conference, edited by I. Taylor & L. Taylor. Harmondsworth: Penguin Books Ltd.

The social supply of cannabis in Australia: Definitional challenges and regulatory possibilities

Simon Lenton, Jodie Grigg, John Scott and Monica Barratt

Abstract

In Australia, as elsewhere, retail markets for most illicit drugs including cannabis are often based upon friendships and occur in closed networks. Yet there is debate about whether 'social supply' should be limited to non-profit making by 'friends', and whether 'minimally commercial supply' is a more apt descriptor as many 'social supply' transactions often involve some small monetary or in-kind benefit. These definitional challenges are of interest in their own right, and also in considering whether and how, 'social supply' transactions could be treated differently in law. In this study, 200 Australian cannabis users aged 18-30 who were recruited from Melbourne, Perth and Armidale were interviewed face-to face, using a mixed quantitative and qualitative approach, to explore their experiences of accessing and providing cannabis. Most participants' experiences of the cannabis market could be captured by the broad notion of 'social supply'. However, definitional specificity was not aided by notions of friendship or profit. The findings have implications for the definition of 'social supply' and how low-level supply offences are addressed in law. Specifically, there may be merit in considering expanding current Australian drug diversion options, which typically include drug information and a brief intervention, beyond simple possession offences to include low-level supply of cannabis and other drugs, but it is unlikely a definition of 'social supply' could be applied in such regulations.

1 Introduction

Cannabis remains the most widely used illicit drug globally (United Nations Office on Drugs and Crime (UNODC) 2014) and in Australia (Australian Institute of Health and Welfare 2014), and it is responsible for the vast majority of illicit drug apprehensions made by Australian law enforcement (Australian Crime

Commission 2015). As such, study of the cannabis market provides a good opportunity to access a sizeable number of both consumers and suppliers in a closed drug market characterised by low-level, not-for-profit, social supply.

There is definitional confusion in the social supply literature regarding the extent to which the term should be limited to non-profit making and/or to non-strangers. For example, Hough et al., (2003: 36) defined social supply as "[t]he non-commercial (or non-profitmaking) distribution of cannabis to non-strangers". In contrast, Potter (2009) distinguished between social suppliers and other suppliers on the basis of *intent* or *motive* – using the term *dealers* for those who were motivated by a desire for profit, while using the term *social suppliers* for those who may make some profit, but were driven by other factors and would continue to supply even if no financial gain were made.

More recently the concept of *minimally commercial supply* has been proposed in recognition that many otherwise 'social supply' arrangements involve some small financial gain through taxing, markup or economies of bulk purchase (Coomber & Moyle 2014 p.160-1). Coomber and Moyle's rationale for proposing the concept of 'minimally commercial supply' was to: (i) more accurately describe the real-life circumstance of the majority of drug supply transactions; and (ii) include the supply activities of addicted user-dealers of Class A drugs, who supply to other addicted users to support their habit but only make limited profit themselves. The core concept here is recognition that much 'social supply', like almost all behaviours, involves some gain to the supplier, ranging from reputational or status gain, such as kudos and prestige, to tangible monetary gain.

1.1 Reflecting these low-level offences in law

While the term 'social supply' may accurately describe a common experience for many participants in various drug markets, there is concern that the term may not be specific enough to be useful in law (See New Zealand Law Commission 2011; Potter 2009). Coomber and Moyle (2014) envisaged the separate graded supply offence of *minimally commercial supply*, similar to the murder/manslaughter distinction, sensitive to real world supply activities and graded according to motivation, harm and intent. Moreover, they suggested that, while some ambiguity would need to be considered in sentencing, future research could potentially delineate the different aspects of *minimally commercial supply* which could inform guidelines covering different roles in social supply behaviour (e.g., 'brokers', 'non-profit motivated sellers', 'nominated group buyers', 'user-dealers') (Coomber & Moyle 2014).

Potter (2009) noted that in a general legal sense there is no difference between one form of supply and another, and it is this rigidity that has been at the heart of the discussion on social supply. However, remarking on the problems of social supply as a legal concept, and reflecting on the UK debates about whether 'drug dealing' and social supply should be distinguished in law, he observed that notwithstanding problems with 'discretion', it may be preferable to keep the law clear (i.e., not try and express 'social supply' in law), but rather maintain discretion on the part of law enforcement agencies and the police (pp. 66-67).-Potter hoped that such discretion can be informed by the scientific understanding of the different nuances and patterns of drug supply (p. 68).

Potter argued that it was thus important that future research explores the nature of the relationship between users and their suppliers, and the economic aspects of such transactions, including levels of profit and getting drugs for free. Further he recommended interrogating the nature of 'friendship' in drug supply relationships, suggesting that determining whether friendship or the dealing relationship came first, might be instructive in separating social supply from true dealing. Underlying the need to clarify the meaning of the concept of friendship in cannabis distribution networks, Belackova and Vaccaro (2013) have highlighted that role-based expectations based on friendship were an important way that trust was engaged to protect the players from the uncertainties of an illicit market subject to undercover law enforcement and other risks. As such, they found that cannabis users, 'middlemen', or dealers could all be described as 'friends'.

Parker (2000) noted that not being in contact with 'real dealers' was one of the central ways young recreational drug users maintain their identity as respectable, recreational drug users. Thus, understanding the true, or real 'dealer' identity is an important part of understanding drug supply in otherwise closed social supply networks. This was explored by Jacinto and colleagues (2008) in their study of people who sold ecstasy in private venues, as opposed to public venues such as clubs or raves. Participants in that study described a dealer as someone for whom drug sales were a main source of income, or who moved large quantities of drugs, or distributed in public settings, or who reinvested their earnings in drug purchases and maintained a stash for future sales (Jacinto et al. 2008). It is also possible that those involved in supplying drugs to their friends may adopt ways of seeing or describing their own behaviour which could be considered techniques of 'neutralisation' (see Sykes & Matza 1957; Maruna & Copes 2005). Thus, by distancing one-self from a 'true dealer' identity, the internal conflict between one's behaviour, and the stigma associated with the societal condemnation of that behaviour (in this case 'drug dealing'), can be reconciled allowing the behaviour to be maintained.

This chapter draws on the qualitative and quantitative data from our Australian study of cannabis social supply (Grigg et al. 2015) to: explore the importance of friendship and profit motive in these cannabis 'social supply' transactions; to explore what constitutes a 'real dealer'; to consider implications for the definition of 'social supply'; and to consider the implications regarding how low-level supply offences might be addressed in law.

2 Method

The project, which was based on the earlier work of Coomber and colleagues (Duffy et al. 2007; Coomber & Turnbull 2007; Duffy et al. 2006), recruited cannabis users aged between 18 and 30 years of age at three project sites. Eighty participants were recruited to participate in a detailed 1-2 hour quantitative and qualitative questionnaire-based interview in both Perth (P) and Melbourne (M) and half this number in Armidale (A), a regional centre in New South Wales. Participants must have used cannabis at least monthly in the three months prior to interview, and/or had brokered access to or sold cannabis within the six months prior to interview. The method has been described in detail elsewhere (Grigg et al. 2015; Lenton et al. 2015). The questionnaire included a standardised measure of cannabis dependence, the Severity of Dependence Scale (SDS) (Gossop et al. 1992), using a previously validated cut-off for cannabis dependence (Martin et al. 2006). Participants were asked a range of questions related to their involvement in the exchange of cannabis, which included giving, brokering, swapping or selling. *Scoring* or obtaining cannabis was defined as an occasion where participants purchased it, grew it, or were given it where it became their property, as opposed to simply sharing with someone at a social gathering (e.g., someone passing them a joint). *Selling* was defined as exchanging cannabis for goods or money. *Brokering* was defined as buying cannabis for others without making a profit. *Giving* was defined as supplying cannabis to another person, where it ceased to become their property and became the recipient's property. The project was approved by Human Research ethics Committees at both Curtin University (HR 172/2011) and The University of New England (HE12-155).

3 Results

3.1 Demographics

The median self-reported age of the sample was 22 years (Interquartile Range (IQR) = 20-25 years) and 71% were male. There were no significant demographic differences between study sites in terms of age and gender. The majority of the sample (60%) described their ethnic background, as opposed to nationality, as 'Australian or New Zealand' followed by 'North West European' (27%). Only 1% identified as being of an 'Aboriginal or Torres Strait Islander' ethnic background. The participants were generally well educated for their age, with 61% of the sample reporting having 'completed a tertiary qualification'. Some 55% cited 'employment' as their main income source, 26% 'pension or allowances', 12% 'family', whereas only 4% said 'the sale of drugs' was their main income stream. Some 54% reported they lived in rental accommodation and 32% in their parent's home.

3.2 Cannabis use

Forty percent of the sample reported they were 'daily' cannabis users and 41% were using 'more frequently than weekly, but not daily'. The most commonly reported form of cannabis used was 'hydroponic' (72%), followed by 'bush' (soil grown) (63%), with only 9% reporting 'hash or resin'. Overall, results showed cannabis to be an important and embedded aspect of the lives of most of these participants. Participants reported primarily using cannabis to 'relax or have fun', yet 62% of the sample scored as cannabis dependent on the SDS, which is relevant to suggestions (below) for how low-level social supply-type offences could be dealt with in law. Participants reported that they spent on average 50 Australian Dollars (AUD) per week on cannabis for personal use for an average of 5 grams of cannabis. The main stated source of funding for their cannabis was 'wages' (61%) or 'government benefits' (16%) with only 6% nominating 'the sale of cannabis' as their main source of funding for their own personal use.

3.3 Obtaining Cannabis – Friends and profit motive

3.3.1 Obtaining cannabis – Friendship

Overall, participants reported that they mostly obtained their cannabis from a median of three different people. The most frequently reported description of these people was 'a friend gets it from a seller (brokered)' (70%), followed closely by 'a friend who sells' (58%) and then 'directly from a seller or grower' (58%). In this study, 'a friend who sells' implied that the person who cannabis was obtained from was primarily considered *a friend* over *a supplier*, whereas 'directly from a seller or grower' implied that the relationship was primarily for the purpose of supply. However, when asked to rank according to who they *most commonly* obtain from, the most often reported were 'directly from a seller or grower' (35%), 'from a friend who sells' (31%) and then 'a friend gets it from a seller (brokered)' (21%). Together these results suggest that in these samples, even though obtaining cannabis via brokering was experienced by most buyers, scoring 'directly from a seller or grower' (i.e. a dealer), and 'from a friend who sells' was how most scores occurred.

Analysis of open ended responses found that although participants often described their cannabis supplier as 'a friend', whether they first came into contact as 'friends' or 'for the purpose of supply' varied, with roughly three-fifths reporting a friendship first, and two-fifths reporting a supply relationship first. However, whether they were friends first or became friends after a dealing relationship, didn't seem to distinguish much about the nature of the relationship in the present. For example:

> "Friendship came first, yeah. I've known him since I started high school which would have been year 8, so 2008 and yeah the year he started dealing on the regular in 2011 so I'd known him for all that time and he always gave me good sized bags and that so I just bought and made him my main dealer because he's actually really nice and reliable." [P81, male, 18yrs]

> "I met him through a friend of mine. I met him for the purposes of buying dope, but we've actually become good friends outside of our business relationship. Yeah, because at first it was just a business kind of thing. You just go in, buy your dope, and get out. But we have a lot of stuff in common outside of smoking pot, like favourite movies, favourite music or favourite video games. It became more of an actual friendship than a business relationship." [P07, female, 23yrs]

3.3.2 Obtaining cannabis – profit and motive

The participants' qualitative accounts of what happened last time they scored or obtained cannabis provided rich descriptions of the relationships and processes of obtaining cannabis for these young users. Some described friends *giving them cannabis. Giving,* although not discussed further here, usually involved friends who grew cannabis with the intention of giving or sharing it with their friends.

The most common descriptions of friends who brokered cannabis involved friends that picked up extra when they are obtaining their own supply, friends that are heavy smokers who bought in bulk and were willing to broker small amounts, and friends who had access to cannabis when their friends didn't.

> "I bought through a friend, who's a far more frequent and heavy user than myself, a colleague from work. I gave him - I only bought a half ounce. I gave him $180. He gave me the weed the next week." [P08, male, 20yrs]

There were a variety of descriptions provided for *friends who sell*, ranging from friends that sold to cover some or all of their own use (i.e., so they could smoke for free), friends that sold to make some extra cash and friends that sold cannabis as their full-time job (i.e., it was their main form of income). This latter group would, by most definitions, not qualify as social suppliers because their profit was large and their motive profit-making. More common were participants who described friends who bought in larger amounts (e.g., ounces) so they could act as the source of cannabis for their close group of friends or people within their social network.

> "Yeah. He either has plants that he has grown himself or has a contact. I know that, amongst our circle of friends, I'm not the only person who he supplies to. He's our kind of little mini-hub for a lot of us." [M81, female, 26yrs]

There were a variety of different types of *dealers* described. Again, these were distinguished from *friends who sell* because the relationship was primarily centred around cannabis supply. They included people that sold cannabis to cover their own use, people that sold to get a bit of extra cash, and people that sold cannabis as their main form of income.

Analysis of transactions according to whether it was from a friend or a dealer and whether it was sold, brokered, or swapped provided comparisons of use of relevance to how the concept of social supply is defined. Overall, transactions that occurred through friends were described as more informal and often occurred in relaxed, often private, social settings. The expression 'killing two birds with one stone' was quoted on several occasions, suggesting that the interaction involved both social interaction and obtaining the cannabis, although the relative importance of these functions probably varied between people and occasions. Transactions that occurred with dealers were described as quicker in duration and more formal. For example, they often involved formal protocols, which facilitated more structured interactions. The expression 'strictly business' was frequently reported in descriptions of these transactions.

3.3.3 Obtaining cannabis – types of brokering

There were a few different types of brokering transactions that were described. One typical scenario involved situations where a friend had access to a supplier that the participant did not personally know, therefore, the friend would obtain the cannabis on their behalf. This often involved the participant going with them, but waiting in the car and not handling the sale (i.e., the friend did not act as an intermediary by introducing the buyer to the seller, but rather purchased the drugs on the participant's behalf). This scenario usually occurred when the supplier only wanted to supply to trusted friends, they didn't like having their phone number handed out, or there firstly needed to be a formal introduction. It was also common for buyers to prefer having their friend act as the 'middle man', as they were more comfortable being a step removed and only dealing with their friend.

> "Basically, I spoke to my friend because he knows a drug dealer. So he picks up if I ever need any, or like I go with him. Yeah, I usually go with him. So I asked him if he was free on this Thursday or something. He said 'yep'. So we just – we went together to the house. I gave him some money. He went in, came back out with a quarter. Yeah, that was it." [M42, male, 22yrs]

Another typical brokering scenario involved buying in groups, where at least one other person contributed a certain amount of money, and one person from the group handled the transaction and later divided and brokered it out to their friends. Sometimes only one member of the group had a relationship with the supplier, and by default occupied the broker role, and in other cases the broker role was taken by different people depending on particular circumstances at the time.

> "Generally it alternates between the three of us, whoever's got money at the time will get a lot and then subdivide it off to the others... The most common method would be usually when a friend has got a large quantity and either myself, or someone else will put up for an ounce or something and then we'll split it up. It's usually done

through friends and pooling our money or whoever's got money at the time." [P19, male, 27yrs]

"A group of mates and us chipped in, 50 bucks each or whatever and we got – this is only a couple of weeks ago, we got – I think we got half an ounce this time and... Well my friend has – he knows the people, I don't really deal in the buying side of things but he knows the people, so he says how much we want to get, asks for the money and we just give it to him." [A25, male, 20yrs]

3.4 Supplying cannabis: Friends and profit motive

Almost the entire sample (94%) reported supplying cannabis to another person at some point in their lifetime, whether it be giving, brokering, swapping or selling. The median age at which participants reported first supplying cannabis was 17 years old (IQR=16-18 years). Some 83% of those who reported that they had ever supplied cannabis had also done so in the past 6 months and 64% had done so in the past month (current suppliers). The median length of time recent (past 6 months) suppliers had been supplying for was two years (IQR=12-48 months). The median number of people that participants reported currently supplying cannabis to was four (IQR=3-8 people); however, the median number of people they reported *ever* supplying to was 25 (IQR=10-50 people).

3.4.1 Level of involvement by relationships and profits

Those who currently supplied mostly did so to 'only to friends/family' (55%) or 'friends/family and their friends' (32%) and a smaller proportion supplied to 'friends/family and their friends/occasionally to strangers' (8%). Only 4% reported that their current involvement in supply would be best described as 'I supply to anyone willing to buy, including strangers'. Similarly, when asked about the nature of their *current* supply activity, 21% said 'I give cannabis away – I never broker or sell' and 57% said 'I supply for the same price as originally purchased (brokering)'. A smaller number said they sold for profit that 'covers their own use' (12%) or 'a little bit extra' (6%). Only 3% said their current involvement in supply could be best described as 'I supply cannabis for profit that covers my use plus significant profit'.

3.4.2 Motive through analysis of qualitative accounts

In terms of another aspect of the social supply definitions, *motive*, for those 66% of participants who commented on reasons why they thought their *supplier* supplied, the responses could be recoded into 'sells to make profit' (52%), 'sells to cover some or all of own use' (30%) and 'only brokers' (17%). Of the 57% of the sample who commented on the profit their supplier makes, responses were coded into: 'covers some or all of own use' (35%), 'makes a small profit' (33%) and 'makes a significant profit' (32%).

Participants who had supplied cannabis in the past month (n=120) were asked about quantities they supplied and the profit they made, including the average amount they supply per week in grams and dollars, as well as the average amount they earn per week in grams and/or dollars. Most (16) of those unable to comment, said they couldn't because they were infrequent suppliers. For those who were able to comment (n=104), the self-reported median amount of cannabis supplied in a typical week was three grams (IQR=1-7 grams). The median value of cannabis participants reported selling in a typical week in Australian Dollars (AUD) was AUD45 (IQR= AUD19-AUD100). Some 77% of those who commented stated they received no cash profit during last sale. The median value for those with cash profit (n=24) was AUD25 (IQR = AUD5- AUD275). The median amount earned by suppliers (n=16) per week in the form of cannabis was approximately two grams (range=0.5-7 grams). There were no significant differences between sites in relation to amounts sold or profit made.

Participants who were currently selling cannabis were asked why they did this. Over a third of participants reported that they continued to sell or broker to 'help friends' (38%) and a quarter to 'help fellow cannabis users' (25%). There was considerable overlap between these two categories; however, some suppliers saw it as friendship-based, while for others it was based on an understanding of cannabis use and knowing what it was like to be without it. A number of people also stated they continued because it encouraged reciprocation. A small number of people reported they continued to supply 'out of habit', to 'cover costs of [their] personal use', or for 'occasional, modest or significant financial gain'. The following account illustrates the ideas of reciprocity and helping friends out:

> "As long as I'm going to buy some and as long as some of my friends are not able to do that when I'm able to do that, I don't see any reason why I shouldn't help them. Obviously because I know that they really would do the same for me. That's it. If it's not convenient for both parties, we wouldn't do it. That's the only explanation I can give, because there's no harm and there's no hassle in doing this… I continue to do it because – I don't know – I like to help people out with smoking, and I really love weed, I suppose. I don't mind helping people out with it… I guess it's a thing where

> we mutually understand each other's smoking habits... It is an everyday thing. Because I know, for them, if they're without weed for a while, they'll be in hell as well. It's just better to help them." [M75, female, 22yrs]

This account, which again highlights reciprocity, demonstrates a seller's rationale for selling to cover some or all of their own use:

> "It makes it a lot easier to be able to smoke cannabis because you're able to have that little bit extra to buy and not have to dig into your own money. It's just sort of a self-working cycle, it's just a circle that goes around. So you buy lots, you sell a bit, you've got some left over and then you buy lots, you sell a bit, you've got some left over and then you don't have to buy it yourself and you don't have to waste your own money." [A13, male, 18yrs]

The reasons for supplying cannabis sometimes shifted over time. While many people indicated that there was no change in reasons for supplying, others felt that growing older and maturing changed their reasons for supplying. Several people admitted that they thought it was a 'cool' thing to do when they were younger – they may have supplied for the sake of image, or to make money, but they had since grown out of such reasons, as the risk of sanctions had become more salient (see also Werse & Müller in this volume). For example:

> "Maybe, when I was still at high school or just fresh out of high school, maybe had more of a mentality to make a bit more profit. Back in Perth and when I was younger I would deal to friends-of-friends or friends-of-friends-of-friends and you don't really care about that. Being younger you just want to have money at the time and it's easy and there's a big market for it. I guess these days there's more at risk and I don't want to get caught with it. I don't want to face penalties or criminal records because that's – it's not really worth it." [M18, male, 24yrs]

A quarter of participants claimed that they would no longer supply cannabis if they knew they would no longer profit financially from it. The reasons they provided for discontinuing supply, if there was no profit, included that it was not worth the risk or that it would result in financial loss.

> "No. Yeah no there's no incentive for me then. Like the incentive for when I was selling was to get marijuana. So if I wasn't getting marijuana well then I wouldn't do it. Because the money is good, but it's not worth what happens if you get caught". [A22, male, 22yrs]

> "Not really. You've got to make a little bit, otherwise what's the point in making all the effort in doing the job, you know?" [M77, male, 28yrs]

A similar number of participants stated that they might still supply even if they were not making a profit, many in this situation noting that they would supply cannabis for a friend, but not a stranger.

> "I wouldn't care. If I was helping a mate, I'm more than happy. But for a random person, no, it's not my problem." [A14, male, 18yrs]

> "Well, I'd supply it to my friends just because we have a good time together. To other people, I'm not sure. It just depends on risk and effort versus how that affects me socially and how that affects other people and that sort of stuff." [M73, female, 19yrs]

Although most people who engaged in supply understood that their activities would be regarded as such *in law*, most (78%) did not consider *themselves* to be 'a dealer'. Some recoiled at the thought and others had never really thought about it or were uncertain. Many had ways of thinking about their own cannabis supply activities which reinforced their belief that they were not 'true dealers'.

With regards to issues in the literature, regarding definitions of social supply and 'true dealing', it seems that for many of these cannabis suppliers, the profit motive and the scale of that profit were more central to their notion of dealer than sale to 'non-friends'. Over a third of participants defined a drug dealer as someone who made a financial profit from the sale of drugs. One in six participants also defined dealers as those who sold cannabis in large quantities and/or supplied it as their primary source of income.

> "I see dealing as kind of your main thing. Like if you're a dealer you're always on call; you're not always on call but you've pretty much always got to answer your phone and buy larger amounts. You either grow it yourself or you know – you're higher up in the chain and you'd have a lot of profit… Your main motive, I see as a dealer, is to make money." [M71, male, 22yrs]

Only a small number of participants described dealers as those who supplied cannabis to people other than friends. Over a quarter of participants defined drug dealers in a negative fashion, as someone 'dodgy', criminal, untrustworthy, or likely to deceive them.

4 Discussion

A caveat on these findings is that, despite the relatively large sample size for a mixed methods study of this type, this study is not based on a random sample of cannabis users or suppliers, therefore generalizability from this study needs to be undertaken with caution. Notably, for obvious reasons, larger scale dealers were probably less likely to contact us for an interview than the cannabis users and small scale suppliers we successfully recruited.

Despite this, and whilst noting the contested definition of the term in the literature, the experience of many of the people we interviewed could be encompassed within a broad understanding of 'social supply'. Thus, most described how cannabis access and supply was integrated as an unremarkable part of their normal social interactions, with social capital and reciprocity, rather than profit, being the main benefit of most cannabis transactions. The study addressed a number of Potter's (2009) recommended lines of enquiry for subsequent research on social supply. Most transactions occurred between 'friends' in that most people accessed their cannabis from someone they knew. However, whether 'a friendship' or 'a drug supply' relationship came first varied and which came first seemed to be largely irrelevant to their relationships in the present. Many users were able to distinguish between 'friends who sell' and 'drug dealers' where in the latter case the relationship was primarily about cannabis supply. Even though obtaining cannabis through brokering was experienced by most buyers, the main way of obtaining cannabis was direct from a 'seller or grower' or from 'a friend who sells'. Nevertheless most consumers had a notion of 'dealer' which related to motive, and scale – it was their job, their main activity. This was similar to the findings of Jacinto and colleagues (2008).

Clearly, making substantial profit did not appear to be a major motive for many of the suppliers we accessed, who only made minimal, if any, financial or in-kind profit (e.g. cheaper drugs). However, whilst many would continue to supply to friends, if not strangers, if there was no profit, for others it wasn't worth the bother. In essence, getting something out of it for themselves, even if minimal in dollar value, was considered compensation for the risk or effort.

Although most participants in our study who engaged in supply understood that the law would class their activities as drug supply, most did not view *themselves* as 'a dealer' and many had ways of thinking about their own cannabis supply activities which reinforced their belief that they were not 'true dealers'. Thus, a number reported that they did not consider themselves to be 'dealers' because they often saw their cannabis supply as 'helping out friends', often in reciprocal relationships, and mostly involving none or minimal profit. Although most, when posed the question, acknowledged that what they were doing did constitute cannabis supply in legal terms, many did not seem to engage with the fact that they were potentially exposing themselves to the risk of being apprehended as a drug supplier and receiving a serious criminal charge. Whilst for some participants the risk of detection by the law did seem to emerge as a factor with maturity or changing life circumstances, for the majority the risk of detection did not seem to be a major consideration. For some of these, their explanations or justifications could be considered techniques of 'neutralisation' (Sykes and Matza 1957; Maruna and Copes 2005).

As to Coomber and Moyle's (2014) notion of *minimally commercial supply*, it is difficult to imagine how in practice decisions regarding the large number of cannabis supply charges that come before the courts (compared to murder vs manslaughter which is their analogy) could be explored in legal argument according to motivation, harm and intent. In Australia in the 2013-14 financial year there were 58,201 (87%) cannabis consumer arrests and 8,460 (13%) cannabis provider arrests (Australian Crime Commission 2015). It is unlikely that the police or criminal justice systems could investigate and consider social supply as a mitigating factor in these many cases, particularly when so many are decided under deemed supply provisions based on weight of drugs seized (Hughes 2011). Despite the difficulties of considering social supply for all cannabis related arrests, the scale and the extent to which the activity was vocational or profit-making could conceivably be relevant to judicial decision making. Either way, consistent with both Potter's (2009) and Coomber and Moyle's (2014) recommendations, it would certainly seem possible and worthwhile to brief court and legal officers about the different roles in small-scale supply behaviour (e.g., 'brokers', 'non-profit motivated sellers', 'nominated group buyers', 'user-dealers') which could inform any opportunity to exercise judicial discretion in these matters.

A number of countries have implemented diversion options where, at some point in the criminal justice system (pre-court, pre-trial, pre-sentence) (Ritter & McDonald 2008), those charged, or found guilty of a minor drug offence can elect to attend an educational or treatment intervention rather than receiving a more serious criminal penalty such as a criminal record, a custodial sentence, or a longer custodial sentence. Australia has had diversion options in place for possession of cannabis and a range of other drugs since 1999 (Hughes 2009). Most European countries have some form of diversion options in place (EMCDDA (undated)). Perhaps surprisingly, other countries to have adopted such schemes include Indonesia (since 2011) (Harm Reduction International 2015) and parts of the US where more than 100 such schemes have been documented (The Center for Health and Justice at TASC 2013).

Given that there appeared to be few differences between participants in this study who were engaged in cannabis consumption versus cannabis supply, and noting the high level of cannabis dependence reported by this sample, there may be an opportunity to reflect lower-level supply through expanding current drug diversion options in countries such as Australia where such schemes already exist for personal use offences. Extending diversion options beyond simple possession offences to include low-level supply of cannabis, and perhaps other drugs, would likely require a broadening of the diversion criteria beyond personal use offences and threshold amounts as noted by others (Moyle et al. 2013). However, the advantage of this approach is that it could avoid the problems already described associated with including subjective elements of friendship and profit in a legal definition of social supply. Although based on amount or weight based thresholds, rather than conceptually relevant notions of motive and intent, such reform may provide an improvement on the current situation where there is little room for discretion in how small scale suppliers are dealt with in law.

Diversion options, including those in Australia, typically include some kind of intervention ranging from information and brief intervention (for cannabis offences) through to intensive rehabilitation for other drug possession offences, as the schemes assume the person has an underlying drug problem which should be addressed. While this is clearly an assumption that is not valid for a large proportion of people who are apprehended for a minor drug offence, it is of relevance that almost two thirds our sample scored as cannabis dependent on the SDS. What constitutes 'low-level supply' would need to be defined and legislative change may be needed to allow the diversion schemes to apply to even this level of supply offence. The operational detail of how the schemes would deal with such offences would likely be primarily a regulatory rather than a legislative matter.

There is limited scope to consider in detail here how such reform might work for low-level drug supply offences in practice; however, the operation of programs that divert drug use-possession offenders away from the criminal justice system in Australia provides possible ways forward, including: (i) Limiting consideration of the diversion option to those charged with their first or second low-level supply offence, consistent with the possession scheme operating in the jurisdiction, would seem appropriate; (ii) Specifying weight limits (such as under 30 grams of dried cannabis plant material) to define a low-level supply offence could provide a working legal definition for the purpose of diversion; (iii) Describing in regulations (rather than laws) factors to be indicative of elements of social supply could include descriptions of the typical, but not necessary, features of this kind of drug supply (e.g. often among friends, not profit-driven, involving only minimal financial gain, if any), along with descriptions of the roles of 'brokers', 'non-profit motivated sellers', 'nominated group buyers', 'user-dealers' could help guide decisions regarding eligibility for diversion; (iv) The intervention could include information on drugs and the law, especially the consequences of a further supply charge, along with assessment of dependence and targeted intervention for those individuals assessed as such; and (v) any such program should be subject to evaluation to determine its viability and effectiveness in terms of the individuals apprehended, the workability from a policing point of view, the effects on other stakeholders, such as the drug treatment agencies, and the views of the wider community.

Some may be of the view that social supply offences should not be subject to any penalty. However, in the current Australian context where regulated legal availability of cannabis for recreational use itself seems a far-off reform prospect, applying diversion approaches to low level supply would seem potentially viable. While such an approach would have its limitations and would not take into account the conceptual and definitional details of the existing social supply literature, it may be a practical way forward to mitigate some of the disproportionally high criminal justice consequences which apply to the large number of drug users who get involved in small scale supply as part of their day-to-day participation in the drug market.

Acknowledgements

This chapter is based on an earlier draft paper presented at the Annual conference of the International Society for the Study of Drug Policy, held in Ghent, Belgium, 20th-22nd May 2015. The material presented draws on the technical report on this project (Grigg, Scott, Lenton & Barratt 2015). The project was supported by a grant from the Australian Government Department of Health through the National Drug Law Enforcement Research Fund (NDLERF). Monica Barratt is the recipient of a National Health and Medical Research Council Early Career Researcher Fellowship (APP1070140). The views expressed are the responsibility of the authors and are not necessarily those of the Commonwealth. The authors would like to thank: the anonymous cannabis users who participated in the project; the members of the project reference group; other researchers who worked on the project, specifically Cary Bennett, Vanessa Bible, Dina Eleftheriadis, Tom Fisher, Annie Haines and Tim Hatfield. We would also like to acknowledge Ross Coomber who encouraged us to undertake this research and allowed us to adapt his questionnaire for the Australian context.

References

Australian Crime Commission (2015): Illicit Drug Data report 2013-14. Canberra: Commonwealth of Australia.

Australian Institute of Health and Welfare (2014): National Drug Strategy Household Survey detailed report 2013. Drug statistics series no. 28. Cat. no. PHE 183. Canberra: AIHW.

Belackova, V. & Vaccaro, C. A. (2013): A friend with weed is a friend indeed: Understanding the relationship between friendship identity and market relations among marijuana users. Journal of Drug Issues, 43(3): 289-313.

Coomber, R. & Moyle, L. (2014): Beyond drug dealing: Developing and extending the concept of 'social supply' of illicit drugs to 'minimally commercial supply'. Drugs: Education, Prevention, and Policy, 21(2): 157-164. doi: 10.3109/09687637.2013.798265.

Coomber, R. & Turnbull, P. (2007): Arenas of drug transactions: adolescent cannabis transactions in England—social supply. Journal of Drug Issues, 22: 1-22.

Duffy, M., Schaefer, N., Coomber, R., O'Connell, L. & Turnbull, P. J. (2006): Cannabis supply and young people 'It's a social thing'. London: Kings College London.

Duffy, M., Schaefer, N., Coomber, R., O'Connell, L. & Turnbull, P. J. (2007): How do young people obtain cannabis? A snapshot view from a large city and rural villages. York: Joseph Rowntree Foundation.

EMCDDA ((undated)): Treatment as an alternative to prosecution or imprisonment for adults. Lisbon: EMCDDA. http://www.emcdda.europa.eu/html.cfm /index13223EN.html (Accessed 06.07.2015).

Gossop, M., Griffiths, P., Powis, B. & Strang, J. (1992): Severity of dependence and route of administration of heroin, cocaine and amphetamines. British Journal of Addiction, 87: 1527 -1536.

Grigg, J., Scott, J., Lenton, S. & Barratt, M. (2015): The social supply of cannabis in Australia (National Drug Law Enforcement Research Fund, Monograph Series No. 59). Canberra: Commonwealth of Australia.

Harm Reduction International (2015): The Global State of harm reduction 2014. London: International Harm Reduction Association. www.ihra.net (Accessed 17.02.2015).

Hough, M., Warburton, H., Few, B., May, T., Man, L.-H., Witton, J., et al. (2003): A Growing Market: The Domestic Cultivation of Marijuana. York: Joseph Rowntree Foundation.

Hughes, C. (2011): Bulletin No. 18: Legislative thresholds for drug possession and traffic: An overview of State and Territory differences in Australia. (Stage 2) – updated August 2011. DPMP Bulletin Series. Drug Policy Modelling Program, National Drug & Alcohol Research Centre: UNSW.

Hughes, C. E. (2009): Capitalising upon political opportunities to reform drug policy: A case study into the development of the Australian "Tough on Drugs – Illicit Drug Diversion Initiative". International Journal of Drug Policy, 20(5): 431-437.

Jacinto, C., Duterte, M., Sales, P. & Murphy, S. (2008): "I'm not a real dealer": The identity process of ecstasy sellers. The Journal of Drug Issues, 38(2): 419-444.

Lenton, S., Grigg, J., Scott, J., Barratt, M. & Eleftheriadis, D. (2015): The social supply of cannabis among young people in Australia. Trends and Issues in Crime and Criminal Justice, 503. Available at: http://www.aic.gov.au/publications /current%20series/tandi/501-520/tandi503.html (Accessed 15.12.15).

Martin, G., Copeland, J., Gates, P. & Gilmour, S. (2006): The Severity of Dependence Scale (SDS) in an adolescent population of cannabis users: Reliability, validity and diagnostic cut-off. Drug and Alcohol Dependence, 83(1): 90-93. http://dx.doi.org/10.1016/j.drugalcdep.2005.10.014 (Accessed 09.12.2015).

Maruna, S. & Copes, H. (2005): What have we learned from five decades of neutralization research? Crime and Justice: A Review of Research, 32: 221-230.

Moyle, L., Coomber, R. & Lowther, J. (2013). Crushing a Walnut with a Sledge Hammer? Analysing the Penal Response to the Social Supply of Illicit Drugs. Social & Legal Studies, 22(4): 553-573. doi: 10.1177/0964663913487544 (Accessed 09.12.2015).

New Zealand Law Commission (2011): Controlling and Regulating Drugs: A review of the Misuse of Drugs Act 1975. Wellington: NZLC.

Parker, H. (2000): How young britons obtain their drugs: Drugs transactions at the point of consumption. M. Natarajan, & M. Hough (eds.), Illegal drug markets: From research to prevention policy (pp 59-81). Monsey, N.Y.: Criminal Justice Press.

Potter, G. R. (2009): Exploring retail-level drug distribution: Social supply, 'real' dealers and the user/dealer interface. Z. Demetrovics, J. Fountain, & L. Kraus (eds.), Old and new policies, theories, research methods and drug users across Europe (pp 50-74). Lengerich: Pabst Science Publishers.

Ritter, A. & McDonald, D. (2008): Illicit drug policy: Scoping the interventions and taxonomies. Drugs: Education, Prevention and Policy, 15(1): 15-35.

Sykes, G. M. & Matza, D. (1957): Techniques of Neutralization: A Theory of Delinquency. American Sociological Review, 22(6): 664-670.

The Center for Health and Justice at TASC (2013): No Entry: A National Survey of Criminal Justice Diversion Programs and Initiatives. Chicago: Author. www.centerforhealthandjustice.org (Accessed 06.07.2015).

United Nations Office on Drugs and Crime (UNODC) (2014). World Drug Report 2014. Vienna: UNODC.

"Friendly" marijuana markets in the Czech Republic and in the U. S. – drug policy outcomes and risks

Vendula Belackova and Tomas Zabransky

Abstract

A growing body of literature shows the importance of friendship within illicit markets in (recreational) drugs, including cannabis, mostly referred to as "social supply". It is not clear to what extent this phenomenon is policy-responsive and what the risks related to it are. This analysis compares two localities with different drug policies (Florida, USA, as of 2009, and the Czech Republic, as of 2009) by examining the role of friendship and the risks of cannabis use related to it. Marijuana market patterns in the Czech Republic and North-Central Florida were analysed using mixed research methods. The quantitative data consisted of representative surveys (general population surveys with marijuana market modules). For the purpose of the qualitative study, 44 marijuana users and retailers were recruited in North-Central Florida and 66 in the Czech Republic via respondent-driven sampling. The inclusion criterion for the study was the use of marijuana in the last 12 months. Semi-structured interviews, which took 80 minutes on average, followed an interview guide focused on marijuana use, sharing, purchases, sales and growing, with extensive probes into the activities of the respondents' "friends", as they defined them. The quantitative data were analysed using frequency analysis and multinomial logit models. The qualitative data were analysed using inductive analysis. Compared to the Czech Republic, the acquisition of drugs through a "friend" was more prevalent in the U.S./Florida. The qualitative study showed that this "friendly" market pattern might encourage increased cannabis use and might increase the likelihood of driving under the influence of cannabis. The outcomes of the analysis suggest that punitive drug policies could provide incentives for shrinking the market into friendly/social networks and thus impose risks on users. It is therefore possible that a repressive drug policy contributes to harmful patterns of drug use, with illicit markets as significant transmission mechanisms.

1 Introduction

A growing body of literature has highlighted the importance of friendship networks for drug markets, especially for ecstasy and cannabis markets. This is done by demonstrating the mere presence of "friends" as suppliers to the users (Caulkins & Pacula 2006), by describing the definition of "friendship" among marijuana users (Belackova & Vaccaro 2013), or by referring to the so-called "social supply" (Coomber & Turnbull 2007; Potter 2009; Nicholas 2008). The concept of "social supply" involves the acquisition of an illegal drug via one's social network rather than from "proper dealers". At the same time, the concept assumes that no profits are made by friends (Taylor & Potter 2013; Coomber & Moyle 2013). Low quantities being sold, an irregular frequency of sales or no stock on the side of supplying friends can be added to the definition.

There are numerous reasons for the increasing evidence regarding the involvement of "friends" in supply networks. Some individuals tend to be less trusted than others (i.e., young people) and thus have difficulties in gaining access to the market (Jacques & Allen 2014). In addition, dealers or customers might want to distance themselves from one another because of security issues (Parker et al. 1998). Overall, maintaining trusted relationships can serve as an instrument for reducing the risks posed by illegal markets – including the risk of arrest, assault or low product quality (Wilkins 2001). At the same time, some scholars have denoted particular recreational drugs markets as benign (Hamid 1991), partly because of the nature of the substances and their effects, as well as the social context in which they are used (Sandberg 2012).

In any case, the evidence of social supply shows that regular citizens who choose to "help out friends" are often subject to severe criminal penalties. This has opened up a debate about necessary alleviations regarding the drug policy approach towards "social supply" in order to reflect this issue (Moyle et al. 2013).

Notwithstanding the difficulties involved in assessing what is social supply and what is not, the question of the extent to which "helping out friends" is a product of strict drug policies itself remains open. Finding answers to this would help provide an understanding of whether this behavior is policy-responsive or whether it is somehow inherent in the culture of recreational drug use. At the same time, there has been only vague discussion of what the risks and benefits of friendly/social supply are (beyond the criminal risks), and thus what the benefits of alleviating drug policies in this respect would be.

In order to answer these questions, we chose to compare cannabis markets in two countries with contrasting policy approaches to cannabis, the Czech Republic and Florida (U.S.), as of 2009 (see Table 1).

Table 1: Comparison of the drug laws in the Czech Republic and Florida, U.S., with respect to cannabis.

	Czech Republic until 12/2009[a]	**Czech Republic since 01/2010**[b]	**Florida, U.S. 2009**[3]
Possession of "small amount"	< 10 doses no jail or record	< 15 grams no jail or record	< 20 grams MIS - 1 year / 1000 USD
Possession of "greater than small amount"	> 10 doses max 2 years / fine	> 15 grams max 1 year / property loss	> 20 grams FEL - 5 years / 5000 USD
Sale (and production) of cannabis – lowest penalties	max 3 years	1 to 5 years	MIS - 1 year / 1000 USD >20 g 5 years / 5000 USD
Growing marijuana plants and other herbal drugs in a "small amount"		< 5 plants no jail or record	
Growing marijuana plants and other herbal drugs in a "greater than small amount"		max 6 months/fine/loss of property, 6 months to 5 years if to a greater-than-large extent	Marijuana Grow House Eradication Act: 15 years minimum sentence
The highest punishment for sale	15 years maximum	15 years maximum	15 years minimum
Possession of paraphernalia	not criminalized	not criminalized	MIS - 1 year / 1000 USD
Use of undercover informants	NO	NO	YES
Police targeting marijuana use	NO	NO	YES
Civil asset forfeiture	NO	NO	YES

SOURCE: [a] Criminal Code of the Czech Republic no. 140 / 1961, [b] Criminal Code of the Czech Republic no. 40 / 2009; [3] Florida Criminal Code

In the Czech Republic, the possession of cannabis (and any other illegal drug) up to a certain amount (defined by legislation) for personal use is considered an administrative offence. In Florida, and the U.S. overall, federal criminal law treats cannabis possession for personal use as a criminal offence (in this analysis, we look at the Florida state laws in relation to cannabis). At the same time, the penalties applied to those convicted of cannabis crimes are significantly higher in Florida than in the Czech Republic

In this chapter, we look into the characteristics of cannabis markets in both places and assess in which of the localities (i) purchasing cannabis from a "friend" was more prevalent, and has an impact on price, and (ii) cannabis was used with greater risks in relation to the means of acquisition. We also look into different definitions of "friendship" that might occur in both (cannabis) cultures.

2 Study design – a mixed-methods approach

For the purpose of the study, a mixed-methods approach was used, combining qualitative and quantitative research methods. We used quantitative data to assess the prevalence of marijuana use and modes of acquisition in both populations, as well as to assess the influence of friendship on cannabis prices. We used a qualitative research design to reveal any possible causal links between obtaining cannabis and drug policy, as well as between use patterns and the source of cannabis. The qualitative data analysis was also used to interpret some of the quantitative survey findings, and to get a better understanding of what the term "friend" meant among cannabis users in both localities.

2.1 Quantitative study design

The quantitative research design used self-reported data on cannabis markets from general population surveys on substance use conducted in the U.S. and the Czech Republic in 2008 (NSDUH – National Survey on Substance Use and Health, U.S.; CS 2008 – General Population Survey on the Use of Psychotropic Substances and on Attitudes Towards it, CZ). In the framework of both surveys, respondents who had used marijuana in the past 12 months were questioned in detail about the modes of its acquisition. The questions about marijuana markets were implemented in the CS 2008 survey for the first time in 2008, and were designed according to the NSDUH. In 2008, a total of 55,736 respondents participated in the NSDUH survey; 3,776 of them reported buying marijuana in the past 12 months. The sample of the Czech population-wide survey (CS 2008) consisted of 4,500 respondents. 128 respondents in the Czech Republic had purchased cannabis in the last year. The two datasets are described in Table 2.

Table 2: Study populations in the qualitative and quantitative research on marijuana markets in the Czech Republic and in the U.S. (Florida)

Quantitative data (representative of 2008 population)	**Czech Republic**	**U.S.**
Survey title, acronym and year	General Population Survey on the Use of Psychotropic Substances and on Attitudes Towards it (CS 2008)	National Survey on Substance Use and Health (NSDUH 2008)
Sample size	4,500	55,739
Oversampled age	15–29	12–26
Age category	15–64	12 and older
No. of respondents who used cannabis in the last 12 months	734	8,954
No. of respondents who bought cannabis in the last 12 months	128	3,776
Monetary incentive	none	30 USD
Number of questions (complete set)	171	2,964
Qualitative data (semi-structured interviews collected by the authors)	**Czech Republic**	**North-Central Florida**
Sample size	61	44
Period	10/2009–01/2010	03–05/2009
Females	22%	21%
Age (min/mean/median/max)	17/28/28/46	18/29/25/61
Monetary incentive	600 CZK (30 USD)	None
Average length of interviews	69 min	79 min

Simple frequency analysis was used to answer our research questions – comparing the share of "friend-sourced" purchases in both localities. Frequency analysis of the weighted data on the prevalence and frequency of marijuana use was applied when looking into the risks associated with use.

We used multinomial logit models to assess whether friendship was a determinant for price in marijuana purchases. The multinomial logit models were constructed on the baseline of the lowest price category, in order to assess the influence of several factors on purchasing cannabis for two other (higher) price levels.

Collinearity was checked by running OLS regression on the data and using a post-estimation test of the VIF factor.

2.2 Qualitative study design

The qualitative data from the Czech Republic and the U.S. were collected using a semi-structured interview guide. We conducted the interviews from March to May 2009 in North-Central Florida and from October 2009 to January 2010 in the Czech Republic. The same interview guide, translated and adjusted to the local population, was used in both settings. The questions in the qualitative interviews were centered on the topics covered in the quantitative NSDUH and CS surveys. The interview guide for the study was constructed using sensitizing concepts that include loosely operationalized notions providing some initial direction to a study (Patton 2002).

The interview guide covered questions about the participants' experience with psychoactive substances, social experiences with marijuana, such as receiving and sharing marijuana, market experiences with marijuana, such as buying and selling, other situations, such as giving away marijuana for free or trading it for something else, and self-supply (personally growing marijuana). The respondents were asked to provide descriptions of the last time they happened to be in one of the above-mentioned settings, and then they were probed to describe the most usual situation.

The recruitment of the participants for the study followed a two-pronged approach, which included elements of purposeful and snowball sampling (Patton 2002; Biernacki & Waldorf 1981), in order to maximize the level of participant response while minimizing the homogeneity of the respondents. The recruitment techniques, as well as the overall research, were IRB approved by the Florida State University Human Subjects Committee on 14th January 2009 (HSC No. 2009.2196), and the researchers also gained the additional protection of a Federal Certificate of Confidentiality issued by the NIH/NIDA (No. DA–09–017).

In total, 44 interviews were conducted in North Florida and 61 interviews and one focus group were conducted in the Czech Republic. The characteristics of the sample and average interview length are presented in Table 2.

All the qualitative study respondents had used marijuana in the last 12 months, except for four respondents in the Czech Republic and two in Florida (these were heavily involved in the cannabis market, had intensive relations with cannabis users, or were representatives of law enforcement bodies focused on cannabis supply). The duration of marijuana use among the respondents ranged from 1 to 29 years in the Czech Republic and up to 41 years in Florida (the oldest

U.S. respondent was more than 10 years older than the oldest Czech respondent). This also affected the mean length of use – 11 years in the Czech Republic and 13 years in the U.S., while the median length was longer in the Czech Republic by one year (11 years in the Czech Republic, 10 years in the U.S.).

The respondents in the Czech research were less frequent marijuana users, as 48% of them reported smoking (almost) daily, compared to 54% in the Florida research. In both groups, using marijuana was more frequent than alcohol use. The U.S. respondents had more experience with using other illegal drugs during the past year (at least one other drug had been used by 54% of the respondents in the Czech research and 61% of the respondents in the research performed in Florida).

The Czech study captured more cannabis growers (44%, in contrast to 9% in Florida). On the other hand, in Florida, relatively more cannabis sellers were interviewed (32%, in comparison with 21% in the Czech Republic). In the Czech Republic, 83% of the respondents classified obtaining marijuana within 24 hours as very easy, while in Florida, this was only the case for 59% of the respondents. Further experiences of the qualitative study respondents on the marijuana market are presented in Table 3.

Inductive analysis of the data was performed, as were coding and sorting of the data until a coherent picture emerged. The data were analysed with the use of the Atlas.ti software.

Table 3: Experience of qualitative study respondents in the Czech Republic and in Florida, U.S. related to marijuana acquisition.

Characteristics QUALITATIVE	**Czech Republic**		**Florida**	
User (only)	17 persons	28%	24 persons	55%
Grower	27 persons	44%	4 persons	9%
Dealer	13 persons	21%	14 persons	32%
Law enforcement/ Other participants	4 persons	7%	2 persons	5%
TOTAL	61 persons		44 persons	

3 Findings

3.1 Purchasing cannabis from a friend and impact on price

In this section, we look at cannabis prices and other market characteristics, as described in the representative population surveys in both localities. Further, we look into insights from the qualitative analysis to complement these findings. Lastly, we present the outcomes of multinomial logit models that looked at determinants of cannabis prices on the market, including "friends" as a source of cannabis.

3.1.1 Source of marijuana

According to the NSDUH 2008 and CS 2008 data, a significantly larger proportion of U.S. marijuana users reported having purchased cannabis when they last obtained it (43%, in contrast to 18% in the Czech Republic; Table 4). The Czech users, on the other hand, were more likely to have grown their own cannabis (8%, in comparison with 1% in the U.S.) or to have received it for free or by sharing (72%, compared to 55% in the U.S.).[1]

A larger percentage of marijuana purchases between friends or relatives was reported in the U.S. (83% of their last purchases, compared to 41% in the Czech Republic) (see Table 4). In addition, more acquisitions had occurred in private places in the U.S. (56%, compared to 27% in the Czech Republic).

The simple frequency analysis of the survey data suggests that the U.S. cannabis market, in comparison with the Czech one, took place rather in "closed" settings and networks (See Table 4). The qualitative analysis confirmed this finding: it was apparent in the Florida interviews that the dealers from whom users had purchased cannabis were automatically labeled as "friends": "If you meet somebody and they're a good friend of yours for a couple of months, and they go, 'Hey, I have a friend' – that friend is their pot dealer" [Ruth]. Several behavioral expectations were linked to this type of "friendship", as we further explain in Section 3.2.

1 In the CS 2008 survey, unlike in the NSDUH one, the respondents were asked to differentiate their answers between "receiving (marijuana) for free" and "by sharing". For validation purposes, the question was asked twice in the marijuana market module, with the two options being asked in reversed order. The option that was asked first yielded higher results than the one asked later. From this, it is estimated that 23% of the cannabis users in the Czech Republic received cannabis for free the last time they obtained it, while 49% received it from somebody who was sharing (a joint, etc,) with them.

Table 4: NSDUH 2008 and CS 2008 survey data on last purchase situations

HOW DID YOU GET THE LAST MARIJUANA YOU USED?	**CS 2008**	**NSDUH 2008**
Bought it	18%	43%
Received it for free or by sharing	72%	55%
Grew it	8%	1%
Traded something else for it or other	2%	1%
SOURCE OF MARIJUANA ON THE OCCASION OF YOUR LAST PURCHASE[2]		
A friend or relative	41%	83%
A person I know	30%	n.a.
Someone I did not know very well or just met	5%	17%
Other (i.e. dealer)	24%	n.a.
PLACE OF LAST PURCHASE		
Private place (home, seller's place)	27%	56%
Public place (public, school, bar, outside)	72%	36%
Other	1%	8%

SOURCE: NSDUH 2008, CS 2008

At the same time, "friends" who were not dealers themselves were expected to get cannabis for their befriended fellow-users. This would often be because the dealers would restrict the type and number of customers, or, from the user's perspective: "With my friend being the middleman, I prefer that the most because I've had situations where it's hard to get hold of them [*the dealers*], they're really weird" [Nora].

2 In the CS 2008 survey, the answers to the question "Who did you get marijuana from the last time you obtained it" were from: (i) a friend, (ii) a partner or relative, (iii) a person I know, (iv) a person I don't know, (v) a dealer, (vi) on the internet, (vii) by mail, (viii) other, (ix) grew it, (x) friend-dealer (only the answers of those who bought marijuana the last time were selected here). In the NSDUH, the options for the answer to the question "Who sold you the last marijuana you bought" were from (i) a friend, (ii) a relative or family member, (iii) someone I just met or I didn't know very well (unfortunately, there was no answer option for "well-known dealer" or similar). In the CS 2008 survey, options i and ii (see above) were summed for comparison with the NSDUH dataset. In addition, 20% of the Czech users who bought their cannabis the last time they obtained some did so from a dealer and 5% used different means. No respondent chose the answer "friend-dealer".

In the Czech Republic, a usual description of a cannabis source was "a guy with weed on the phone" [Pavel], or, as Samantha puts it, "a guy comes and says you can call him any time". In this sense, it was more common for the Czech respondents to buy their cannabis without the necessity to have established a "friendly" relationship.

The term "friend" in a market setting was used rather in reference to a person who grows and sells cannabis at the same time.

> "I buy from him 'cause he's a friend, and I prefer to give money to him rather than to anyone else. I could be buying at a variety of different places, but that would be a lower quality. Cause he's a remarkable grower." [Hung]

Another respondent explained how he brokered a larger amount of cannabis from his befriended grower to other friends of his:

> "A friend who needed more stuff approached me. And I would never give the phone number of this [grower] friend of mine, that wouldn't be safe." [Vladan]

This shows that "friendly" terms were important in situations where a greater risk (to the supplier) was present.

Last but not least, the Czech respondents were reluctant to call their cannabis acquaintances "friends". A number of them provided accounts in which they referred to "real" or "normal" friends.

> "With these 'friends' on the campus, it is our main activity (smoking). I do normal things with normal friends." [Ondra]

Or, as Lenka said: "There are people, these 'sort of friends' who come by to see whether we've got something. And then you have the real friends, like Zdenek."

To conclude, "friendship" was vouched more commonly among the U.S. cannabis market participants, and among the Czech users who purchased directly from cannabis growers. It was used as a tool to mitigate the risks imposed by cannabis policy. In addition, the interpretation of survey outcomes has to take into account the possibility that the term "friend" could stand as a synonym for both the "dealer/grower" and the "middleman", more so among the NSDUH respondents.

3.1.2 Prices paid per gram and amount of cannabis on the occasion of the last purchase

The price per gram of cannabis was also subjected to our analysis. Prior to presenting the figures for both countries, we will make a remark on the average amounts purchased, as the price per gram tends to reflect the total size of the purchase (Caulkins & Pacula 2006). The majority of purchases made in the Czech Republic were below 5 grams (91%); a comparable amount[3] was obtained by only 56% of the U.S. respondents. An additional 23% of U.S. last-year cannabis users bought an amount between 5 to 9 grams, and 21% bought an amount larger than that (see Figure 1). The rather large quantities purchased by users in the U.S. could reflect the fact that they purchased cannabis for fellow users too. The distribution of cannabis amounts at last purchase is shown in Figure 1.

Figure 1: Amount of marijuana obtained on the occasion of the last purchase in the Czech Republic and in the U.S.

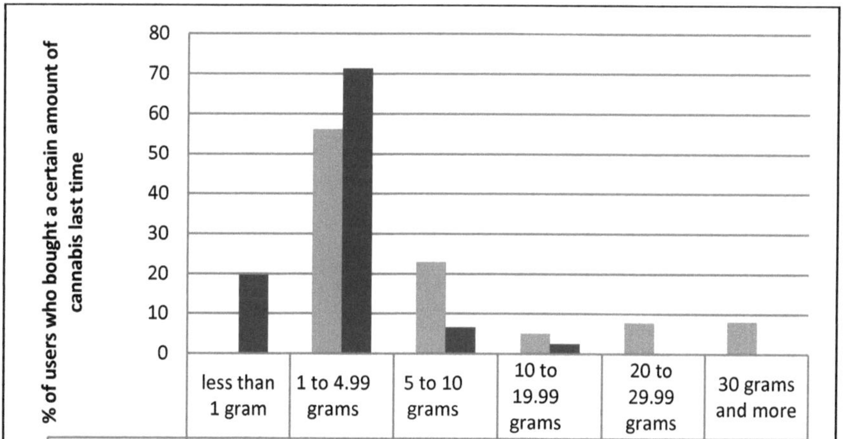

	less than 1 gram	1 to 4.99 grams	5 to 10 grams	10 to 19.99 grams	20 to 29.99 grams	30 grams and more
NSDUH 2008	0	56,14	22,96	5,03	7,79	8,07
CS 2008	19,67	71,31	6,56	2,46	0	0

n (CZ) = 122; n (US) = 4,672
SOURCE: NSDUH 2008, CS 2008

3 It is customary in the U.S. to report purchases in ounces; for the purpose of comparison, ounces were recounted into grams in this study.

The price variable had two extremes for the Czech Republic, (i) one for almost non-marketable marijuana (10% of the respondents who bought marijuana claimed they did not actually pay for it the last time) and (ii) the other one for the market in indoor marijuana (with 21% of the purchases at a cost of 100–149 CZK per gram, equivalent to 5 – 7.5 USD; see Figure 2). One of the Czech qualitative study respondents explained: "If someone sells something, it is indoor stuff. Well, sometimes the outdoor stuff gets sold among friends too [Jiri]."

In the U.S., three price categories could be observed. On the basis of the qualitative data analysis, these could be: (i) low-grade marijuana of Mexican origin ("*regs*"), costing less than 2.5 USD per gram; (ii) outdoor-grown marijuana or lower-quality indoor marijuana of U.S. origin ("*mids*"), costing between 9.99 and 12.49 USD per gram, and (iii) high-quality indoor-grown marijuana of U.S. origin ("*crips*"), costing between 20 and 22.5 USD per gram. Prices and their distribution are presented in Figure 2.

Figure 2: Prices of marijuana obtained on the occasion of the last purchase in the Czech Republic and in the U.S. (the U.S. prices are for amounts up to 30 grams).

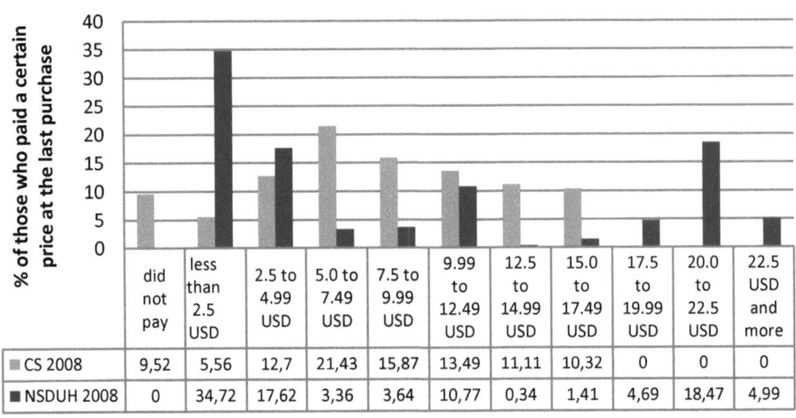

	did not pay	less than 2.5 USD	2.5 to 4.99 USD	5.0 to 7.49 USD	7.5 to 9.99 USD	9.99 to 12.49 USD	12.5 to 14.99 USD	15.0 to 17.49 USD	17.5 to 19.99 USD	20.0 to 22.5 USD	22.5 USD and more
CS 2008	9,52	5,56	12,7	21,43	15,87	13,49	11,11	10,32	0	0	0
NSDUH 2008	0	34,72	17,62	3,36	3,64	10,77	0,34	1,41	4,69	18,47	4,99

n (CZ) = 126; n (US) = 4,672
SOURCE: NSDUH 2008, CS 2008

3.1.3 Receiving cannabis for free

The greater role of free-of-charge acquisition in the Czech Republic in comparison to the U.S. has been outlined above. Here, we take a further look into the characteristics of acquisitions where marijuana was acquired "for free". This option was distinguished from "receiving cannabis by sharing" in the Czech Republic only, and it is embedded in its specific historical and political context.

In the former (communist) Czechoslovakia before 1989, there was no market in cannabis: "I would never buy during the communist regime, no. It'd always be from friends that grew it or something" [Petr, 46].

To many respondents, this perception of cannabis as a non-marketable good persisted until contemporary times. For instance, as Standa put it:

> "I see buying and selling marijuana as a deadly sin; I believe the plant shouldn't be sold, but rather given away."

The relatively large percentage of growers contributes to the situation: "I get it in different ways. Sometimes from friends that grow who give it to you so that you can taste" [Vladan], as well as the fact that marijuana is not a "scarce" good, as Marian suggests: "It's not sold; it's given out, as there is a surplus, sort of."

We looked further into the characteristics of free-of-charge transactions and of those who reported them as the way they got cannabis the last time in the CS2008 survey.

Those who claimed to have received marijuana for free the last time (23% of the last-year cannabis users, on top of the 49% who received it from somebody sharing it with them; see footnote 1), mostly received less than 1 gram (47% of cases) or about 1 gram (32%). However, receiving larger amounts was not uncommon (12% received 1–2 grams, 5% got 3–4 grams and 5% obtained 5 grams or more).

Those who received free cannabis were less likely to have used cannabis in the last 30 days (51%) than those who bought it the last time (80%), and were less likely to be daily users (4%) than those who purchased it (9%).

Regarding the type of marijuana they received, these users were less likely to have obtained indoor-grown marijuana (31%) than those who had made a purchase last time (50%), and more likely not to know the type of cannabis they got the last time (46%) than those who bought it (31%).[4] They were also more likely to have got cannabis from a friend or relative the last time (62% compared to 41% who bought it).

---

4 Overall, the Czech respondents (cannabis users in the last 12 months) were asked to identify the type of cannabis they obtained the last time. More than a third (35%) said they got indoor-grown cannabis, 21% said it was outdoor-grown cannabis, 3% said it was hashish and 33% said they didn't know what type of cannabis it was.

3.1.4 Logit models

In the multinomial analysis, the goals were to explain what determines cannabis prices in each of the places and to examine the role of friendship.

A multinomial logit model (multinomial logistic regression) was used to predict the probabilities of the different outcomes of a categorical variable (in our models, it is "marijuana price per gram paid on the occasion of the last purchase" categorized into three outcomes[5]), given a set of independent variables.

We examined the odds ratios[6] of paying a higher price in relation to the following independent variables: "amount of cannabis obtained on the occasion of the last purchase", "place of last purchase", "obtaining marijuana from a friend in the last purchase situation", sociodemographic characteristics of the customers, their "demand for cannabis" expressed as frequency of use, and the "size of the city of residence". An indicator of cannabis "quality"[7] was added into the Czech model (such a variable was not available in the NSDUH). Thus, we looked at how a unit change of either of these predictor variables multiplied the probability of paying a particular price for cannabis (Hosmer et al. 2013).

This means that we looked at how the likelihood of paying 2.5 USD–14.99 USD per gram instead of less than 2.5 USD in the U.S. changed when a larger amount of cannabis was bought on the spot, cannabis was purchased at a private party, close to home, when the respondent was male, a year older than other respondents, unemployed, was using cannabis more frequently, tried to cut down his/her cannabis use, sold any marijuana last time or lived in a big city. We equally looked at how the likelihood of paying more than 14.99 USD rather than 2.5 USD or less in the U.S. changed given these factors (see Table 5), and at how the likelihood of paying between 100 CZK and 199 CZK instead of 100 CZK or less and more than 200 CZK instead of 100 CZK or less in the Czech Republic was influenced by similar factors (see Table 6).

---

5 The price variable was split into three categories in each dataset, based on its percentile distribution. In the U.S., it was 1 – less than 2.5 USD per gram, 2 – 2.5 USD to 14.99 USD, 3 – 15 USD or more. In the Czech Republic, it was 1 – less than 100 CZK (equivalent of approx. 5 USD), 2 – 100 CZK to 199 CZK (equivalent of 5 USD–10 USD) and 3 – 200 CZK (equivalent of 10 USD) or more. Those respondents who said they did not pay for their cannabis on the occasion of their last purchase (in the Czech Republic) were excluded from the analysis.

6 In Stata, the mlogit command was used with the ",rrr" option, which provides exponentiated coefficients – the relative risk ratios, commonly interpreted as odds ratios. See the Stata webpage for more information about the function: http://www.ats.ucla.edu/stat/stata/output/stata_mlogit_output.htm.

7 "Indoor" (grown) marijuana, commonly understood as an indicator of higher potency among the Czech respondents.

3.1.4.1 Cannabis price determinants in the U.S.

In Table 5 we present a model that explains about 8% of the variation in the prices paid per gram of cannabis in the U.S. In determining the cannabis price in the U.S., the amount on the occasion of the last purchase was a significant factor, as were the place of purchase, relationship with the seller, intention to cut down cannabis use, selected socio-demographics (age, gender, employment status, size of the city of residence) and the question of whether the respondent had sold some of the marijuana he had bought the last time.

Those respondents who purchased their cannabis in a private setting and who were male and/or older had a significantly higher likelihood of paying more for their cannabis than the price we set as a baseline (2.5 USD or less). This was especially the case when cannabis was purchased from a friend or a relative (respondents were 48% more likely to pay between 2.5 and 14.99 USD per gram of cannabis than below 2.5 USD, and 74% more likely to pay over 15 USD).

On the other hand, respondents who were unemployed, who had tried to cut down their marijuana use in the last 12 months or who lived in a city with over 1 million inhabitants were significantly more likely to have paid a price lower than 2.5 USD per gram of cannabis on the occasion of their last purchase.

Several variables yielded inconsistent results in terms of influencing the chance of the respondent falling into either of the two higher price categories on the occasion of their last purchase. While purchasing higher amounts of cannabis reduced the likelihood of paying over 15 USD per gram, at the same time it increased the likelihood of paying 2.5–14.99 USD. Also, purchasing cannabis close to home was a significant predictor of paying 2.5–14.99 USD per gram of cannabis, but not for paying more than that. Those respondents who claimed that they had sold any of the cannabis they bought the last time were 77% more likely to have paid over 15 USD per gram.

Table 5: Determinants of cannabis prices paid on the occasion of the last purchase in the U.S.[8]

	2.5 to 14.99 USD		15 USD or more	
BASE OUTCOME: price per gram lower than 2.5 USD	Odds ratio	Standard error	Odds ratio	Standard error
Amount of last cannabis purchased (*categorical variable*)[a]	1.206***	0.059	0.441***	0.028
Bought cannabis the last time at a private place, home or party	1.475***	0.119	1.738***	0.155
Last cannabis purchase was close to home	1.211*	0.096	1.149	0.099
Last cannabis purchase was from a friend or relative	1.647***	0.171	1.914***	0.227
Gender: male	1.413***	0.115	1.591***	0.141
Age (*continuous variable*)	1.079***	0.014	1.194***	0.017
Social status: unemployed	0.628***	0.066	0.473***	0.059
Demand for cannabis/frequency of cannabis use in the last 12 months (*categorical variable*)[b]	1.037	0.033	1.017	0.035
Tried to cut down on marijuana use in the last 12 months	0.847*	0.066	0.685***	0.059
Sold any of the marijuana bought last time	1.067	0.146	1.773***	0.276
Population size in the place of residence over 1 million	0.821*	0.064	0.669***	0.058
Constant	0.172***	0,036	0.235***	0.054
Prob > chi2	0.0000			
Pseudo R2	0.0838			
N	4067			
Log likelihood	-4081.36			
* p<0.05. ** p<0.01. *** p<0.001				

[a] Categories coded as 1 – less than 5g, 2 – 5 to 10g, 3 – more than 10g

[b] Categories coded as 1 – last year but not last month, 2 – last month but not last week , 3 – once a week or more often, 4 – several times per week. 5 – every day or almost every day

SOURCE: NSDUH 2008

The fact that purchases made from a "friend" were at a higher cost than otherwise is rather surprising. The findings of the qualitative analysis showed that a "friend"

8 If not stated otherwise, the independent variables are binomial, coded as 1 – positive outcome, 0 – negative outcome.

was expected to get cannabis for "friends" from the dealer with no mark-up on price, as Matthew explained:

> "I would say that if you can serve as a middleman for a friend, the rule is you should do it without any attempt to make a profit."

Some respondents did indeed claim that having a friendly relationship with the dealer meant a better price:

> "Yeah, for a long time he (friend / dealer) wouldn't tax[9] me. And he would just tax everyone else." [Kristen]

The most plausible explanation of the fact that receiving cannabis from a friend was associated with higher prices is the missing variable that would control for cannabis quality; in this respect, price was also a proxy of cannabis quality in the U.S. dataset. It can be assumed that the "closed", "friendly" market was supplying higher-grade cannabis, which was more expensive. This was explicitly formulated by one of the respondents:

> "For example, we don't have any real open-air markets here in the town. Just like I said, a smaller city. Um, but in the bigger cities where you do have an open-air marijuana market...um, that is definitely the lower-quality stuff. Whereas the separate market for the higher-quality stuff usually comes from, uh, you know, a personal household. A friend or a drug dealer you know on a personal level."

Disadvantaged cannabis users, on the other hand, might be buying lower-grade cannabis for lower prices. Many cannabis users, however, would be getting medium-quality cannabis in their neighborhood at discounted rates in rather large amounts (possibly when supplying their friends as "middlemen").

3.1.4.2 Cannabis price determinants in the Czech Republic

In Table 6, we present a model, which explained about 18% of the variation in prices paid per gram in the Czech Republic. In determining the cannabis price in the Czech Republic, the amount obtained on the occasion of the last purchase was

9 The quote was referring to the fact that in Florida, two levels of prices were commonly mentioned by the respondents – 50 USD per 1/8 of an ounce as a standard or original price, and 60 USD for the same amount as a "taxed" price that entered the market at some point in 2008 or 2009. The advantage of having a friend could then mean that one was charged the standard price instead of the inflated one.

a significant factor, as well as whether the respondent purchased indoor cannabis, felt any risk during the last transaction, grew his own marijuana or if he/she had tried to cut down on cannabis use in the last 12 months.

Table 6: Determinants of cannabis prices per gram paid on the occasion of the last purchase in the Czech Republic[10]

price per gram:	**100 to 199 CZK**		**200 CZK or more**	
BASE OUTCOME: price per gram < 100 CZK	Odds ratio	Standard error	Odds ratio	Standard error
Amount of last cannabis purchased (*categorical variable*)[a]	0.527	0.303	0.304*	0.180
Last time got indoor marijuana	2.032	1.201	4.146*	2.537
Did not feel any risk during last purchase	0.089**	0.070	0.064***	0.051
The buyer initiated contact last time	3.030	1.733	2.476	1.482
Last time got marijuana in a private place, home or dealer's place	0.743	0.480	0.575	0.386
Got marijuana from a friend, relative or somebody he knew	0.281	0.192	0.267	0.191
How many of the people you know sell but do not grow marijuana (*continuous var.*)	1.025	0.070	1.041	0.071
Last time got indoor marijuana/ grew himself	0.375	0.395	0.038*	0.055
Gender: male	0.647	0.476	1.968	1.633
Age attained last birthday (*continuous var.*)	1.019	0.034	1.024	0.035
Social status: unemployed	1.697	1.569	0.881	0.851
Demand for cannabis/frequency of cannabis use in the last 12 months (*categorical var.*)[b]	1.170	0.316	1.567	0.440
Tried to cut down cannabis use in last year	1.938	1.095	5.575**	3.342
Population size in the place of residence over 1 million	0.893	0.927	1.076	1.160
Prob > chi2	0.0039			
Pseudo R2 (McFadden)	0.1800			
N	138			
Log likelihood	-118.28			
* p<0.05, ** p<0.01, *** p<0.001				

[a] Categories coded as 1 – less than 5g, 2 – 5 to 10g, 3 – more than 10g
[b] Categories coded as 1 – last year but not last month, 2 – last month but not last week , 3 – once a week or more often, 4 – several times per week. 5 – every day
SOURCE: CS 2008

10 If not stated otherwise, the independent variables are binomial, coded as 1 – positive outcome, 0 – negative outcome.

Overall, when the respondent felt no risk, s/he was more likely to pay a price corresponding to the lowest category than either of the higher prices (100–199 CZK or more than 200 CZK).

Apart from that, there was no significant difference between the likelihood of paying below 100 CZK and of paying 100–199 CZK per gram.

At the same time, purchases for more than 200 CZK were about four times more likely to occur if the type of cannabis was “indoor” and 5.5 times more likely if the respondent had wanted to cut down on cannabis use in the last 12 months. On the other hand, the respondents were less likely to pay this price if they purchased in larger quantities, or if they were cannabis growers themselves.

The outcomes of the multinomial analysis of the Czech survey data on cannabis markets demonstrate that only higher-grade indoor cannabis has a fully developed market with discount mechanisms. In other transactions, a network of free-of-charge acquisitions or low-priced outdoor cannabis prevails.

While the Czech cannabis users get better prices in situations where no risk is perceived (presumably, when dealing with trusted individuals), the term “friend” was not found to be significant in general cannabis market situations.

To conclude, the analysis suggests that while in both places, the cannabis price is somehow influenced by the risks taken in the purchase situation, it had more features of “social supply” or “friendly terms” in the U.S. (the place with more punitive drug policy in our analysis). The norms were as follows:

> “Not bringing friends over when you’re picking up, unassociated friends that the dealer wouldn’t know...” [Andrew]

This resulted in a situation in which marijuana users often make purchases on behalf of fellow-users. This norm served the purpose of reducing the risks. Jamel explained:

> “If you get too many people going in and out of your house and you start dealing with people that you don’t know very well… They might come in with a gun and say: give me your money.”

For those accepted by the seller, it means that friendly manners have to be manifested and maintained, including using cannabis with the dealer. We will discuss the risks in the next section.

3.2 Cannabis use risks in relation to means of acquisition

The percentage of last-year cannabis users in the population aged 15–64 was higher in the Czech Republic than in the U.S. (15 % had used cannabis in the past 12 months in the Czech Republic in contrast to 12 % in the U.S. in 2008). As Table 7 depicts, despite the overall lower last-year prevalence of cannabis use, the U.S. last-year users tend to use cannabis more frequently (2 % had used it daily in the U.S., in contrast to 1 % in the Czech Republic).

A number of situations were described by our U.S. respondents in which cannabis use was present in 'friendly' market situations, as well as in social settings where there was a risk of not being able to get cannabis the next day.

For instance, in order to be able to call a dealer 'a friend', certain rules had to be followed, such as "hanging out" with the dealer, at least in order not to induce a flow of people coming in and out of the house at short intervals, and thus lowering the risk of the dealer being detected.

Table 7: Frequency of marijuana use in the Czech Republic and in the U.S. according to 2008 population surveys (weighted outcomes).

The Czech Republic			United States		
	of total	of last year	of total	of last year	
every day or almost every day	1%	5%	2%	15%	20-30 days a month
several times per week	1%	9%	1%	10%	6-19 days a month
once a week or more often	3%	18%	2%	13%	3-5 days a month
once a month or more often	4%	24%	3%	22%	1-2 days a month
last year but not last month	7%	44%	5%	41%	less than once a month
LAST YEAR	15%	100%	12%	100%	*LAST YEAR*
used in their LIFETIME but not last year	19%		37%		*used in their LIFETIME but not last year*
NEVER used marijuana	66%		51%		*NEVER used marijuana*
TOTAL	100%		100%		*TOTAL*

SOURCE: CS 2008, NSDUH 2008

The normality of dealer-friendship relationships was witnessed by the respondents, making a non-friendship business model a special case:

> "Sometimes it's sort of refreshing when you deal with someone you don't have to hang out with. You know it's going to be a quick deal. Sometimes it's easy, 'cause you don't really want to hang out." [Truman]

At the same time, for most cannabis users, smoking with their dealer at the point of purchase in order to comply with social norms related to the dealer-friendship relationship meant driving home under the influence of cannabis:

> "So not only did I just buy an illegal substance, but now I'm high off of that illegal substance. And now I'm going to drive home. You know, like, I don't feel very good about that." [Rodney]

Second, being the middleman, although not a monetarily rewarded one, could bring "benefits" in further smoking situations, i.e.:

> "I'm getting it for them; they will definitely smoke with me. And they appreciate it. It's nice to do things for people you know." [Kristen]

Another possible benefit of being a middleman was getting more cannabis for oneself.

> "These two girls, they smoke a lot more than I do, so I don't mind introducing you to them so that way I don't have to worry about it, you know... but he was, like, no; I trust you, so I think you should go ahead and continue to play the middleman role. Whenever you do, I'll make sure to give you something to smoke." [Douglas]

Last but not least, friendship networks in cannabis-related social situations produced certain norms about sharing cannabis that could lead to greater-than-normal use. The role of cannabis sharing seemed to go beyond altruism, rather ensuring that over the course of the time, when a disruption in the market happened, "*friends*" would be able to help one another out:

> "You know it's not really that available but if you can get your hands on some then, you know, we'll share it like that." [Frank]
> "And you're, yeah, so you're able to share with your friends, knowing that they will do the same for you later." [Roy]

The users described numerous situations in which reciprocity resulted in a circle of sharing situations that reinforced one another, using the term "to smoke somebody out" for situations where they offered their own marijuana to share with someone who did not have it on him (see also Werse and Bernard in this volume):

> "It's kind of, like, I smoke you out, you smoke me out, that kind of thing. With people that you're going to hang out with more than once, that's usually how it is." [Pamela]
> "I've had friends, like, they almost feel guilty if I smoke them out too much if they don't. They're like 'oh, I haven't smoked you out for like…'" [Andrew]

Truman provided a similar account, stating that his friends actually served to compensate for him not buying marijuana, since he was trying to cut down:

> "I used to be, but not lately. I used to be a fairly regular smoker. It was pretty good that I was only buying it, like, half the time. So it seems to work; I think you know. It's only fair that you have friends that you get high and then they get you high." [Truman]

4 Discussion and conclusions

We showed that purchasing cannabis from "a friend" is a more common feature of cannabis markets in the U.S. than in the Czech Republic. Sourcing cannabis from a "friend (dealer)" was a significant factor influencing the price of marijuana on the U.S. market. While it was an insignificant factor in the Czech Republic, the qualitative analysis suggests that "friendly" terms are important in acquisition settings where there are more risks (to suppliers). This would suggest a greater appearance of 'social supply' or purchases from 'friends' for a lower price in the country/state where cannabis policy is stricter (as of the year 2008).

Apart from the finding that in the U.S. "friends" are expected to purchase for other "friends" on demand, our qualitative study revealed the term 'friend' as a synonym for 'dealer' (highlighting the problems with identifying actual 'social supply'). An unknown proportion of dealers can thus be expected to appear in acquisitions from 'friends', as well as in situations in which a higher price was paid. Social supply per se, users acquiring cannabis for fellow users, manifested itself as a drug policy outcome as dealers tried to avoid meeting new, unaccredited customers in the U.S. where drug policy is stricter.

In the U.S. the prevalence of cannabis use was lower than in the Czech Republic. On the other hand, a greater proportion of the respondents was using cannabis on a daily basis. We found several mechanisms through which strict drug policy could influence this pattern, as well as other risks associated with cannabis use. Among them, using cannabis with the dealer to manifest 'friendly' behaviour and to lower the risks of detection was an important issue (while, at least in some cases, it created the risk of drugged driving). In addition, cannabis users supplying their friends were rewarded by free smoking, and the very common habit of cannabis sharing would help sustain one's supply when there was a shortage on the market.

In the Czech Republic, users were paying significantly lower prices for cannabis in situations where they "felt no risk" – unrelated to whether the seller was labelled as a 'friend' or not. This demonstrates that 'safer' markets might exist in places with less strict drug laws. At the same time these might be less embedded in closed social networks or in what is referred to as "friendship" or "social supply". In addition, given the specific tradition of the country and the long-term tolerance for outdoor cannabis cultivation, a distinct social supply environment where cannabis is given away for free emerged in the Czech Republic. As a result, the last-year prevalence of cannabis use is higher in the country where cannabis use is more tolerated by the law. However, the frequency of use among these users is somewhat lower – part of this might be due to the absence of using cannabis as a means to mitigating drug policy risks.

Our analysis suggests that the more punitive the drug policy is for users, the more likely they are to integrate into closed use-supply networks. These social networks are demanding on users with respect to specific patterns of use that require sharing, reciprocity, and thus more frequent use in order to secure supply chains. This is in line with the fact that there is no evidence that drug policies have an impact on the prevalence of drug use (Reinarman et al. 2004), but rather on the extent of the harm resulting from substance use (Reuter & Stevens 2007). The illicit market and its mechanisms were shown in our study to be a transmission mechanism from drug policy to the harms of drug use.

References

Biernacki, P., & Waldorf, D. (1981). Snowball sampling: Problems and techniques of chain referral sampling. *Sociological Methods & Research, 10*(2), 141-163.

Caulkins, J. P., & Pacula, R. L. (2006). Marijuana markets: Inferences from reports by the household population. *Journal of Drug Issues*, 36(1): 173-200.

Coomber, R., & Turnbull, P. (2007). Arenas of drug transactions: adolescent cannabis transactions in England—social supply. *Journal of Drug Issues, 37*(4), 845-865.

Coomber, R., & Moyle, L. (2013). Beyond drug dealing: Developing and extending the concept of 'social supply' of illicit drugs to 'minimally commercial supply'. *Drugs: Education, Prevention and Policy*, 21(2): 157-164.

Hamid, A. (1991): Crack: new directions in drug research. Part 1. Differences between the marijuana economy and the cocaine/crack economy. *Substance Use & Misuse*, 26(8): 825-836.

Hosmer, D.W., Lemeshow, D. & Sturdivant, R (2013). Applied Logistic Regression, 3rd Edition, John Wiley & sons. 528 p.

Jacques, S., & Allen, A. (2014). Bentham's Sanction Typology and Restrictive Deterrence: A Study of Young, Suburban, Middle-Class Drug Dealers. *Journal of Drug Issues*, 44(2): 212-230.

Moyle, L., Coomber, R., & Lowther, J. (2013). Crushing a walnut with a sledge hammer? Analysing the penal response to the social supply of illicit drugs. *Social & Legal Studies*, 22(4): 553-573.

Nicholas, R (2008). The Impacts of Social Networks and Not-For-Profit Illicit Drug Dealing on Illicit Dug Markets in Australia, Hobart, Tasmania: National Drug Law Research Fund.

Parker, H., Aldridge, J. & Measham, F. (1998). Illegal leisure: The normalization of adolescent recreational drug use. Adolescence and society series. London: Routledge.

Patton, M. Q. (2002). Qualitative Research & Evaluation Methods. Thousand Oaks: Sage Publications.

Potter, G. (2009). Exploring retail level drug distribution: Social supply, 'real' dealers and the user/dealer interface. T. Demetrovics, J. Fountain, & L. Kraus, (eds.), Old and New Policies, Theories, Research Methods and Drug Users Across Europe. Lengerich: Pabst Science Publishers.

Reinarman, C., Cohen, P. D. A., & Kaal, H. L. (2004). The Limited Relevance of Drug Policy: Cannabis in Amsterdam and in San Francisco. *American Journal of Public Health*, 94(5): 836-842.

Reuter, P., & Stevens, A. (2007). An Analysis of UK Drug Policy. A Monograph Prepared for the UK Drug Policy Commission. London: UK Drug Policy Commission.

Sandberg, S. (2012). The Importance of Culture for Cannabis Markets Towards an Economic Sociology of Illegal Drug Markets. *British Journal of Criminology*, 52(6): 1133-1151.

Taylor, M., & Potter, G. R. (2013). From "Social Supply" to "Real Dealing": Drift, Friendship, and Trust in Drug Dealing Careers. *Journal of Drug Issues*, 43(4): 392-406.

Wilkins, C. (2001). A "new institutional economics" approach to the reliability of street-level drug transactions. *Contemporary Drug Problems*, 28(4): 679-693.

"The distribution of illicit drugs" (TDID) – general results. Quantitative findings from a study on socially inconspicuous drug users and dealers in Germany

Bernd Werse and Christiane Bernard

Abstract

This chapter presents a mainly quantitative overview of the German mixed-methods research project "The Distribution of Illicit Drugs". The main objective was to explore the profit and non-profit driven distribution of illicit drugs in socially inconspicuous settings and thus in a field that makes up a much bigger proportion of the phenomenon than the much-discussed public, socially conspicuous drug scenes. In total, 214 drug users of whom the majority had also distributed drugs, were interviewed.

The results indicate that dealing activities within networks of recreational drug users are, to a large extent, not profit-driven and often carried out as a favour to friends. However, even among those who had made at least some money by selling drugs, gaining profit was usually not the priority. Only a small minority of retail sales was carried out with the intention to make as much money as possible. It has to be noted, though, that a substantial part of drug distribution activities is completely free of charge – in the form of shared drugs and gift giving. This high significance of (often mutual) sharing, social supply, and minimally commercial supply appears to be driven by the particular conditions of the illegal market.

1 Introduction

The following results are based on a research project focusing on the retail level of drug distribution. Unlike stereotypical images of drug dealers and users in public settings, regular recreational drug users appear to be more likely to obtain drugs in private surroundings rather than street markets (e.g., Murphy et al. 1990; Caulkins & Pacula 2006; Harrison et al. 2007; Werse 2008a). Furthermore, a substantial proportion of drug distribution seems to be carried out on a not-for-profit basis as a mutual supply of illicit substances by fellow users – a phenomenon commonly referred to as "social supply" (Coomber & Turnbull 2007). To shed more light on this largely unexplored group of users as well as this level of the drug market and its situation in Germany, the research project "The distribution of illicit drugs" was set up, funded by the German Research Foundation (DFG). In contrast to most research on illicit drug acquisition and distribution that aim at marginalised users, our study explicitly focused on illicit drugs users with a relatively high socioeconomic status who do not meet any criteria for problem drug users (PDUs). In doing so, the project aimed to gain insights into the typical structures and procedures of drug acquisitions and sales among this specific group – a subject on which there is little research internationally (see above, plus, e.g.: Jacinto et al. 2008, Duffy et al. 2008, Potter 2009, Belackova & Vaccaro 2013, Taylor & Potter 2013, Jacques & Allen 2014), let alone in German-speaking countries (only: Werse 2008b, Genterczewsky 2008, Bernard & Werse 2013).

Drawing mainly on quantitative data, this paper presents general findings on the non-profit distribution of drugs, characteristics of profit-driven dealing activities, intersections between both segments, and specifics of drug purchases. In the discussion section, we use some quotes from the qualitative interviews to illustrate and assess our quantitative findings.

2 Methods

The target group were current recreational illicit drug users, in particular persons experienced in distributing drugs. Participants had to be experienced illicit drug users with several years of use *and* use of any illicit substance within the last 12 months. In order to exclude problem drug users and to ensure social inconspicuousness, participants had to meet the following additional criteria:

a. having a fixed abode,
b. having never utilized harm reduction or treatment services associated with the setting of street drug scenes, and
c. having finished an apprenticeship or university degree, several years of steady employment and/or parental home duties, or currently in training/apprenticeship/university.

The study aimed to recruit at least 200 recreational illicit drug users, especially users with experience in dealing drugs. Participants were recruited through snowball or chain referral sampling (Waldorf & Biernacki 1981). Interviewees were compensated 20 Euros for their time and participation in the study. Adopting the element of the incentive system of "respondent-driven sampling" (RDS) (Heckathorn 1997), those interviewees who successfully referred other respondents, were paid 10 Euros for each recruited respondent. Experienced social researchers conducted most of the interviews, while some interviews were conducted by social science students. Due to the high significance of intensive fieldwork for the recruitment process, three interviewers (two qualified researchers and one student) carried out the vast part of the interviews.

The interviews consisted of two parts: A guided qualitative biographical interview focusing on the development and context of drug use, drug acquisition and, if applicable, drug distribution, was followed by a standardised questionnaire, which contained detailed questions on:

- socio-demographic data,
- prevalence and patterns of use of licit and illicit drugs,
- sharing and gift-giving of drugs,
- drug purchases,
- distributing drugs, with or without profit (including motives, avoiding criminal prosecution, etc.) and
- other criminal behaviour.

Applying this procedure, we collected both, detailed quantitative data on modes of drug distribution as well as a large qualitative database on the same issue, including its context such as the setting and social background, as well as changes, developments, and turning points within careers of recreational drug users. Taken together, this information allowed for specific qualitative analyses from a biographical point of view (see Werse in this volume). In addition to general information on socio-demographics, the prevalence and patterns of use of different drugs and the prevalence of different modes of drug acquisition and supply, we mainly utilized the quantitative data for comparing different groups of drug users with regard to various distribution aspects.

Data collection took place between November 2010 and March 2012. A total of 214 persons were interviewed, mostly in Frankfurt or other places in the Frankfurt/Rhein-Main metropolitan area (39% respectively). All interviews were conducted face-to-face and were audio taped with consent. Most interviews (83%) took place in the respondents' home, while some were conducted in an office room at the university, in public places such as parks or cafés or at the respondent's workplace.

On average, the interviews lasted 76 minutes, with a range of 30 to 180 minutes. All interviews were transcribed verbatim. To ensure confidentiality, any information that could identify participants was removed from the transcripts.

Quantitative data was analysed using SPSS (20), applying standard statistical procedures. The qualitative interviews were analysed with content analysis in accordance to Mayring (2000) using MaxQDA.

3 Sample description

76% of the 214 respondents were male. The average age of the interviewees was 29.9 years, ranging from 16 to 58 years. The educational level of the sample was very high. This is most likely due to the mode of recruitment and the fieldwork itself which was mainly carried out among students and other persons with an academic background: 84% of participants had finished their secondary school with a university-entrance diploma (German “Abitur”), 12% had left secondary school with a level I certificate (“Realschulabschluss”), and 2% with the lower “Hauptschulabschluss”. Only two persons (1%) had not graduated at all. Almost a third (31%) were enrolled at a university at the time of the interview (most of them in social science, economic sciences or law), 53% worked full- or part-time (including self-employment) and only 6% were unemployed. There is a clear tendency towards social and educational occupations (social workers, teachers, etc.), which accounted for 20% of the whole sample. 11% of the participants had a commercial occupation, 10% worked in the service sector (e.g., IT, advertisement, design), 6% in gastronomy (cook, hotel staff etc.), and 5% could be classified as blue-collar workers or craftsmen. 95% had a German citizenship – a relatively high number compared to the general population (91.8%)[1].

Regarding the marital and relationship status, 45% were single and unmarried. 41% were unmarried, but lived in a steady relationship, only 7% were married and 3% divorced (others: 4%). Among the 20% respondents with own children, 64% lived with their child(ren) in the same household.

4 Results

4.1 Drug use

All respondents had used cannabis and more than 90% other illicit substances in their lifetime (see table 1). Almost all were current illicit drug users (use in the previous 30 days): more than four in five respondents had used cannabis and half had used at least one other illicit substance in the last month (amphetamine/speed

1 http://www.crp-infotec.de/01deu/einwohner/auslaender.html, 10-15-2013

being in this regard the most prevalent drug, followed by cocaine and ecstasy/MDMA)[2].

Table 1: Prevalence of lifetime, past year and past month use of different drugs among the sample (%; n=214)

	Lifetime	Past year	Past month
Cannabis	100	95	83
Illicit drugs other than cannabis	92	70	51
Amphetamine	82	58	36
Cocaine	80	57	23
Ecstasy/ MDMA	79	44	22
Psychedelic mushrooms	72	17	3
LSD	50	18	5
GHB/ GBL	25	9	1
Ketamine	17	12	7
Heroin	14	1	0.5
Crystal Meth	14	4	1
Crack cocaine	5	0	0
Opium	12	*	*
Salvia Divinorum	11	*	*
"Spice"/synthetic cannabis/synthetic cannabinoids	17	*	*
Other new psychoactive substances/research chemicals	8	*	*

* no information (lifetime prevalence derived from open question in the questionnaire)

As shown in table 1, there are also high proportions for lifetime use of LSD and psychedelic mushrooms, as well as significant proportions of respondents who had used drugs such as ketamine[3], heroin, crystal meth, opium, salvia divinorum, and new psychoactive substances.

Relatively large proportions of respondents were frequent users: 43% used cannabis on a (nearly) daily basis (20 times in the last month or more)[4], and 13%

2 Since there are only significant sub-samples of experienced users who provided information on purchasing and trading these four substances, the following results are restricted to these drugs.

3 The relatively high amounts of last-year- and last-month-prevalence for ketamine (compared to lifetime use) mainly result from a subsample of respondents from the Frankfurt-based dance party scene, where ketamine was somewhat popular at the time of the interviews.

4 20% of the respondents, respectively, used cannabis either 1 to 5 times or 6 to 19 times a month.

used other illicit substances more than 5 times in the last month[5]. All of these results indicate that the sample mainly consists of subjects with a relatively strong leaning towards drug *use*.

With regard to gender differences, women showed a slightly lower lifetime prevalence of drugs other than cannabis (80% vs. 96%, $Chi^2=12.6$, $p<0.001$), but an almost identical rate for the use of these substances during the prior month (women: 51% vs. 50%, $Chi^2=0.0$, n.s.). Current cannabis use (past month) was less prevalent among women (73%) than among men (86%; $Chi^2=4.8$, $p<0.05$). In addition, less women than men were frequent cannabis users (more than 20 times in the prior month: 29% vs. 47%, $Chi^2=4.7$, $p<0.05$). The gender difference for frequent use of drugs other than cannabis (several times a week) showed no statistical significance, due to the small sub-sample (8% vs. 15%, $Chi^2=1.6$, n.s.).

According to their frequency and experience in drug use, we defined four similar sized groups of respondents: 1) 'Experimental users' (24%) were participants who had either never used any illicit drug other than cannabis *or* who had not used any other illicit substance other than cannabis more than five times in their life. 2) 'Experienced users' (23%) were defined as individuals who had used any illicit substance other than cannabis more than five times but less than 40 times in their life. The group of 3) 'skilled users' (23%) was defined as having consumed any illicit substance other than cannabis for at least 40 but less than 200 times in their life, whereas respondents who had used any illicit drug other than cannabis for 200 times or more in their life were defined as 4) 'intensive users' (29%).

Although the sample consists of individuals who had used different illicit drugs, and this sometimes rather frequently, even when compared to other drug-experienced populations (Kemmesies 2004), it has to be pointed out again that none of the interviewees could be categorised as a marginalised problem drug user (as required in the eligibility criteria).

4.2 Drug acquisition

Half of the cannabis users stated to (mostly) buy this drug themselves; while about one fifth said that they mostly receive it for free from others who share their cannabis with them. About one fourth reported to buy cannabis or use it free of charge equally often (see table 2). In contrast, only about one third of the amphetamine,

5 Of these respondents, four persons (2% of the whole sample) reported using either speed or cocaine 20 times or more in the prior month. Another 38% used at least one illicit drug other than cannabis in the last month, but none of these substances more than five times.

cocaine and ecstasy users mostly purchased the respective drug, while roughly two fifths mainly obtained it for free (table 2). These higher rates for free participation of these substances seem to reflect the fact that amphetamine, ecstasy and cocaine are, on average, consumed far less often than cannabis. Consequently, there was a significant positive correlation between drug purchase and frequency of use in the last month (see 4.1), both for cannabis ($\tau_b=0.237$, $p<0.001$) and for the most prevalent ‚other' illicit drug amphetamine ($\tau_b= 0.252$, $p<0.01$). Our results suggest that moderate drug users are likely to acquire a considerable part of the substances they use free of charge through participating in other users' drug supplies.

Table 2: Modes of acquisition of the four most prevalent drugs (percentage of respondents)

	Mostly buying	Buying and receiving for free equally often	Mostly receiving for free
Cannabis (n=214)	50	28	22
Amphetamine (n=138)	32	30	38
Cocaine (n=119)	33	23	44
Ecstasy/ MDMA (n=117)	36	26	38

Considerable differences were observed between male and female respondents: women were more likely to receive cannabis (almost) exclusively for free than men (26% vs. 8%, $Chi^2=11.2$, $p<0.01$). A similar correlation appeared for ecstasy (28% vs. 11%, $Chi^2=4.4$, $p<0.05$), while the less pronounced gender differences regarding the acquisition of cocaine (33% vs. 18%) and amphetamine (23% vs. 17%) showed no statistical significance. With regard to all drugs being acquired, 28% of the female respondents stated to receive all of them mostly for free, while this is true for only 6% of the males ($Chi^2=17.7$, $p<0.001$). These differences cannot just be explained by the (slightly) less frequent patterns of use by the women in the sample – thus, female drug users seem to be generally more likely to receive drugs for free.

The high significance of sharing drugs among recreational drug users also becomes apparent with regard to the question whether the respondents share their own drugs with others: 74% of the cannabis users stated that they do so often or almost in every case. A similar percentage rate was observed for amphetamine (67%), while ecstasy (54%) and cocaine (55%) were shared slightly less frequently. According to the high percentage rates, receiving and sharing drugs for free appear to be a mutual behaviour, i.e. those who receive free drugs from others are also likely to share their own drugs.

Free drug use not only comes in the form of sharing, but also as gift giving: 92% of all respondents had ever received drugs as a gift, and the same percentage was observed for the lifetime experience of giving drugs as a gift. 34% received drugs as gifts in the prior month, while 39% reported giving such gifts in the past month. The highest proportions of respondents who had ever received or given drugs as gifts were observed for cannabis (receiving: 88%, giving: 89%), followed by amphetamine (66% & 68%) and ecstasy (56% & 55%). Probably due to its relatively high price, cocaine, in contrast, was far less likely to be received (31%) or given (25%) as a gift[6]. The vast majority of gift giving took place between well-known persons: 95% of those who had ever received cannabis as a gift got it at least once from friends, acquaintances or partners, while 8% had received free cannabis from dealers and 2% from strangers.

When it comes to the actual purchase of drugs, friends and acquaintances play an outstanding role: As table 3 shows, nearly every respondent had bought cannabis from a person he/she knew well at least once and for nearly two thirds, this was the (almost) exclusive mode of cannabis supply. Similar proportions were observed for the three other frequently used illicit drugs amphetamine, ecstasy/MDMA, and cocaine. Beyond friends, only private dealers[7] played a significant role as a regular source for purchasing drugs: About one quarter of the respective users bought cannabis and other drugs almost exclusively from private dealers, while only small proportions had never done so (see table 3). Street markets were, to some extent, only relevant for purchasing cannabis: About two thirds of the cannabis users had ever bought from a street dealer, while the respective proportions for amphetamine, ecstasy/MDMA and cocaine were much lower. However, only one respondent stated that buying cannabis in public settings was his (almost) exclusive way of purchase. Apart from that, considerable proportions had ever grown their own cannabis or had bought the substance in a Dutch "coffeeshop", while very few used these options (almost) exclusively. When looking at synthetic drugs, the purchase in semi-public club settings was somewhat relevant: more than half of the amphetamine and ecstasy/MDMA users had ever bought from a club dealer. Again, very few of the synthetic drugs users reported this to be their regular mode of purchase (see table 3).

6 Percentages refer to those who have ever used the respective drug and gave an answer to these questions.

7 During the interviews, it was sometimes hard to distinguish between "friends" and "private dealers" (e.g. when friends sold drugs for profit or dealers turned into friends over time; see also Belackova & Vaccaro 2013). In these cases, usually a distinction was made depending on the question whether respondents also spend leisure time with sellers with no drug dealing being involved.

Table 3: Modes of drug purchase (%, percentages refer to those who had used the respective drug and gave information on the mode of purchase)

	Cannabis (n=212)		Amphetamine (n=131)		Ecstasy/MDMA (n=115)		Cocaine (n=113)	
	ever used	(almost) always	ever used	(almost) always	ever used	(almost) always	ever used	(almost) always
Friends/ acquaintances	98	64	97	62	90	58	90	50
Private dealers	84	27	66	24	60	22	62	27
Street dealers	64	0.5	8	0	3	1	14	2
Club dealers	*	*	60	2	66	3	24	3
Dutch "coffeeshops"	60	1	*	*	*	*	*	*
Home growing	51	1	*	*	*	*	*	*

* answer option not available

Generally, it can be concluded that among socially integrated drug users purchasing drugs in public spaces seems to be the exception rather than the rule. The proportions of regular illicit drug users who mostly buy from friends or acquaintances are remarkably high: e.g., even 54% of the *daily* cannabis users almost exclusively buy from this kind of persons. Hence, fellow users within peer groups appear to play a crucial role for the distribution of illicit drugs among recreational users. However, Belackova & Vaccaro (2013) stressed that the definition of 'friendship' in networks of recreational drug users often works as a (symbolic) measure of social control and protection against legal consequences, so that some 'friendships' only exist as a stable relationship for the procurement of drugs (see also Belackova & Zabransky in this volume).

This observation fits into the respondents' answers to the question for strategies to reduce the risk of criminal prosecution regarding drug purchases[8]: for two thirds, the exclusive purchase from friends or acquaintances was in this regard an important strategy, and 35% mentioned having a steady supplier as a protective measure. However, the most frequently stated way of reducing these risks associated with buying drugs was to avoid talking about drugs on the telephone (75%). A majority of respondents (59%) also reported the exclusive purchase within private surroundings (e.g. apartments). Only one respondent referred to the anonymity of purchases in public settings as a protective measure.

8 The questionnaire allowed for multiple answers to this question.

Buying drugs from a regular supplier (e.g., 72% of the cannabis users stated to mostly buy from a steady dealer) not only provides some protection against legal consequences, but may also ensure the quality of drugs. Since 57% of the respondents had ever purchased fake drugs, this seems to be a significant issue. The majority of such fake purchases were reported for cannabis: 44% of those who had ever bought the substance had obtained fake cannabis at least once. In comparison, the proportions for amphetamine (20%), ecstasy (19%) and cocaine (10%) were much lower. Fake drugs were mostly bought from unknown persons in public: e.g., 69% of those who had ever purchased fake cannabis got it from a street dealer or another stranger. In 72% of the cases, faked amphetamine and ecstasy were purchased from a dealer in a club or at a party. These uncertainties when it comes to buying drugs in (semi-) public settings may largely contribute to the fact that the vast majority of users prefer to purchase within private settings.

4.3 Drug dealing

Roughly four out of five respondents (79%) had ever distributed illicit drugs and nearly one third (31%) had done so in the prior month. With the exception of one respondent, all had ever supplied others with cannabis and 55% with other illicit substances at least once (41% amphetamine, 36% ecstasy or MDMA, and 28% cocaine) in their life. However, 55% stated their dealing activities to be mostly or exclusively not profit-oriented and roughly one quarter (23%) had never made any profit from selling drugs. Therefore, it has to be noted that the term “drug dealing” is somewhat misleading, since a considerable part of these transactions is carried out with no profit as social supply among fellow users.
Table 4 shows the extent of “dealing” experience for the four most prevalent drugs. The distribution of cannabis was much more prevalent than the sale of other drugs. Furthermore, the average number of times the respondents sold drugs was much higher for cannabis than for amphetamine, ecstasy/MDMA or cocaine.

When compared to the other three illicit substances, the much higher number of cannabis sales might have also contributed to the fact that cannabis was less likely to be sold without profit. While only every fourth supplier reported an exclusively non-profit-oriented sale of marijuana or hashish, the respective proportions for cocaine (39%), ecstasy (33%) and amphetamine (32%) were significantly higher. It can be said that most of those who had ever distributed cannabis simply had more opportunities to gain at least some profit through selling.

Table 4: Frequency of distributing drugs in lifetime (%; percentages refer to all respondents who ever sold any illicit drug)

	Cannabis	Amphetamine	Ecstasy/MDMA	Cocaine
Never	1	59	64	72
1-10 times	10	10	12	15
11-50 times	24	14	10	8
51-200 times	22	9	5	1
More than 200 times	44	9	8	5

The extent of using illicit drugs except cannabis, as well as the frequency of current cannabis use correlated with drug dealing: e.g., only 37% of those who had never used any substance other than cannabis more than five times, had ever made any profit through selling drugs, while this was true for 77% of those who had used at least one 'other' illicit drug more than 200 times ($Chi^2=22.4$, $p<0.001$). 49% of the daily cannabis users had sold drugs in the prior month, while this only applied to 22% of the non-daily users ($Chi^2=16.3$; $p<0.001$).

Male respondents were not only more likely than females to buy drugs (see 4.2), but also to sell drugs: while 87% of the male participants had ever sold illicit substances, this was true for only 53% of the females ($Chi^2=27.3$, $p<0.001$). Regarding profit-oriented dealing activities, the gender differences were even more pronounced: 71% of the male respondents had ever made profit, this compared to 27% of the females ($Chi^2=31.1$, $p<0.001$). 66% of the men who ever sold drugs and 33% of the respective women stated that they mostly (or exclusively) sold drugs with profit ($Chi^2=10.3$, $p<0.01$). Regarding the types of drugs being sold among the dealing-experienced respondents, no significant gender differences were found. In addition to the general lower proportion of women who had ever sold drugs, the extent of their dealing activities was significantly lower than for men: 21% of the dealing-experienced women had never sold any type of drug more than ten times, this compared to only 5% of the respective men. And while 51% of the male respondents who had ever dealt any type of drug had done so more than 200 times, this was only true for 25% of the females ($Chi^2=12.7$, $p<0.05$)[9].

When asked about the motivational background for distributing drugs (fig. 1), the vast majority agreed to the motive "friendly turn" (81% chose 4 or 5 on a five-item-scale ranging from 1 "absolutely disagree" to 5 "absolutely agree").

9 At least one drug more than 10 times, but no drug more than 50 times: men: 20%, women: 29%; at least one drug more than 50 times, but no drug more than 200 times: men: 24%, women: 25%.

Among those who did not sell for profit, this was usually the only motivation stated.

Figure 1: Motivations for dealing, (scale with five items; %; percentages refer to all respondents who ever sold any illicit drug)

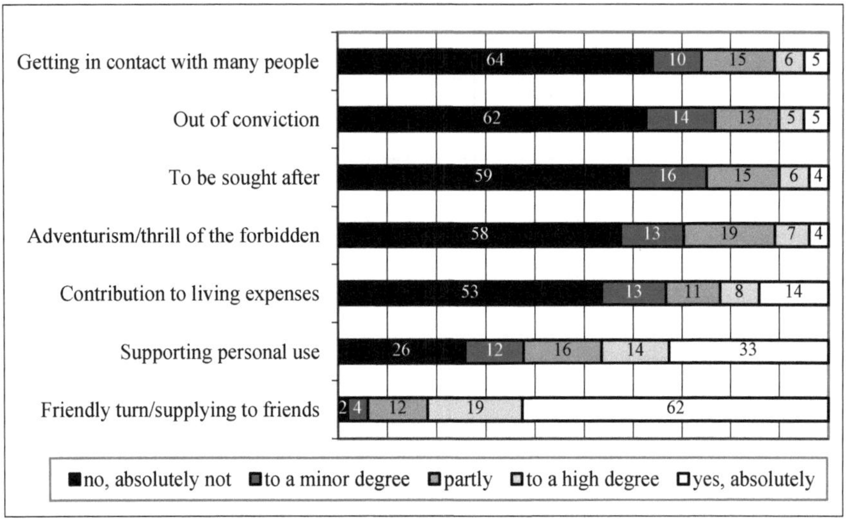

47% of all respondents who had ever sold drugs reported "supporting personal use" to be a relevant motive. Every fourth supplier stated that the financial gain acquired through dealing served as a contribution to living expenses. The other four motives displayed in figure 1 played a role for only about one tenth of the respondents, respectively. These motives refer to attitude/ideology ("adventurism", "out of conviction"), or status ("to be sought after", "contact with many people"). These four motives strongly correlate with each other (all correlations: $p<0.001$).

Consequently, as an opposite pole to those who "drift into dealing" without own efforts, there seems to be a small group who is intrigued by the status of a drug dealer; similar to Katz's "seductions of crime" (Katz 1988). This applied particularly to respondents who had escalated to higher levels of dealing: we found strong correlations between the degree to which respondents agreed to these motives and the revenue they made in their most profitable month ("to be sought after": $r=0.3$; $p<0.001$; "contact with many people": $r=0.6$; $p<0.001$; "conviction", and "adventurism": $r=0.5$; $p<0.001$). In addition, respondents who stated that their dealing activities were mostly geared to make profit, were significantly more likely to agree to these four motives. The results indicate that, the more people earn (or have earned) through distributing drugs, the more they identify with the role of a drug dealer. However, these correlations do not touch the question whether these attitudes were developed before becoming a 'real' dealer or whether they can be rather regarded, in the form of a differential reinforcement (Akers & Burgess 1966), as a result of being a dealer (see Werse & Müller in this volume).

In accordance with "friendly turn" as the most important motive, more than two-thirds of those who had ever sold cannabis (70%), amphetamine, or cocaine (71%, respectively), whether with or without profit, stated that all of their customers were friends or acquaintances. A slightly lower percentage (62%) was observed for those who had ever sold ecstasy/MDMA. Whereas between 18% (cocaine) and 25% (cannabis) reported to mainly sell to steady customers, the sale to a variety of customers (including strangers) was rare. Those selling ecstasy reported the highest proportion of selling to non-steady customers (16%), this compared to only 5% of the large group of cannabis distributors. Thus, the supply side data appear to confirm the notion that the distribution of illicit drugs on the users' level mainly takes place within social networks of fellow users. However, this mainly applied to small-scale transactions, while a higher number of respondents with larger trade volumes were selling drugs to people who did not belong to their network. Among those who had ever earned more than 2,000 Euros a month by dealing drugs, 44% had also sold to non-steady customers, while none of the respondents with revenues less than 50 Euros had done so (Chi^2=43.1; $p<0.001$).

While 45% of those who had ever distributed drugs stated that they had never gained any financial profit, a wide range of revenues showed up for those who had ever made any money by selling drugs: The profit obtained in their most profitable month varied between 2 and 30,000 Euros. On average, they had earned 2,305 Euros in their most profitable month (median: 600 Euros). Taking into account that these data refer to the top-selling month, the typical monthly profit was usually much lower. This is also indicated by the 23 respondents (11% of the total sample) who had also made profit in the previous month, with less than half of them earning more than 200 Euros in this time period (median: 200 €; mean: 621 €; min.: 1 €, max.: 5,000 €).

Furthermore, a relevant proportion of those who had ever sold drugs (17%) stated that they never earned money, but had profited in other ways (mainly by receiving free drugs) at least once. Among all respondents who had ever received free drugs as profit (53% of those who had ever sold drugs), these earnings amounted to 277 Euros on average (median: 120 €) in the most profitable month. Taken together, 24% of those who had ever made profit with dealing drugs had earned up to 100 € (money + free drugs) a month, 27% had earned up to 500 €, and 17% either up to 1,000 € or up to 3,000 €. Only 15% reported revenues of more than 3,000 € in their most profitable month.

Consistent with the general findings pointing to a smaller proportion of female respondents who had ever sold drugs, their profits gained in their best-selling month (money + free drugs) were lower than those made by male respondents. However, due to the small sub-sample, this difference was not statistically significant (AM: 616 € vs. 2,193 €, SD: 1,050 € vs. 4,469 €, median: 175 € vs. 550 €, ANOVA: 1.7, n.s.).

The *relative* profit gained at the last dealing occasion (among those who made any profit at this last occasion) revealed a wide range of percentages. For cannabis, they ranged from 1.3% of the purchase price up to 300%, with a mean of 41% (SD: 39; median: 33; n=67). 25% of those who had made profit with their last cannabis deal did not gain more than 20% of the purchase price. Thus, this part of the retail cannabis market usually reaches relatively moderate margins. Slightly higher values were observed for cocaine (min.: 17, max.: 112, AM: 48, SD: 28, median: 38; n=18). It has to be mentioned, though, that the average purchase price for a gram of cocaine (48.30€) is about seven times higher than the price for cannabis (6.70€), thus the *total* profit made from selling a certain amount of cocaine exceeds by far the profit made from a respective amount of cannabis. The profit margins for synthetic drugs were considerably higher: while the 19 respondents who gave information on the profit of their last amphetamine transaction almost reached one hundred percent on average (min.: 25, max.: 257, AM: 97, SD: 69, median: 67), relative profits from selling ecstasy were even higher, with an average of 176% (min.: 47, max.: 525, SD: 142, median: 100; n=13). Hence, at least within this present subsample of retail drug distributors, synthetic 'party drugs' appear to be the most profitable commodities.

However, when asked about purchase price and sales price of the last occasion for selling cannabis, almost half (48%) of these transactions were without any profit. This supports the notion that social supply is of high importance for this commodity. With 37%, the respective proportion for amphetamine was somewhat lower, while the proportions for those who did not gain profit at their last occasion selling ecstasy (19%) or cocaine (14%) were much lower. However, the low (absolute) numbers of those who provided this kind of information on the last dealing occasion of these substances has to be taken into account (see above).

When looking at the drugs being sold in the most profitable month, 65% of the respondents stated they had only sold cannabis at that time, 12% had only dealt with synthetic drugs, and 2% had exclusively sold cocaine. Another 16% had dealt with cannabis plus cocaine and/or synthetic drugs, while 3% had sold drugs other than the aforementioned. When compared to our findings regarding the frequency of types of drugs distributed in life (table 4), these results indicate that respondents did not significantly tend to turn to ‘harder’ drugs when they had reached the peak of their dealing activity.

With regard to the amount of drugs being bought for retail distribution at the most recent occasion, the average value for cannabis was 242 grams (median: 20g, min.: 1g, max.: 8kg). For amphetamine, this value was 88 grams (median: 10g, min.: 1g, max.: 1kg,), for cocaine 103 grams (median: 7,5g, min.: 1g, max.: 1kg) and for ecstasy 748 pills (median: 100 pills, min.: 1 pill, max: 10,000 pills). The discrepancies between mean and median suggest that, on the one hand, a large percentage of those experienced in dealing drugs only bought relatively small amounts for selling (e.g., 41% of those who ever acquired cannabis in order to sell it did not buy more than 10 grams at the last occasion). On the other hand, some respondents reported the acquisition of extremely large amounts for retail sale – consequently, this applies exclusively to profit-oriented dealers.

Thus, within our sample a wide range of experiences with supplying drugs exists. However, the vast majority of the respondents limited their distribution activities to social supply without making any profit or with only marginal mark-ups. Some of the interviewees, though, had proceeded to higher levels of the drug market. For example, 43 of respondents (25% of those experienced in selling) reported having earned a minimum of 1,000 Euros (money *and* free drugs) at least in one month. While female respondents were generally less likely than men to sell drugs at all, their extent of dealing activities as well as their maximum revenues tended to be lower, too. These results suggest that, even in a sample comprising of relatively frequent drug users (including female respondents), women are much less likely to be involved in distribution activities of these drugs.

4.4 Encounters with law enforcement and strategies to avoid prosecution

43% of those who had ever sold drugs had been charged with a drug offence at least once (mostly due to driving under the influence of drugs or drug possession). However, in half of these cases charges were dropped, a common procedure in Germany when someone is caught with small amounts of cannabis for personal use. Not surprisingly, those involved in dealing activities bear a greater risk of criminal prosecution than drug users not involved in distributing drugs: Only 22% of respondents who had never distributed drugs got into any drug-related conflicts with the law. Besides, it has to be noted that only 14% of the respondents who had sold drugs (and 7% of those who had not) had been charged with a non-drug-related offence, mostly because of minor property offences or traffic violations. Hence, respondents did not seem to be overly likely to be involved in criminal activities other than drug use and drug selling.

For participants who had sold or were still selling drugs, the most common strategy to reduce the risk of criminal prosecution was the exclusive sale to friends or acquaintances (81%). Other important precautions included "no drug talk over the phone" (75%), "limiting the amount of drugs distributed" (60%), "use of code words" (56%) and "limiting the number of customers" (47%). These answers roughly corresponded with those given when asked about precautions for drug purchases (3.3). To some degree, these strategies depended on the profits gained through selling drugs: Whereas almost all respondents who had never earned more than 500 Euros per month stated to exclusively sell to friends, the same only applied to half of those who had earned higher profits. While, consequentially, limiting the quantities was mainly mentioned as a precautionary measure by those with rather low profits, this did (surprisingly) not apply to the limitation of the number of customers. On the other hand, stashing drugs outside the own home was only relevant for respondents trading greater volumes of drugs (more than 500 € per month: 40%; other drug-dealing experienced respondents: 5%). This indicates a certain degree of professionalization of dealing activities, similar to the more specific precautions of some other respondents who reported selling drugs on the middle level: e.g. carrying out drug transactions at special places outside private homes or frequently changing mobile phones or SIM cards. However, it has to be pointed out that even among those with larger trading volumes, the private character of drug dealing still played an important role. Thus, limiting the distribution of drugs to social networks is not only a feature of the lowest distribution level, but also seems to be common among more profit-oriented dealers.

5 Discussion

The present study provides a wide range of data regarding drug distribution activities on the users' level among recreational users, with a strong focus on regular and frequent users, including a substantial proportion of current users of illicit drugs other than cannabis.

With regard to the use-distribution-nexus among recreational users, the sharing and gifting of illicit drugs seem to be common practice – the latter especially applying to the large number of occasional users, who, according to representative surveys (e.g., Pabst et al. 2013; see also Werse 2008b), make up the largest group among current drug users. However, sharing drugs also seems to be common among regular users. According to the high rates of respondents who stated to both buy and share drugs, a high reciprocity of these acts can be assumed, not only for cannabis, but obviously also for amphetamine, ecstasy and cocaine. Yet still there appears to be a certain imbalance for frequent users who seem to be much more likely to provide free drugs to others but less likely to receive drugs free of charge.

Since female users are more likely to receive drugs as a gift than males do, it can be assumed that it is not uncommon for men to share their drugs with their girlfriends or other female friends as some kind of 'gentleman behaviour', similar to paying for drinks (see also Werse 2008b).

In addition to sharing and gift giving, many frequent users also sell drugs to their drug-using friends, although they only partly benefit from these activities (monetarily or in the form of free drugs): While some of these suppliers do not charge friends extra, others add a mark-up to the retail price. This is often justified by the higher risk someone has to take when buying larger amounts of drugs (and consequently fearing harsher punishment when caught by the police): "I do not really earn anything, but I get paid for taking the risk" (Cornholio, 33 years, business economist). Frequently, these persons emphasise that they do not intend to make 'real' money with those deals: "Perhaps one or two Euros per gram, at most. Say, I didn't make a twenty-Euro-rate out of a ten" (Daniel, 28 years, apprentice). This phenomenon has been described as "minimally commercial supply" (Coomber & Moyle 2014, Coomber et al. in this volume).

Particularly regular small-scale dealing within networks of friends is frequently justified by the intention of supporting personal use. Taking into account that prices are considerably lower for larger amounts of drugs, this can be easily put into practice with just a few regular customers.

Our respondents showed a wide range of experiences with social supply as well as minimally and proper commercial supply. This variety was also sometimes observed within our respondents' individual careers: switching from one mode to the other, depending on opportunities, friendship status or other conditions, was quite common. Many respondents had experienced a peak period regarding profit making. Sometimes this was associated with selling illicit drugs other than cannabis, particularly synthetic drugs, that provided the highest profit per sale, but high earnings were also often reached by selling larger amounts of cannabis.

A crucial finding concerns the significance of social networks for drug distribution on the users' level. A large part of drug distribution is carried out among friends, acquaintances or established and long-lasting connections to private sellers. This seems to be largely attributed to the illegality and the limited availability of drugs, which is compensated through social networks of users and the willingness of some, with (temporary) better access, to provide drugs for others. Especially occasional users seem to benefit from this, as they can avoid having to build up relationships with 'real' dealers – a relationship that might be perceived as unpleasant not only because of the deviant character of these relationships but also because dealers often appear to be interested in a 'private' character of these relationships:

> "Then he invited me, and we talked to each other, and, in some way, it was kind of two different worlds clashing. He, the criminal, er, and me, sort of, non-criminal, yeah, an apprentice who does not do any wrong apart from smoking pot. (...) And then, in a sense, you couldn't just leave. Because I didn't want to offend him by saying: 'Look, I can't be arsed to hang around with you! Erm, I just want to get some drugs and leave!' That was simply not possible" (Blueberry, 26 years, craftsman).

The urge of drug dealers to build up friendship-based relations to their customers might be an additional explanation for the crucial role 'social supply' plays among friends: Particularly occasional users seem to have no interest in establishing a 'friendly' relationship to a 'real' dealer. Instead, they prefer trading transactions to take place casually during non-dealing related private encounters.

As mentioned above, the privacy of drug purchases functions as an important protective measure against legal prosecution, both for users and dealers. Just like users are usually not interested in buying drugs of unknown quality from unknown people in public, dealers, especially those working at the bottom end of the drug market, are not interested in serving unknown customers. Moreover, these vendors usually do not want to expand their number of customers, since this goes along with increased conspicuousness and thus an elevated risk of getting caught (for a more theoretical perspective on this aspect, see Vlaemynck in this volume). Hence, most drug dealers researched in this project did not conform to the common rules of market economy (particularly with regard to profit maximisation), and, as implied, are not in line with the stereotype of the greedy 'pusher' who is constantly trying to attract new customers. The existing negative stereotypes that are often associated with the (English) term 'dealer' in German common speech, might be a reason why even most of the respondents who had gained profits through selling drugs rejected this term as a self-description (see also Jacinto et al. 2008; Werse & Müller in this volume).

Generally, most of our respondents did not conform to the motives usually associated with a stereotypical 'dealer': neither a special status within a deviant network nor the acquisitions of larger profits were of significant importance. Much more relevant were motives that referred to the illegality of drugs the distributors mostly used themselves. Apart from (often mutual) 'friendly turns', this mainly refers to supporting personal use. According to the information given by the respondents, the need of social inconspicuousness, along with the desire to separate oneself from criminal surroundings, seems to be very pronounced – not only for mere users, but also for social suppliers and small-scale dealers. Those respondents stating a different motivation were, in contrast, more likely to proceed to higher market levels and/or sold larger amounts of drugs.

Women, on the one hand, are more likely than men to use drugs someone else had bought. On the other hand, and even as regular user, they are less likely to supply drugs, either in the form of non-commercial 'social supply' or as profit-oriented dealing. While men are generally massively overrepresented among regular and frequent drug users, this overrepresentation appears to be even more pronounced with regard to distribution activities[10] (for further information on gender issues of the TDID project, see Bernard in this volume).

To conclude, the presented findings confirm the notion that, to a large extent, the retail level within networks of recreational drug users does neither follow common rules of market economy nor does it usually have direct connections to criminal settings. Regarding socially inconspicuous users (who are by far the largest group of illicit drug users), this is a reasonable feature, since those users are usually respectable people with no criminal records, who wish to stay away from any deviant behaviour other than using illicit drugs:

> "I never had anything to do with people carrying weapons or were somehow part of some mafia-like circles. I think that I know people who know such people, but myself, I never had anything to do with, let's say, professional drug pushers or, how you might imagine, some Moroccan gangs, or Turkish gangs, or whatever, with this kind of people, I have never… there was always… always some kind of social interaction involved apart from drug use. Thus, it was always like you got invited to a birthday party, and generally had contact on a private basis, too" (Homer, 39 years, tradesman).

References

Akers, R. L. & Burgess; R. L. (1966). A Differential Association-Reinforcement Theory of Criminal Behavior. Social Problems, 14 (2), 128-147.

Belackova, V. & Vaccaro, C. A. (2013). "A Friend With Weed Is a Friend Indeed": Understanding the Relationship Between Friendship Identity and Market Relations Among Marijuana Users. Journal of Drug Issues 43(3), 289-313.

Bernard, C. & Werse B. (2013). Die andere Seite des Drogendealens: Eigenbedarfshandel und „Social Supply". Monatsschrift für Kriminologie und Strafrechtsreform 2013, 96(6), 447-460.

Caulkins, J. P. & Pacula, R. L. (2006). Marijuana Markets: Inferences from Reports by the Household Population. Journal of Drug Issues, 36 (1), 173-200.

10 A similar gender imbalance was found in a sample of cannabis home growers (Potter et al. in this volume).

Coomber, R. & Turnbull, P. (2007). Arenas of Drug Transactions: Adolescent Cannabis Transactions in England – Social Supply. Journal of Drug Issues, 37 (4), 845-865.

Coomber, R. & Moyle, L. (2014). Beyond drug dealing: Developing and extending the concept of 'social supply' of illicit drugs to 'minimally commercial supply'. Drugs: Education, Prevention, and Policy, 21 (2), 157-164.

Duffy, M., Schafer, N., Coomber, R., O'Connell, L., & Turnbull, P. (2008). Cannabis supply and young people: "It's a social thing". York, England: Joseph Rowntree Foundation.

Genterczewsky, C. (2008). Kokaindealer im bürgerlichen Milieu. In B. Werse (Ed.), Drogenmärkte. Strukturen und Szenen des Kleinhandels (pp. 149-185). Frankfurt a.M.: Campus.

Harrison, L. D.; Erickson, P. G.; Korf, D. J.; Brochu, S. & Benschop, A. (2007). How much for a dime bag? An exploration of youth drug markets. Drug and Alcohol Dependence, 90, 27-39.

Heckathorn, D. D. (1997). Respondent-Driven Sampling: A New Approach to the Study of Hidden Populations. Social Problems, 44 (2), 174-199.

Jacinto, C., Duterte, M., Sales, P., & Murphy, S. (2008). I'm Not a Real Dealer: The Identity Process of Ecstasy Sellers. Journal of Drug Issues, 38, 419-444.

Jacques, S. & Allen, A. (2014): Bentham's Sanction Typology and Restrictive Deterrence. A Study of Young, Suburban, Middle-Class Drug Dealers. Journal of Drug Issues, 44, 212-230.

Katz, J. (1988). Seductions of Crime – A Chilling Exploration of the Criminal Mind. New York: Basic Books.

Kemmesies, U.E. (2004). Zwischen Rausch und Realität. Drogenkonsum im bürgerlichen Milieu. Unter Mitarbeit von B. Werse. Wiesbaden: VS.

Mayring, P. (2000). Qualitative content analysis. Forum: Qualitative social research, 1 (2), Art. 20. http://www.qualitative-research.net/index.php/fqs/article/view/1089/2386). Accessed 01. Oct 2015.

Murphy, S., Waldorf, D. & Reinarman, C. (1990): Drifting into Dealing: Becoming a Cocaine Seller. Qualitative Sociology, 13 (4), 321-343.

Pabst, A., Kraus, L., Gomes de Matos, E. & Piontek, D. (2013). Substanzkonsum und substanzbezogene Störungen in Deutschland im Jahr 2012. Sucht, 59 (6), 321-331.

Potter, G. R. (2009). Exploring retail-level drug distribution: Social supply, "real" dealers and the user/dealer interface. In Z. Demetrovics, J. Fountain, & L. Kraus (Eds.), Old and new policies, theories, research methods and drug users across Europe (pp 50-74). Lengerich, Germany: Pabst Science Publishers.

Taylor, M., & Potter, G. R. (2013). From "social supply" to "real dealing": Drift, friendship, and trust in drug-dealing careers. Journal of Drug Issues, 43, 392-406.

Waldorf, D. & Biernacki, P. (1981). Snowball Sampling. Problems and Techniques of Chain Referral Sampling. Sociological Methods and Research, 10 (2), 141-163.

Werse, B. (2008a). „Gib mir'n korrekten Dreißiger" – Erwerb und Kleinhandel von Cannabis und anderen illegalen Drogen. In B. Werse (Ed.), Drogenmärkte. Strukturen und Szenen des Kleinhandels (pp.91-129). Frankfurt a.M.: Campus.

Werse, B. (2008b). Retail markets for cannabis – users, sharers, go-betweens and stash dealers. In: D.J. Korf (Ed.), Cannabis in Europe. Dynamics in Perception, Policy and Markets (pp. 106-123). Lengerich: Pabst.

Drifting in and out of Dealing - results on career dynamics from the TDID project

Bernd Werse and Daniela Müller

Abstract

This chapter examines the ways in which people got in and out of profit-oriented drug dealing. 114 respondents from the German TDID research project gave information about getting into the selling of illicit drugs, while smaller subsamples were analysed for the intensification, reduction and/or cessation of their dealing activity. All respondents were recreational drug users.

Three modes of entry into drug dealing described in Murphy et al.'s paper "drifting into dealing" (1990) also emerged in our analysis (*stash-dealer, go-between, connoisseur*). In addition to these, four more significant types were examined (*supply guarantee, adventurer, money-driven, dealer fame*). A significant part of the respondents showed a combination of several motives for their entry into drug dealing.

Reasons why respondents intensified their dealing activities were *demand-pull increase*, *money-driven*, *supply-induced*, *stress reduction,* and *dealer-fame*. The modes of entry as well as the modes of intensification could be mostly described as a drift: a vast majority successively got into regular deviant behaviour, often rather unintentionally.

The notion of drift is even more important for the ways of exiting drug dealing: A vast majority described it as a rather fluid process in the context of "maturing out" of regular illicit drug use, usually including several motives such as changes in life course, fear of discovery, social stress, changes in relations with friends and business partners, or self-perception. A minority referred to one crucial experience for stopping dealing activities, this was mostly related to law enforcement activities.

A remarkable feature of the drifting process is that for many respondents, progressions from drug use to social supply, to making profit, to increasing sales volumes were not regarded as a further step into "real" deviance. Only a few subjects developed a "real" deviant identity, some of them cherishing the status in a deviant setting.

1 Introduction

Murphy et al. introduced the concept of "drifting into dealing" into social drug research by their paper of the same name from 1990. Referring to Becker's (1963) general career-oriented view on the self-concept of deviant and, in particular, drug-using persons, and Matza's (1964) concept of drift in and out of deviant behaviour among young delinquents, they examined careers of cocaine sellers with regard to their modes of entry. Most of these subjects had other intentions than making profit when they started to sell the drug (see 3.1), but then drifted into the role of a drug dealer successively. This concept of 'unintentional' drug dealing is heavily opposed to traditional views of dealers as greedy 'pushers'.

A number of more recent papers have revisited this concept. E.g., in an analysis of ecstasy dealers – a different drug, usually taken in different settings –, Jacinto et al. (2008) concluded that apart from several non-profit motives mentioned by Murphy et al., "profit was the primary motivation for Ecstasy sales" (ibid.: 427) for about one third of their subjects. However, a much larger proportion than among Murphy et al.'s cocaine sellers rejected the label 'drug dealer', primarily by using techniques of neutralization (Sykes & Matza 1957), including the limitation of their circle of customers and selling only in private settings. Limitation of the dealing activity by "restrictive deterrence" was the main focus in a work by Jacques and Allen (2014): "Restrictive deterrence is the process whereby offenders limit the frequency, magnitude, or seriousness of their offenses to avoid pain" (ibid.: 1). They found that mainly (formal) political sanctions (law enforcement), moral sanctions (negative reactions from persons of their personal network), and sympathetic sanctions (e.g. "regret, shame, and embarrassment for psychologically, physically, or financially hurting a parent, lover, or friend"; ibid.: 8) were responsible for the restriction of drug selling. Taylor and Potter (2013) examined "the borderline area between 'social supply' and the 'real dealer'" (ibid.: 6). By analysing a sample of respondents who had started out with non-profit supply, they point out that due to the nature of the market, the process of drift might take place quite quickly, and that those dealers who had drifted into the business were "the least likely to perceive themselves as 'real dealers', and often fail to see the risks associated with being caught due to their self-perception of their activities as being nondeviant" (ibid.: 4).

Although these publications examine different stages of the drift and identity process, including self-restraint, none actually explored the drifting *out of* deviance, a stage originally included in Matza's (1964) concept of drift. The interviews from the TDID project (see Werse & Bernard in this volume) provide a large source of data for analysing social suppliers and dealers of cannabis, synthetic drugs, and cocaine with respect to their modes of entry, and thus for re-examining Murphy et al.'s categories in a different sample. Additionally, a closer look is taken with regard to the modes of exit from drug selling, primarily by describing the motives for the cessation or reduction of dealing activities.

2 Methods

The present analysis was carried out as part of the project "The distribution of illicit drugs" (TDID), funded by the German Research Foundation (DFG). The main goal of this project was an exploration of the structures of distribution and sale of illicit drugs at users' level, within networks of recreational users; an area of research that is largely unexplored in German-speaking countries. For this purpose, we conducted a large number of qualitative-quantitative interviews with drug users and dealers. For more information about interview settings, methods and a detailed description of the sample, see Werse & Bernard in this volume. For this chapter, we analysed the in-depth interviews, which focused on the development and context of drug use, acquisition and selling. The 214 guided interviews were recorded and transcribed. Our analysis explores the motives for entering the drug trade, as well as changes in drug selling activities. It focuses on career dynamics, among respondents who had ever made profit with drug dealing. The particular research questions for this paper are:

- What are the motivational conditions for persons who start selling illicit drugs?
- Which motives influence the careers of drug suppliers who ascend to higher levels/trade volumes vs. dealer careers that end early?
- What are the crucial factors for the decrease or cessation of dealing activities?

To answer these questions, we largely applied the methodology of qualitative content analysis (Mayring 2000, 2014), using the MAXQDA software. With regard to the research questions, qualitative content analysis supports the exploration of new evidence. This was a main factor in order to gather all aspects concerning the topics 'entry into drug dealing' and 'change of dealing activities'. Orienting on our specific research questions, we decided to choose an inductive approach for the application of categories, taking into account the categories described by Murphy et al. (1990). The analysis of the qualitative material included a constant, ongoing process of verification and modification of the category system, including additional sub-categories. The last step was the qualitative and quantitative interpretation of this category system following the research questions.

The number of respondents analysed in each chapter differ according to the research question: while 114 respondents reported about their modes of entry, 40 respondents described reasons for the intensification of the selling activity, and 86 persons referred to their modes of exit or decrease. Due to the large number of interviews, the following analyses also contain some quantitative analyses of the qualitative data.

3 Results

3.1 Modes of entry into drug dealing

In order to give answers to the question for motivational conditions for entering the drug business, we based the process of categorisation on the five basic ways of entry into drug dealing described by Murphy et al. (1990). Three of these five modes were relevant within our sample: (1) *stash-dealer*, (2) *go-between,* and (3) *connoisseur*. In addition, we identified four more significant types in our data: (4) *supply guarantee*, (5) *adventurer*, (6) *money-driven* and (7) *dealer fame*. Overall, 114 respondents (53% of all interviewees or 67% of those who had ever sold drugs) described their way of entry into drug dealing according to at least one of those types. In the following analysis of paths of entry and their characteristics, percentages refer to the respective proportion of the total number of respondents whose path(s) of entry could be identified by examining the qualitative data. Since some of the respondents fell in more than one category, the given percentages sum up to more than 100%. The other two categories described by Murphy et al. did not occur, since no single respondent mentioned *apprenticeship* as the primary mode of entry (however, to some degree, this category occurred as a mode of increasing dealing activity). *Expansion of product line* could not be an option by definition, because our analysis refers to the initial entry into dealing with any illicit drug (mostly cannabis being the first one). Generally, a large number of the dealing-experienced respondents sold different drugs (mainly cannabis, speed, ecstasy, and/or cocaine), in different modes and frequencies. Thus, all of those who had sold different drugs did at some point expand their product line. There was no general difference between the specifics of sale of different substances, except that unlike other drugs, synthetic drugs were sometimes sold in club surroundings, and except for differences in prices, amounts and profit margins (see Werse & Bernard in this volume).

With 53%, the category *stash-dealer* was the most frequently occurring mode of entry in our sample. Following Murphy et al., a stash-dealer is a person who sells illicit drugs in order to support his/her own drug use. The dealing activities are directly linked to the personal drug consumption. The typical stash-dealer does not sell for financial profit; he/she just wants to cover the expenses for his/her use:

> "For me it was not about the bucks, but rather to fund my own use." (Veltins[1], 32 years, social worker)

One reason for this type being the most prevalent one in the sample was probably the fact that most respondents had started to use drugs regularly as (post-) adolescents, at a time when they had few money available:

> "It was all about paying less for my weed. I couldn't be bothered paying so much money for my own stuff. I was a student at that time and I had little money available. I don't know, I just thought: you can't spend so much money on smoking pot. In this sense, it was kind of intentional" (Tylor Thun, 29 years, journalist).

> "Back then, regarding smoking weed, it was like, I was a teenager, I didn't have so much money, and just funded my own use with that." (Kater Murr, 29 years, trainer)

While a large part of the stash-dealers referred to that motive, other respondents appeared to have developed an attitude that they simply did not want to pay for their own use, no matter what their financial situation was.

> "The point was, I didn't want to spend money anymore on my own use. I wanted to have that funded. Simply, this was money that could easily be earned." (Hans, 32 years, hotel employee)

The last-mentioned sentence points to an interesting perception by many of the small-scale dealing respondents: They find it relatively easy to make at least some money with selling drugs. This might be linked to the fact that most recreational users of cannabis and/or other drugs are part of a social network of fellow users.

Social motives are crucial for the second largest group, the *go-between* (32%). A typical initial situation for this type of entry is a person with, on the one hand, a group of friends who want to buy and use drugs, and, on the other hand, a 'good connection': contact to a trustworthy dealer who offers good prices and quality. The initial motivation (and in many cases the main motivation) of these

1 To protect the identity of study participants, they were asked to choose a codename.

respondents referred to 'friendly turns', favours for their friends. This can be regarded as the usual non-profit-oriented social supply (Coomber & Turnbull 2007) mode among fellow users. Consequentially, regarding our whole sample, quite many go-betweens never made any profit with these transactions:

> "Well, I often buy something for friends, but I don't earn anything. Simply because they do not know the people or they aren't nearby." (Van Nelle, 18 years, student)

Those who *did* start making profit out of their transactions mostly justified this turn with some compensation of higher risk and/or higher expenditure:

> "At some point I thought: no, I'm the one to obtain that every time, riding back and forth with a giant packet, and then I started to add a relatively small profit. This increased slightly, because people came around, who were not necessarily part of my circle of friends, but had contact with my friends. Well, I've made sure that I wasn't with complete strangers..." (Lolle, 29 years, social education worker)

This quote perfectly illustrates the process of drifting, if the go-between does not really restrict the number of his clients. At the same time, it contains a subjective neutralization of the respondent's own behaviour: By insisting that his clients were no "complete strangers", but at least "friends of friends", he still referred to some kind of go-between behaviour. However, the respondent used the notion that these persons are not *really* friends as a justification for gaining more profit from his dealing activity.

Interestingly, the category *money-driven* as a motive for initiation did not appear among the middle-class dealers examined by Murphy et al., while it was the third largest group in our sample (28%). Most of the persons in these category strived for money to realise a specific lifestyle. The pursuit of luxury was the mainspring of their dealing activities:

> "Money. My parents did not give me what I needed, you could say that. I always wanted to have more. I wanted to buy wicked clothes, pants for 150 euros, a playstation. Yes, and I couldn't afford that from my pocket money. That was the biggest motivation." (Neo, 24 years, student)

Often, the narration of 'quick money' was a major driver for the actions of the dealer:

> "Yes, we wanted to make lots of money fast." (Mr Pink II, 27 years, teacher trainee)

As stated above, it seems relatively easy to make money with drug dealing, if the user is part of a network of other users. If someone has the will to make money, this effect might increase substantially, particularly if the respective person knows someone with considerable experience in dealing:

> "And then one thing lead to another. I already had this connection, someone who could obtain quite large amounts, but I always just purchased something from him for my own use or for a few buddies. He already sold to me on tick. And it was him who explained to me the incentives. He said: 'Sell this, and you will get loads of money. You can always come and take as much as you want'. This offer was simply alluring, and it was all too simple. I just had to link one thing to another. I didn't even need any seed capital." (Hustler Hard, 34 years, betting shop employee)

To some degree, this respondent followed the *apprenticeship* mode of entry mentioned above, but, obviously, his intention to make money was the main driver in this case.

While the 'luxury' motive was crucial for a majority of those whose initiation in drug dealing was 'money-driven', some of the respondents started to sell illicit drugs for the purpose of debt reduction. They didn´t strive for the 'big money', they started out of financial distress:

> "I knew that, this is a deal, if it works, I´m saved. I was totally broke. My accounts have been completely overdrawn." (Lumumba, 34 years, student)

As mentioned above, none of the middle-class cocaine dealers interviewed by Murphy et al. entered dealing motivated by financial gain. Instead, only the four respondents who were street sellers did so, invariably out of financial distress. Thus, this substantial difference between our sample and Murphy et al.'s cocaine sellers might be explained in part by the fact that our sample included more respondents who could not exactly be classified as 'middle class' (although not all 'money-driven' respondents grew up with a lower economic status).

The motivation of the respondents in the category *supply guarantee* (17%) referred to the need to ensure one's own drug supply. It gives them a comforting feeling to store large amounts of drugs at their home. Profit orientation certainly plays a role, but the primary impulse is the coverage of their own supply over longer periods of time:

> "It was not the case that we passed on everything, we already retained a big part for us. Just because I thought it would be nice to have some stock at home, so that I won't be bothered with that for a while." (Richie, 39 years, freelancer in the film industry)

The category 'supply guarantee' might be understood as a specification of stash-dealer, because both are concerned about their captive consumption. However, the stash-dealer is concerned about funding his/her own use, while the 'supply guarantee' dealer aims to always have some drugs in stock. Moreover, this motive resembles the 'connoisseur' mode of entry, since it is all about the provision of a proper, reliable source for the drugs used by the seller (see below).

The interviewees' motivation in the category *dealer-fame* (8%) is based on the desire of increasing prestige and recognition, which can be regarded as a strategy to gain social gratitude:

> "…to gain appreciation of people. Bringing myself in a certain position. Not necessarily as the great, cool guy, but as the one who is part of something, who plays a particular role in the system. This was a strategy to make me feel better." (Etikett, 42 years, student)

Belonging to a group and having some kind of important status might be action-guiding factors for some subjects following this entry mode. In addition, many of the respondents in this category said positive things about the everyday life of a dealer:

> "Nah, to be cool, of course, is indeed some factor… because you… because, it was fun when the beeper beeped continually, or the phone ringed, or something. Then you regard yourself as a bit important... So, then just something was going on. Somehow action and stuff. I don´t know, being under stress, a bit. Then you have to meet there, on the playground, and there, and 1000 people, babble babble." (Jay, 34 years, social education worker)

As we can see in this quote, this mode of entry is not just a matter of taking a specific function within a group and enjoying the resulting prestige, it is also about the positive experience of the obligations associated with that function, which structures everyday life. The following quote illustrates the megalomaniac self-perception that some of these prestige-driven dealers develop:

> "It sounds stupid, but I thought it was cool, sitting at home, the bell rings, you always meet new people, you do not need to care about anything, because they come to you and they kind of suck your dick, to get something from you. I just thought that was cool. You've just met a bunch of people without any efforts." (Sid Vicious, 29 years, unemployed)

It has to be noted that the significance of 'dealer-fame' not only concerned only a minority as a mode of entry, but there were also few sellers who gave this aspect any importance in later stages of their career.

The *connoisseur* (4%) is driven by the desire to buy high quality drugs. As Murphy et al. describe, the connoisseur buys larger amounts of drugs to ensure a higher quality of the product. Afterwards he/she sells and/or shares the high-quality drugs to/with his/her friends:

> "But that's just such a thing, that you just know that you can find good grass here. Because it wasn't like that before, like the stuff with the bird sand, I didn't want this any longer. For this reason, we arranged it that way." (Willsten Habbe, 24 years, warehouseman)

Following this quote, the motivation was actually not due to particularly high quality of the product, but mainly to avoid low quality. The fact that very few respondents reported that, at a certain time, only adulterated drugs were available might explain why the 'connoisseur' mode of entry was rare within our sample. Instead, there were several respondents who followed the 'supply guarantee' mode (see above).

The smallest category is the *adventurer* (3%). These are persons who sell illicit drugs for the purpose of thrill. This can include curiosity for the experience of 'being a real drug dealer':

> "Just to see how it is. I already observed people selling something, and I wanted to experience what was going on. I wanted to see how it is, socially. Who comes your way and so on." (Laura, 30 years, teacher)

Others appreciated the feeling of risk and excitement:

> "But on the other hand, as a teenager, it was exciting for me. Many people had been paranoid in these days, hiding their stuff in the forest and so on. You already went to jail for one night even for a small amount. And then it has been about the thrill to do it nevertheless." (Mr. Pink, 31 years, artist)

Similar to 'dealer-fame', this mode of entry refers to some incentive of deviant behaviour: living an exciting and dangerous life, including virtually unlimited resources of money and drugs. The observation that only few persons followed these modes of entry suggests that the vast majority did not have a 'criminal' or at least 'adventuresome' intention in a narrower sense.

3.2 Combined modes of entry into drug dealing

Overall, 114 respondents expressed their motives for the entry into drug dealing. By taking a closer look on the quantitative distribution of different routes of entry, we can distinguish between people who reported only one initial motivation (67 persons) and respondents who described a combination of different motives (47 persons). Within the group that shows only one initial motivation, more than a third (37%) found their way into dealing exclusively as *stash-dealers*. The second largest category were the *go-betweens* (30%) followed by *money-driven* (18%) and *supply-guarantee* (6%). Only 3% described their initial motivation as a *connoisseur*. The *adventurer* does not occur as a single initial motivation. 41% of the dealing-experienced respondents found their way into dealing based on a combination of different motives. Within this group, the combination of stash-dealer with at least one other motive is the most frequent one (77%). Therefore, we will focus on the presentation on two of these specific combinations. 13 persons showed a combination of stash-dealer and go-between motivation when they entered dealing:

> "That was no conscious decision. However, this goes along with, say, you're getting this straight somehow: Hey, now I earn something by selling, respectively… in the beginning, it was not about the profit, but it was more about funding my own stash, to some degree… and then, I'd say, you kind of acquire a taste for it (…) Well, someone asks you: oh, when you go there, couldn't you bring me some too? And then you do that, and if you do that for the second or third time, then you think: Why should I take the risk for free, so to speak, to walk out of the dealer's place with a larger amount, across the streets, to your place? Yeah, and then you ask yourself, if you shouldn't get paid for that risk, by, what I think is absolutely legitimate, selling it a bit more expensive." (Alfred, 38 years, education sector)

Although only a minority of respondents explicitly stated that a combination of these motives was crucial for their entry into 'real dealing', this quote is somehow typical for the sample. Most interviewees had a considerable need for *stash* in their initial phase, and, at the same time, a considerable network of fellow users who were also in need for stash. Since almost every respondent started selling to friends, it is likely that, to some degree, a combination of these two modes of entry is relevant for a large part of the dealing-experienced respondents. The quote also illustrates the drift of action going along with some drift of conscience in the initial phase: The respondent realizes that he is doing some kind of work he should be paid for, a work mainly consisting in taking a higher risk than those he sells to. Referring to Murphy et al. (1990) and their reference to Becker (1963), this marks a tipping point for the second step in the deviant career, the development of deviant motives and interests. The respondent had already become involved in some kind of regular deviant behaviour (first step: the regular use of illicit drugs), and now, earning some money, at least to cover the cost of own use, became an option. Interestingly, this second step is not really a huge one, subjectively. Instead, the respondent regarded it as a completely logical and legitimate move.

While this interviewee did not think about making money by dealing at that time, other subjects did so, even if this was not mentioned initially. In the following quote, the underprivileged status obviously did not only lead to a certain willingness to make profit (money-driven), but also to improve self-esteem (dealer-fame). However, the first motive mentioned for entering drug dealing referred to the stash-dealer type.

> "The subject of using and selling was similar, except that I did not start really big in the beginning. However, I wanted to fund my own use. I then started to sell pills and speed in clubs [*stash-dealer*] (...) I had a single mother. Me and my brother, we simply wanted to have a certain standard of living. We wanted to keep up with the others, like video games and stuff [*money-driven*] (...) Dealing also helped me strengthening my self-esteem. This has become a kind of social thing, with me as the central person. I pulled all the strings [*dealer-fame*]." (Kaiser Soze, 27 years, unemployed)

Characteristically, and different from the vast majority of dealing-experienced persons, this respondent started his dealing activities straight away within public settings, instead of selling drugs to friends in private surroundings. These observations indicate that users with personal shortcomings might be more vulnerable to develop motives related to status and money and thus becoming a 'real dealer' in a quite short period.

It has to be kept in mind that most of those respondents who ever made profit by selling drugs restricted their activities to their private network and rather low profits, thus we could characterise them as social suppliers or minimally commercial suppliers (see Werse & Bernard in this volume). However, it is worth looking at the significant subsample of those who escalated to greater revenues and/or higher levels.

3.3 Intensification of dealing activities

To answer the question on the motivational conditions for changes in dealing activities, we start with a closer look on the five different types of motivations for an increase in sales: (1) *demand-pull increase*, (2) *money-driven*, (3) *supply-induced*, (4) *stress reduction*, and (5) *dealer-fame*. Overall, 40 respondents described an increase in their trading activities, which corresponds to 31% of those respondents who had ever made profit with drug dealing. The following percentages indicate how often a category could be identified in the subsample of 'advanced' dealers. Since some of these respondents showed more than one reason, the percentages given add up to more than 100%.

Demand-pull increase was the category that occurs most often (62%). These respondents pointed out that the intensification of their trading volume mostly did not follow a conscious decision. Instead, the increase can be described as a self-perpetuating consequence of their own actions:

> "Of course, more and more people have noticed that I had a good source. This got around, and, accordingly, people came to me and said: 'Bring me some of the delicious stuff'." (Phillip, 31 years, chimney sweep)

Other respondents reported that their volume of trade increased even though the number of customers remained the same or even decreased:

> "And the point was, that I [had] (...) at the end almost even fewer customers, but these were customers whom I knew, I can get from them... like, there is something going on, you know? Here I sell for 50 €, there I sell for 100 € and er, and I will get the money, and er, I regularly supplied them, yes, and then it worked. And before that, I perhaps had more customers, but er, that was not so profitable, because some of them took only small amounts." (Mr. Nice, 32 years, student)

However, this seller, who restricted his transactions to customers who bought, on average, larger amounts, was not typical for the sample. Increasing the circle of customers without own efforts was much more common. As mentioned above, this was often due to the fact that it had become widely known that the respondents were selling "good grass at good prices." (Peter Positiv, 29 years, student), as well as other personal dealer qualities, like being a "decent dealer with good prices" (Lola, 26 years, student; see Bernard in this volume).

While the category *money-driven* plays some role for the entry into the drug trade, it is much more important for intensifying dealing activities: 55% of the respective subsample referred to this motive. Many of these respondents admitted that this motivation is attributable to a wish for luxury and money. In this respect, drug dealing could be a means to an end for escaping from the conventional wage labour life:

> "Not having to work has always been the greatest luxury for me." (Manfred, 48 years, driver)

Some of the respondents reported that, after they had already been selling for a while, they recognized that the sale of illicit drugs is a lucrative business:

> "And at some point I just thought to myself, you can also make money with this" (Puma, 26 years, warehouseman).

> "At that time, you just simply stood there, thinking, you are the king of the world. Because you were able to buy everything with the money you gained." (Felix da Housecat, 35 years, artist)

In the latter case, the respondent had already progressed to a further stage of deviance and dealer identity, triggered by the fascination of 'easy money'. This is a feature that applies to most of those respondents who had progressed to higher levels of drug dealing. The desire to earn money with drug dealing was partly justified by the perception that selling certain drugs, e.g. cocaine, entails a higher risk than selling cannabis:

> "At some point there was the idea that you have to earn money, especially in the case of cocaine. I funded my own use, but I also thought that if I already deal with cocaine, which is another level, then I have to earn money with it. Then, when I go out on weekends, the whole party has to be paid, or also my food in the refrigerator, or luxury goods." (Peter, 30 years, social worker)

The category *supply-induced* is, with 30%, the third most common in our subsample. For these respondents, the increase of dealing activity and/or trade volume was due to stimuli from the own source of supply. To some degree, this mode of extension resembles the "apprenticeship" mode of entry described by Murphy et al. Again, it is striking that most of these respondents referred to others as primary drivers for the increase in selling:

> "I hadn't thought about it and hadn't planned it. (…) It started out that he always left me a bit more. (…) And then the quantities started to get bigger and bigger and that's how it happened." (Grüner Elefant, 25 years, sociology student; see also Bernard in this volume)

Another typical pattern for this category was a situation in which the own source forwarded the respondent to the next level. At this stage, the minimum amount is usually higher than at the previous one, so that, to some extent consequentially, the trade volume has to increase:

> "Following this hierarchical structure, that you are always getting one step higher. You just knew the dealer and then you just bought from the dealer who sold to your dealer." (Godzilla, 31 years, student)

But, as several respondents stated, this only works if "you know enough people" (Soul, 31 years, IT engineer), meaning higher-level dealers and potential buyers. No respondents mentioned own efforts to make the acquaintance of such persons. Some interviewees reported very lucrative offers they could hardly refuse: "...because it simply sounded like a wonderful deal" (Lasershow, 20 years, waiter).

Another remarkable factor for an increase in trading volume was the attempt to reduce the stress that arises with the frequent dealing of smaller volumes. Statements of this kind we classified as *stress reduction* (13%):

> "I was fed up with it then, because every idiot is calling you, at any time of the day. And at some point it really annoyed me. Therefore, in principle, I stopped it, to sell small small. Then, I decided only to sell starting at 50 grams, or whatever, 100 grams." (MiuMiu, 31 years, student)

Permanent availability is an important feature of being a 'good' and 'reliable' dealer. If the number of clients increased over the time, the number of phone calls, daily visits, etc., also increased. This and the partly intrusive behaviour of some customers led to a permanent increase of the daily stress level. In these cases, a smaller customer base with higher quantities ordered immediately reduces stress. The dealing activity decreases, while at the same time the trading volume increases. The category of stress reduction is closely related to the category demand-pull increase, as growing demand is an almost necessary condition for a growing stress level.

The category *dealer-fame* as a motivation for increasing dealing activities was relevant for two persons (5%) only. These respondents felt attracted to the reputation they earn for being a big dealer:

> "I already was the king, and, in addition, with selling [larger amounts], I was the absolute king. I was the centre of attention." (Phillip, 31 years, chimney sweep)

It should be noted that nobody in our sample raised his/her dealing activities *only* for being a famous dealer. The desire for fame is relevant for only few members of networks of recreational users and private dealers, and if so, it can usually be regarded as a side effect only. One of the respective two respondents in our sample (Phillip, see above) linked the fame motive to some lack of family attachment, while the other one had a longer history regarding appreciation and status in the drug-using world: When he started using cannabis at the age of fifteen, he was the only higher-educated boy from a wealthy family in a group of lower-educated users who had cheated him several times when he aimed to buy cannabis. So when he got into dealing later, he described his status-related motive as some kind of payback:

> "And then I turned the tables on them. I sold to all these other guys who had sold to me before, who had cheated me before, and I could charge high prices, since I had built a monopoly somehow… it actually was some kind of revengefulness that drove me." (Cornholio, 33 years, business economist)

It should be noted that those respondents whose trading activity and/or volume had increased because of a demand-pull increase and/or had been supply-induced, rarely made a conscious decision to go deeper into drug dealing. This means that, at least, more than every second respondent *drifted* into increased dealing activities. Following Murphy et al., this phenomenon can be understood as a long-term process, which in most cases is not based on a conscious decision. However, most of these persons *did* consider aspects of conspicuousness and other issues regarding the risk of being subject to law enforcement.

Concluding this section, we give some other typical examples for drifting, which illustrate how different incidents, motives and significant others may interact with regard to an increase of dealing activity:

> "It was because I paid a good price for that. There already were many people in my surrounding, and thus, this was no problem at all. I then just bought higher amounts." (Manfred, 48 years, driver)

> "It was never like, I have to earn money with that. (…) I just knew these people and I had the option. I also was asked if I could give them more. Yes, and I had the opportunity. It was this typical thing, it doesn't really matter if I'm going to get 100 grams or 200 grams, and the others [customers] were also like that, it didn't make a big difference if they took 50 or 100. Yeah, and then all of a sudden, there were many of them who wanted 50 or 100, and then I was going to get more and more." (Soul, 31 years, IT employee)

> "I don't know how this all happened. Megalomania, but I also had a comfortable life, and I had the options for that. But then, also megalomania came up. You got money, everyone wants something from you, you get more and more popular. At some point, however, you think, you don't need to have more. Then I selected five or six guys, and I gave them 500 grams per week on tick." (Theo, 28 years, mechanical engineering student)

As shown in these quotes, drift may take place on all levels of drug dealing, however, with different implications: The higher the amounts being sold, the more the dealer is likely to be intrigued by the financial gain and the status of being a big player in the business. Nevertheless, higher profit and larger networks of suppliers and customers are also associated with higher risk, which was an important reason for many respondents to limit their dealing activity (Jacques & Allen 2014). The general risk of discovery and punishment is also a main driver to cut down or stop, but, as shown in the next section, there are also many other reasons for drifting out of dealing.

3.4 Reduction or cessation of dealing activities

A majority of those respondents who have ever made profit with drug dealing did not currently sell drugs: 34% had not dealt in the last 12 months and another 25% sold drugs in the last 12 months, but not in the preceding 30 days. Among those 41% who did sell drugs in the last month, 28% did not make any monetary or non-monetary profit, while the other 72% showed a wide range of earnings, but no single respondent had earned nearly as much money with drug dealing as in his/her most profitable month before. That means that all dealing-experienced respondents had, at least to some degree, reduced or stopped their dealing activity. In a way, this is no surprise, since this reduction mostly goes along with a reduction of own drug use when growing older and taking more responsibility at work and/or in the family. This phenomenon of "maturing out" (Winick 1962)[2] of regular illicit drug use among recreational users has been documented for a similar population in Kemmesies 2004 (see also Bernard and Lenton et al. in this volume). Furthermore, the reduction or cessation of dealing activities mostly took place in a casual way, without particular efforts, so that it can also be described as *drifting*. Particularly with regard to persons who had reached higher levels of drug dealing, this notion does not fit in popular images of the commitments associated with regular criminal activity, including threats and violence against "dropouts". Hence, the modes of exit or reduction deserve a closer look.

Compared to the modes of entry, more different reasons for exiting could be identified, and they are also less clear-cut, which is obviously due to the rather casual mode in which the reduction or cessation took place. In the majority of the cases, several motives played a role for this process. Thus, we could do only a rough quantitative ranking of the existing qualitative data, without percentages.

2 Different from the persons discussed here, Winick introduced his concept with regard to the self-recovery from heroin addiction.

Overall, 86 persons gave at least some information about their motives for the cessation or reduction of their drug dealing efforts. In descending order, these motives include (1) *changes in life course*, (2) *crucial experiences*, (3) *risk of discovery*, (4) *social stress*, (5) *lack of cost-effectiveness*, (6) *changes in the commercial relationship*, (7) *self-perception*, (8) *changes in relation to friends and/or customers*, and, as the least prevalent motive, (9) *moral concerns*.

The most frequently mentioned motive is the one that is most directly linked to the concept of "maturing out" mentioned above: *changes in life course*. Sometimes these changes take place simultaneously to turning points in the personal career. E.g., several respondents stopped their dealing activity after finishing their studies and starting their first 'real' job. Another respondent stopped dealing when he moved in with his girlfriend ("...and then, I didn't want some guys to come and ring the doorbell"; Horst II, 38 years, producer), and another one referred to the birth of his child as the moment of exiting the drug trade. However, such explicit points in time for cessation were rather the exception than the rule. Much more respondents described a longer process of getting more into the 'conventional life' and successively reducing the use and the selling of illicit drugs:

> "Well, erm, marriage, family, and simply... working. Above all, really getting into my profession, commuting, and many private changes and activities, and therefore, it simply wasn't... it was simply a different phase. I mean, I still smoked weed at that time, but I... simply did not contact these guys anymore in order to ask them: do you need something?" (Walter, 37 years, civil servant)

For some other respondents, there was a direct link between a more conventional life and some kind of weariness regarding regular drug use and particularly drug-infused partying:

> "At some point, it is, however... somehow the euphoria has worn off for all this techno-dance-whatever-fuss, and then starting a family, and some other things, simply by... coming of age, I'd say quite carefully." (Fruchtzwerg, 40 years, civil servant)

As this quote illustrates, the explicit notion that retreating from drug use and drug selling can be regarded as part of the process of getting older is quite common among the respondents. Retrospectively, they regard the time period when they took and sold drugs regularly as an extension of their adolescence.

Relatively many respondents reported a *crucial experience* that motivated them to cut down or end their drug-selling activity. The most frequently mentioned incident was getting caught by the police:

> "I got busted then once, and, thank god, I only had a little trouble because of that, except for some hours of community service. But then, I also lost my driving licence (...) and those were just a bit too many things going wrong at that time. And then I definitely didn't want any more contact with the police." (Lilli, 34 years, kindergarten teacher)

Several other respondents mentioned heavier sanctions such as suspended prison sentences. In some cases, abstinence from drug dealing only lasted as long as the time of probation, but for other respondents, it had a permanent effect:

> "Meanwhile, I don't dare anymore. The arrest really preyed on my mind. I also don't want to bring some stuff to others. I try to avoid that." (Giovanni, 37 years, social worker)

It should be mentioned, though, that only a minority of those profit-oriented dealers who were charged for drug offences stated that it had an impact on their dealing behaviour.

For some other respondents, the imprisonment of related persons (customers, suppliers or friends) was the crucial experience that led to a decrease or cut-off of their own dealing activity:

> "...because someone from my closer network got caught, and then I thought... I became scared shitless, and this was also because of my job." (Schorsch, 37 years, lawyer)

In this case, the respondent had at least two reasons for quitting: Firstly, the arrest of his friend, and secondly, concern about his job and social inconspicuousness in general – a typical feature of people with a higher professional status, particularly legal practitioners (see also Kemmesies 2004). Some of the respondents intimidated by the sentencing of others even weighed up (financial) benefits and potential costs:

> "Well, my colleague, with whom I had built this purchasing cartel (...) got into a routine traffic check and got caught with 200 grams of hashish. He lost his driving licence, and barely got away with a large fine. Almost got probation for that. And then I thought, this is not worth the risk. The profit made from several orders wouldn't even suffice for paying the fine. And then you'd also be stigmatised. You'll lose your driving licence, you'll be labelled." (Gordon, 23 years, sociology student)

A few of the respondents reported a particular crucial experience related to their self-concept and others' perceptions of drug dealing:

> "[*Expansion of the*] circle of customers... not really. I wasn't up for that at all. I stopped that completely, after some guy who I had never met before knocked on my door and asked me if he could have something. So to speak, this was a wake-up call, after which I just stopped it." (Tylor Thun, 29 years, journalist)

These respondents realised that they were perceived as a "real" dealer, and that this label spread even among persons they did not know. An incident like that might have been significant for most of our dealing-experienced respondents, since only few of them regarded themselves as drug dealers (see also Jacinto et al. 2008). However, this kind of experience not only refers to self-concept, but also to conspicuousness, which is, of course, related to the risk of discovery by law enforcement (see below). For a few other respondents, informal sanctions from their loved ones were obviously more important than formal consequences, since they quit dealing after family members had found out about it:

> "It was the revelation that my family got to know about it. That was the crucial factor. The imprisonment alone would not have been sufficient for me to quit." (Ganja Mania, 31 years, social worker)

A significant proportion of those who had quit or cut down their selling activities referred to the *risk of discovery* as the main reason. This could either be simply due to diffuse feelings of discomfort. Such feelings could be more or less serious. In severe cases, they even led to significant mental problems:

> "I was scared shitless. I stopped everything then, became depressive, I got treatment and medication for that. Every day I thought, now the cops will come and pick me up."(Neo, 24 years, student)

In other cases, such fears were combined with perceptions described above as crucial experiences, like strangers asking them for drugs, or related persons being imprisoned. Here, these incidents were not the crucial factors, but contributed to the perception that the risk has become too high. Often, this process could be described as drifting, influenced by different factors:

> "And then it just so happened, I didn't intend to do so, it was like, he [*her supplier*] didn't have anything for a while or something like that. Then I quit for one or two months, and after that, they busted him. That was a close shave for me." (Grüner Elefant, 25 years, sociology student; see also Bernard in this volume)

Frequently, such drifting processes that mainly referred to the chance of discovery were also fuelled by changes in life course ("...if I'd get caught, particularly with selling, I don't know, perhaps I'd even get some kind of occupational ban"; Hans

III, 23 years, social worker), which confirms the 'maturing out' scheme mentioned above.

A significant proportion of respondents who had dealt with drugs regularly stopped because of *social stress*. This particular phenomenon of small-scale dealers can be brought to the point with the following quote:

> "At some point, I was simply fed up with this permanent bell-ringing and all these people coming in every time." (Alfred, 38 years, education sector)

While for a few others, frequent contact with many different customers contributed to status and a positive (deviant) self-perception (dealer-fame, see 3.1 & 3.3), it was the reason for quitting for quite many respondents. An important aspect of this stress is the notion that many customers expect the dealers to be available every time, which interfered with other, non-deviant activity:

> "Somehow, I wanted to do my studies. But they came at every time of the day. When I was in the lecture room, they called me to ask when I'll return home finally. Yeah, and then, I even did this, went home, and then this guy only wanted to buy for ten Euros. Fantastic." (IC Wiener, 30 years, student)

As many of these respondents emphasized that this stress or weariness, subjectively, came up after a considerable period of dealing, it is obvious that this motive might often also be rated as part of a maturing-out process.

Another important aspect that functions as a reason to quit dealing is *lack of cost-effectiveness*. Some respondents stated that they had the feeling that they just did not make sufficient profit:

> "Then I earned… two Euros a gram, I mean, not even, and this is like, which I realized quite quickly, simply nothing. All the stress coming up, and all the expenditures… it never did for me, I never thought: oh my god, now you have a lot of money in your pocket, or, now you can really smoke a lot, or whatever. And for this reason I thought: hey, sorry, that's too much for me, I'm not gonna do that job anymore." (Karsten, 25 years, filling station attendant)

It should be mentioned, though, that these persons who referred to this motive mostly only sold small amounts of drugs, to a small number of customers, and as making profit was not their main intention, they also made no efforts to charge higher prices from the customers or to get better purchase prices from vendors. So this motive can mostly be regarded as part of a drifting-in-and-out process, which included other aspects (e.g. worries about the risks, or social stress) and sometimes did not last very long (e.g., a few months, as in the case quoted above).

Another mode of exit mentioned by some respondents can be summarized as *change in the commercial relationship*. Sometimes this change could also be classified as a crucial experience, e.g. when suppliers were caught by the police, however, the reason for quitting in these cases was not the fact that the respondents were impressed by the seizure, but simply the fact that they had no supplier anymore. Some other respondents lost their supplier for other (not specified) reasons, and a few dealers successively lost their circle of customers, which can often also be seen in the light of maturing out:

> "...but, in recent times, this has declined, particularly because here, in my current circle of friends, the people smoke less cannabis." (Mister XY, 23 years, administrative officer)

Only one person (Lola, 26 years, philosophy student) reported that she (temporarily) quit dealing after she was threatened by competing dealers (see Bernard in this volume). Remarkably, this was the only case in which some kind of 'criminal' behaviour of others played a role in the cessation of selling activities. On the other hand, no single respondent mentioned getting in significant trouble with business partners when s/he decided to quit dealing.

One motive for exiting that obviously plays a role for many respondents, particularly for those with rather few drug dealing experience, but explicitly mentioned only by some, is *self-perception*. As stated above, a vast majority of the dealing-experienced persons did not regard themselves as dealers, and, as a consequence, some stopped their dealing activity because of this self-perception. In some cases, this was intrinsically tied to others' perception of them, often because of a crucial experience in which they felt labelled as a "dealer" (see above). Other respondents stated that they stopped dealing just because "this has never been my concept of life" (Kater Murr, 28 years, trainer). Such persons were often those who had sold drugs just occasionally or for a short period of time. Sometimes, the conflict between self-perception, common expectations and specifics of drug dealing was more complex, as shown in the following quote:

> "At some point, I stopped this, deliberately. (...) I said: I'm fed up with that. I can't get used to the money. (I: What do you mean by that: can't get used to the money?) Well, because this was no real money. For me, it was no money which I could build upon. It could be gone from one day to another. And you get used to a standard of living that you haven't earned. (...) It came up with, with some Hollywood films, I don't know, when you saw these careers, or also from other examples, such careers... they always got money, and from one day to another, like 'pop', it's gone. And suddenly, everything is fucked up... Not getting into this vicious circle, I didn't want

> this somehow. You might get dependent... you have a criminal record... and whatever." (Jay, 34 years, social education worker)

Although this respondent decided to cease all of a sudden, he describes a process in which the decision to stop arose gradually. As self-concept, risk of discovery and stigmatization, common images of dealers and financial issues came together to make this decision, this respondent being a good example for many others whose exit was not linked to only one reason.

Some respondents reported reducing or quitting their dealing activity because of changes in *relations to friends and/or customers*. Some respondents were annoyed by former friends who had turned into mere customers, always expecting to buy drugs from them. Others were bothered simply by the number of customers (who had not necessarily been friends before), which is heavily related to the category "social stress" shown above. Another feature of this reason for exit is the way their customers behave, e.g.

> "...I felt uncomfortable with these people, who permanently came and were, like, pseudo-friendly, but only wanted to buy something. I found that double-faced and disgusting, to curry favour with me like that. It was boring and irksome, finding myself in such an environment." (Laura, 30 years, teacher)

While this respondent referred to the behaviour of customers, such unpleasant experiences were mixed with actual social stress and the number of customers in other cases:

> "This thing, that you sit together, after someone bought something, and smoke a joint, this annoyed me at some point. I didn't want to smoke and chill so much anymore at some point. It was because of word-of-mouth recommendations. Eventually, also friends of friends came, which I didn't want. Someone permanently bringing along someone. Eventually, this someone of someone of someone also brings along someone. These were dimensions that I couldn't control anymore." (Godzilla, 31 years, student)

In a way, this respondent decided to stop dealing because he had unintentionally drifted more and more into it, triggered by a demand-pull increase. Although in this quote, his friends' habits were the first thing to complain about, it was also the number of customers that made him decide to stop selling (with regard to 'unintentional' cannabis use, see Belackova & Zabransky in this volume).

Two persons decided to quit because of *moral concerns* regarding their dealing activity, both related to crucial experiences with customers. While one of these was a less severe case of a mental disorder, the other one referred to a suicide, for which he felt responsible:

> "A friend of mine killed himself. He suffered from schizophrenia, however, it was under control at that time, but because of all the ecstasy I gave him, it broke out. It broke out again, and then he committed suicide. And that was something that really gave me food for thought. Because in part, I felt responsible for that. I just thought, I should have pulled the rip cord earlier." (Cornholio, 33 years, business economist)

4 Conclusion and discussion

Following our three research questions, we start our conclusion with the *most important motivational conditions for persons who start selling illicit drugs*. The most frequent mode of entry was the intention to fund own drug use by selling (*stash-dealer*). The mere frequency of occurrence as well as quotes from many of the respondents show how easily and common it is for users to follow this mode, often in a casual way. The second most common category in our sample was the *go-between.* A characteristic of these persons who started with 'collective orders' for friends is a reasoning process setting in after a while leading to the desire of 'getting paid for the risk'. A considerable proportion of respondents (however, still a minority) had the intention to make money with drug dealing right from the beginning (*money-driven*), which distinguishes them from those who 'drifted' into dealing like most of the go-betweens and stash-dealers. Profit orientation was mostly associated with the pursuit of luxury. Because of the intentional aspect, these respondents were much more likely to ascend rapidly to higher levels of the illicit drug trade. A relatively low number of respondents referred to some kind of *supply guarantee* or a *connoisseur* motive as the primary mode of entry: they sold drugs to ensure their constant supply with drugs of good quality. Few dealers stated that *dealer-fame* or even an *adventurer* motive were the crucial reasons for getting into selling drugs. Particularly those who entered the business primarily for fame were most likely to adapt the identity and an everyday life structure of a stereotypical 'drug dealer'.

Referring to Murphy et al. (1990) and their reference to Becker (1963), earning at least some money or free drugs by selling drugs marks a tipping point for the second step in a deviant career: the development of deviant motives and interests, after the subject had already become involved in some kind of regular deviant behaviour (first step: regular use of illicit drugs). Interestingly, this second step is not really a big one, subjectively. Instead, many respondents regarded it as a completely logical and legitimate move. This might explain why a majority of the profit-oriented dealers *drifted* into this kind of behaviour: The use of cannabis, synthetic drugs, cocaine etc. is already a (formally) deviant act, but, at the same time, a common behaviour within a network of fellow users. The same is true for the purchase of these substances, which often takes place in a rather casual mode between friends (social supply). However, there is no legal difference between social supply and 'dealing proper', which, in turn, also affects the perception of the suppliers: The step between using and selling drugs subjectively is a rather small one, while at the same time, it is a big one regarding (formal and informal) deviance. It appears that every progression regarding profit, sales volume and circle of customers is not really regarded as a 'real' further step into deviance. However, only a minority of those who started drifting into profit-oriented dealing proceed to higher levels or even to the development of a dealer identity, due to mechanisms of "restrictive deterrence" (Jacques & Allen 2014).

With regard to the second research question on the *motivations for proceeding to higher levels vs. dealer careers that end early*, we firstly refer to the last-mentioned type. Since go-between behaviour or social supply seems to be a basic feature of networks of recreational drug users, the go-between mode of entry is also the most frequent one of those who end their career as 'real dealers' quite early. Usually these persons heavily rejected the label 'drug dealer', and many of them went back to (occasional) non-profit social supply after a short period of profit-oriented dealing. However, there were also respondents whose self-concepts made them more inclined to increase their selling activity. Remarkably, in the majority of these cases, the crucial factors for such an increase could also be classified as typical 'drifting' factors: The most prevalent factor is *demand-pull increase*, which either refers to a growing circle of customers and/or growing demand by the existing customer base. On the other hand, impulses from the supply side (*supply-induced*) often contributed to a further increase in sales, which can also mostly be categorized as part of a rather unintentional process. In contrast, the category *money-driven*, the second most frequent one for an increase in the dealing activity, is usually an intentional one. This motive frequently occurs among persons with low economic status and/or other social deficits, who mention an explicit desire for luxury. In this respect, these respondents resemble the young adult migrants researched in Bucerius 2007, living in the same region as most of the respondents of the present study. In line with the results from these analyses, such respondents were also most likely to develop a deviant identity, including the 'criminal' fame associated with the dealer status. However, the seductions of money and deviant identity are not restricted to 'compensatory' behaviour of the underprivileged: sometimes, respondents started identifying with the role of a drug dealer after a long process of rather unintentional drifting.

The motive *stress reduction*, mentioned by only a few, can be regarded as an ambivalent one: on the one hand, respondents tried to reduce conspicuousness and thus the risk of law enforcement. On the other hand, they did so by increasing the average amount being sold, and thus, increasing the potential sentence. It should be noted that, with regard to this motive, but also to the rather unintentional ones described above, subjects must already have developed some further stage of deviant identity to follow these motives and thus increase their dealing activity. It cannot be cleared with the existing data whether this might also be due to patterns of drug use, but since the extent of selling activities was significantly linked to the extent of use (see Werse & Bernard in this volume), it is likely that there might be some kind of reciprocal effect.

The notion that the drifting process might take place relatively quickly (Taylor & Potter 2013) can be confirmed with some of the present data. As mentioned above, this can be related to special (social and psychological) conditions of the respondent, the will to make money and an early adaption of the dealer identity. However, in some cases, this could merely be linked to favourable terms of the business, e.g., reliable supply, good quality and good prices which might rapidly increase the circle of customers. In summary, the development of a deviant (drug dealer's) identity is one of the most important factors for the progression to higher levels. Conversely, persons who strongly reject the role of a dealer are most likely to stop their selling activities quite soon.

Finally, the *reasons for the decrease or cessation of dealing activities* were, on average, more ambiguous than the reasons for entry or increase. In the vast majority of the cases, respondents successively drifted out of dealing and showed several different motives. This process could mostly be described as "maturing out" of drug selling, often along with maturing out of (regular) illicit drug *use*. While the processuality of the exit applies to a large part of profit-oriented dealers, a significant minority stopped selling more immediately because of a *crucial experience*, either because of (own or others') experiences with law enforcement or other incidents in their personal surrounding. Generally, the most important reason for drifting out of dealing was a *change in life course* (job, family, etc.), followed by the *risk of discovery*. These two factors often go along with each other, as it is perfectly illustrated by the following quote:

> "Then, some day, I finished my studies, and with my degree, or somehow, it occurred to me, the idea, 'hey, you've really got something to lose now'. Before, it was kind of this student highlife thing, like, I have nothing to lose if I'd get caught now, what the hell. And then somehow I flipped the switch and I realised that I don't want this anymore." (Cornholio, 33 years, business economist)

Social stress was another motive for cutting down or quitting dealing activities, which, in a way, can be regarded as the opposite to the stress reduction motive for increasing sales. This motive also fits well into the maturing-out pattern: while it might be acceptable to have many customers ringing the doorbell and hanging around at the dealer's home in a highly drug-related phase of life, respondents grew weary of it when getting more and more involved in a conventional lifestyle.

Other reasons for cutting down that were important for at least some respondents were *lack of cost-effectiveness* and *changes in the commercial relationship*, both related to specifics of the business. However, while the first mentioned of these motives usually applied to persons who had few interest in making profit anyway, the second one (usually the loss of a supplier) might also not necessarily be a reason for quitting, if the seller is involved in a network of users and other dealers. Thus, both motives can usually be regarded as one impulse for a change of mind that had already started.

Another reason that obviously plays a role for many, but was explicitly named only by a few, is *self-perception*. While, like in other studies on this issue (Jacinto et al. 2008, Taylor & Potter 2013), relatively few respondents would regard themselves as 'drug dealers' anyway, particularly those whose 'dealing career' ended early were most likely to be deterred by the 'dealer' label. They usually returned to non-profit-oriented go-between behaviour. Furthermore, few respondents referred to *relations to friends and/or customers,* mostly in the form of annoyance regarding their behaviour, which was regarded as typical for a drug dealer's customer. And finally, *moral concerns* played a role only for very few, exclusively related to cases of mental problems of customers. Generally, none of the (other) respondents would regard their behaviour as condemnable, because the acts of selling take place by mutual agreement, and often, customers are the driving force for an increase in sales. Thus, subjectively, the sellers have no reason for moral concern.

Many quotes from our interviews indicate that entering drug dealing did not require significant efforts. Particularly when looking at the descriptions of the beginning of stash-dealing, the words "easy" or "simple" were used quite often, as in the following example:

> "With my buddy, I realized that you can easily make money with that, and then I thought: 'Like this, you can fund your own use'." (Herbie, 27 years, hotel employee)

This notion that particularly frequent or heavy users might drift quite easily into drug dealing can be explained by the nature of illicit drug distribution which is directly linked to prohibition: the fact that there is no licit supply, together with a considerable demand for these drugs, creates a wide network of social supply, minimally commercial supply, and profit-oriented supply, in which a large part of the users are involved to some degree. Since the average user might usually be happy if s/he knows a reliable seller within his/her personal network, someone who is willing to adopt this role (usually some quite frequent user from this network) is usually welcome. Thereby, prohibition contributes to heavy use, since the legal conditions make it easy to fund it.

On the other hand, as observed by Jacques & Allen (2014), prohibition also plays a role with regard to the restriction of dealing activity. Particularly those with a rather conventional life-concept (apart from their use of illicit drugs) are heavily affected by the threat of being subject to law enforcement. In many cases, these worries had a growing impact when the person 'came of age' in a wider sense (however, this does not necessarily mean that these people stopped social supply activities, which are generally regarded as less risky). At the same time, a less conventional self-concept, e.g. among socially deprived persons, might lead to a higher likeliness of increasing the selling activity and adapting a deviant identity, including stereotypical ideas about the glamorous and dangerous lifestyle of a drug dealer. While most of those who made money with selling drugs in their earlier, 'carefree' days will mature out of dealing at some point, 'stereotypical' dealers are obviously much less likely to cease.

As a consequence, we can conclude that, while prohibition keeps law-abiding people from getting too deep into the world of drug dealing, it is a nearly perfect condition for making quick illegal money, if a person has the will to do so (which is true only for a small part of the respondents presented here).

References

Becker, H.S. (1963): Outsiders: Studies in the Sociology of Deviance. New York: The Free Press.

Bucerius, S.M. (2007): "What Else Should I Do?" Cultural Influences on the Drug Trade of Migrants in Germany. Journal of Drug Issues, 37 (3): 673-697.

Coomber, R. & Turnbull, P. (2007): Arenas of Drug Transactions: Adolescent Cannabis Transactions in England – Social Supply. Journal of Drug Issues, 37 (4): 845-865.

Jacinto, C., Duterte, M., Sales, P. & Murphy, S. (2008): I'm Not a Real Dealer: The Identity Process of Ecstasy Sellers. Journal of Drug Issues, 38 (2): 419-444.

Jacques, S. & Allen, A. (2014): Bentham's Sanction Typology and Restrictive Deterrence. A Study of Young, Suburban, Middle-Class Drug Dealers. Journal of Drug Issues, 44 (2): 212-230.

Kemmesies, U.E. (2004): Zwischen Rausch und Realität. Drogenkonsum im bürgerlichen Milieu. Unter Mitarbeit von Bernd Werse. Wiesbaden: VS-Verlag.

Matza, D. (1964): Delinquency and Drift. New York: Wiley.

Mayring, P. (2014): Qualitative content analysis: theoretical foundation, basic procedures and software solution. Klagenfurt: online. (http://nbn-resolving.de/urn:nbn:de:0168-ssoar-395173)

Mayring, P. (2000): Qualitative Content Analysis [28 paragraphs]. Forum Qualitative Sozialforschung/ Forum: Qualitative Social Research, 1(2), Art. 20: online. (http://nbnresolving.de/urn:nbn:de:0114-fqs0002204)

Murphy, S., Waldorf, D. & Reinarman, C. (1990): Drifting into Dealing: Becoming a Cocaine Seller. Qualitative Sociology, 13 (4): 321-343.
Sykes, G. & Matza, D. (1957): Techniques of Neutralization. American Sociological Review, 22 (6): 664-670.
Taylor, M. & Potter, G.R. (2013): From "social supply" to "real dealing": Drift, friendship, and trust in drug-dealing careers. Journal of Drug Issues, 43 (4): 392-406.
Winick, C. (1962): Maturing out of narcotic addiction. Bulletin on Narcotics, 14 (1): 1-7.

Women as social suppliers and retail dealers – qualitative results from a German sample

Christiane Bernard

Abstract

Drawing on a subsample of socially integrated female drug users, this paper looks at the participation and experience of women on the retail level of the drug trade. It aims to better understand the processes and factors, which encourage or hinder women's involvement in drug dealing activities.

In contrast to most research, the focus lies on private drug markets rather than street markets. Furthermore, it centres on socially inconspicuous female drug users whose involvement in the illicit drug economy is mostly limited to small-scale distribution activities. In total, 51 female drug users participated in structured face-to-face interviews. All women were recruited from out-of-treatment settings through snowball sampling.

Paying close attention to the respondents' points of view as they were expressed in the interviews, the women's strategies for acquiring and financing drugs as well as their involvement in drug distribution activities are explored.

Regarding their use, the majority of women were regular cannabis users but used other illicit substances (mostly party drugs) rather frequently as well. Most acquired drugs through friends or private dealers whom they had known for years.

Their financial resources for illicit drugs mainly came from legal sources. More than half of the interviewees had supplied drugs at least at some point in their life. Nine women were still involved in dealing activities at the time of the interview. Fourteen women had ever made any profit through supplying drugs, thus only a minority of the sample had ever dealt drugs in a genuine term.

Initiation into dealing was rarely a profit-driven choice and most interviewees distanced themselves from the identity of a drug dealer. The majority managed to maintain a non-deviant identity: together with their social responsibilities this played a significant role for reducing and maturing-out of dealing drugs.

1 Introduction

Research on drug markets rarely pays attention to gender as a factor in studying drug dealers. Traditionally, drug dealing has been viewed as a male activity with studies either focusing exclusively on men (e.g. Topalli et al. 2002, Taylor & Potter 2013, Bucerius 2007) or including only a small number of women (e.g. Jacques & Allen 2014), usually without analysing differences between female and male participants. In line with the common perception of the drug trade being a men's world, most studies suggest that due to the gender-stratified nature and hierarchy of the drug economy, women remain confined to marginal, low-level and passive roles. Their participation in distribution activities is regarded as being limited by men and their perception of women as unreliable, untrustworthy, and lacking the necessary abilities (most importantly: employing violence) to become a successful drug dealer (Maher & Hudson 2007, Adler 1985, Steffensmeier 1983).

Newer research, however, has challenged this limited view of women's participation in the drug trade, arguing that these gender differences are effects of the traditional research focus on male drug dealers resulting in "narrowly masculinist conclusions about the nature of the operations, resources, and skills involved in drug dealing" (Denton & O'Malley 1999, 514). These more recent studies, predominantly conducted by female researchers, have provided a more distinct picture, pointing to a more active, independent and powerful role of female drug dealers, describing them as skilful and competent actors (Denton & O'Malley 1999; Morgan & Joe 1996; Taylor 1993). Despite these findings, researchers still agree on the assertion that the drug economy is a highly male-dominated labour market that favours men and puts women at a disadvantage. It has been viewed as a place where the key to acquiring and holding a position as a dealer is to enact masculinity (Dunlap et al. 1997).

Yet, these findings are based on research on street markets characterized by the compulsive use of hard drugs, social and economic marginalisation and structural violence and where drug dealing can be understood as a survival strategy. Therefore, these findings cannot be transferred to other drug markets, especially not to recreational drug markets which usually lack a violent, organized crime-like structure (Taylor & Potter 2013, Coomber & Turnbull 2007). Research has described markets for recreational drugs as largely relying on social networks of friends; especially for cannabis but also for other party drug markets, the importance of friendship is a well-documented feature (Belackova & Vaccaro 2013, Taylor & Potter 2013, Coomber & Turnbull 2007, Caulkins & Reuter 2006). Also, the concept of "social supply", whereby friends supply illicit drugs to other friends at cost or with a modest mark-up, has been largely linked to lower-level recreational drug markets (Comber & Turnbull 2007, Taylor & Potter 2013, Potter 2009). Even though various definitions of social supply exist within the academic field, the term is usually applied to the "non-commercial" supply of recreational drugs between "friends" (Potter 2009). Thus, social supply blurs the line between end users and retail dealers and is regarded as a level of distribution that is below retail dealing but above the level of the end consumer (Taylor & Potter 2013). To date, there is no study within the growing body of research on recreational, middle-class drug markets and social supply that has paid specific attention to the role of women within this area of drug supply. This paper aims to address this research gap by drawing attention to women as social suppliers and retail dealers.

2 Methodology and sample description

The results presented here are based on a subsample of a larger study on socially integrated drug users of whom most had supplied drugs to others at some point in their lives. All participants were interviewed using a guided biographical interview followed by a standardised questionnaire. In order to ensure that all respondents included were socially integrated as well as experienced and current drug users, different criteria were set at the beginning of the study (for a detailed description of the methodology, see Werse & Bernard in this volume). After respondents had given consent to participate, they were asked to choose a code name. To further ensure anonymity, any information that was given in the interviews and could have identified respondents was removed from the verbatim transcripts.

A total of 214 respondents were recruited through snowball sampling, among them 51 women. The median age of the 51 female participants was 27 years, ranging from 16 to 38 years. Most had a higher-educated background: Nine out of ten respondents had the German Abitur (comparable to A-levels) and more than a fifth had earned a university degree. Half of the women were still enrolled at a university and a third had a regular full time or part time job. Only 4% were unemployed. Almost half (n=24) lived in a steady relationship (including three women who were married), and nearly one in four (n=12) had children. Almost all mothers lived together with their children: three were single mums, six lived together with the children and their father and two had joint custody where they shared the lodging and care of the children with the father.

Regarding their drug use, all women had used cannabis and 80% other illicit substances at some point in their life, with ecstasy being the most common (73%), followed by cocaine (69%) and amphetamine (67%). Nearly three quarters had used cannabis and half other illicit substances in the prior month, most often amphetamine (39%) and, to a lesser extent, ecstasy (26%) and cocaine (24%). A third consumed drugs on a regular basis: 29% used cannabis almost daily and 8% took other illicit drugs at least a few times a week. Other substances than the aforementioned not only played a very marginal role (if any role at all) for the use patterns of the interviewees but also for their distribution activities.

3 Results

3.1 Acquiring and financing drugs

Obtaining drugs for free was very common among the sample: Depending on the substance, between half and three fifths of the women stated that they mostly acquire drugs as a gift from other users. This was especially true for cocaine while it was a bit less common for cannabis. Furthermore, one in six reported to almost never pay for drugs. In this regard, most interviewees agreed that it was much easier for women than for men to get drugs for free, typically from other male users.

> "I always got invited. As a girl you rarely have to bother about getting a hold of drugs." (Erna[1], 38 years)

> "As a girl you don't have to spend much [*on drugs*], that's the good thing." (Nina, 34 years)

One important reason for this seems to be that men prefer the company of women when taking drugs.

> "They don't wanna smoke alone, or wanna be high alone. And they are always grateful when a girl is around, it gives them more pleasure than when there are only guys around." (Nina, 34 years)

Not only did a majority of the interviewees receive drugs for free, many also shared their drugs with others. Two thirds stated to often share their own cannabis or amphetamine with others, half often shared their own ecstasy and a third shared their own cocaine. Conversely, only between a tenth (amphetamine) and a third

1 To protect the identity of study participants, they were asked to choose a codename.

(cocaine) said that they never share their own drugs with others. Hence, the sharing and gift giving of drugs can be understood as a common and reciprocal phenomenon among socially integrated recreational drug users.

> "Among friends it's common to treat others to a line from time to time, because you know they will return the favour." (Maria, 26 years)

> "I have to say, when I have drugs, I always share with others. It's not a big deal to me because it is mutual. If someone shares with me, I share with him. It's no big deal." (Alice im Wunderland, 20 years)

Interestingly though, women seem to be more likely to be treated to the rather expensive drug cocaine and less likely to share their own cocaine with others.

While, in general, only a minority of the respondents predominantly purchased their own drugs – for cannabis this was true for one third of the women, and for amphetamine, cocaine and ecstasy for one quarter, respectively – almost all (with one exception) had purchased drugs themselves at least once at some point in their lives. In this regard, friends were the first choice: All respondents had ever purchased drugs from friends, whereas three quarters had ever bought from private dealers, half from street dealers and 45% from a dealer in a club. Nearly three out of four cannabis users, three out of five cocaine users and more than half of the amphetamine and ecstasy users almost exclusively bought from friends. This finding highlights the importance of friendship networks for purchasing recreational drugs.

Private dealers, on the other hand, were an almost exclusive source for only one in ten cannabis users and about one fifth of the ecstasy and amphetamine users. With one quarter of the respondents, cocaine was the drug most likely to be bought exclusively from a private dealer. No interviewee reported to almost always buy drugs from a street or club dealer.

Buying drugs from friends also worked as a strategy to protect oneself against unknown or bad drug quality, elevated prices and the risk of prosecution.

> "That has always been my principle: never buy drugs from people you don't know. I have heard and experienced too many horror stories. That's why I only buy from friends." (Miss Marple, 27 years)

> "Friends don't sell you shit." (Eule, 30 years)

Many had experienced negative situations when buying drugs in public from an unknown dealer.

> "I know where I can buy weed in public. But you get ripped off. It's a terrible price-quality ratio. You pay double the price. They rip you off in terms of quantity, make a huge profit and in the end it turns out to be of crappy quality." (Maria, 26 years)

> "These were the situations when I got ripped off. Generally, you get less and a worse quality than when buying in private settings. (…) I only did it when I had no connection and couldn't get a hold of drugs in any other way." (Sonne, 26 years)

> "I have heard many weird stories. You can never know… the guy might be a plain-clothes cop." (Josefine, 26 years)

Among the 26 cannabis users who mostly bought their own cannabis or at least purchased it and received it for free equally often, all stated to have a steady dealer. On average these relationships had been lasting for 3.5 years. The amphetamine, cocaine and ecstasy users, in comparison, were not only less likely to purchase these substances themselves but were also less likely to have a steady dealer: only 29% of the ecstasy users, 40% of the amphetamine users and 50% of the cocaine users who at least sometimes bought these drugs had a steady dealer. On average they had had a steady cocaine dealer for 2.3 years and a steady amphetamine and ecstasy dealer for 1.7 years. Having a steady dealer was usually related to a more regular use of the drug in question.

The money for buying drugs most often came from legal sources: primarily from full or part time employment and students' jobs, but also from pocket money and, to a far lesser extent, from savings or borrowed money. Only six interviewees stated that they either used to finance or that they were still financing their drug use through illegal activities: one of them through petty theft, one through running errands for a drug dealing friend and four through selling drugs.

Even though only four women financed (or had financed) their drug use through dealing activities, a total of 27 interviewees (53%) had ever distributed[2] illicit drugs in a non-profit or profit-oriented way. The following sections focus on these women.

3.2 Initiation into distributing drugs

All 27 women had ever dealt in cannabis and 15 (56%) in other illicit substances as well, most commonly amphetamine, followed by ecstasy and cocaine. None had ever dealt in 'street drugs' such as heroine or crack cocaine.

2 This includes selling drugs to others at cost, with a marginal mark-up or higher profits, but excludes sharing or gift giving.

The median age for distributing drugs for the first time without profit was 16 years (range: 13 to 23 years), and for selling with profit 19 years (range: 14 to 33 years). Most interviewees described their initiation into selling to be more of a coincidence than a conscious decision. Some simply found a new 'connection' they could purchase larger amounts from, knowing that it would be easy to find enough customers among their friends.

> "Well, I would say it was a bit of a coincidence. If I hadn't met this source, it probably would have been different now. I wouldn't have sat down, thinking about dealing drugs and then start to look for a source. Definitely not." (Sina, 33 years)

Others were motivated by friends who knew about the women's drug connection and asked if they were willing to buy drugs for them.

> "Two things came together. Friends asked me, because they knew I knew someone who was selling. Because of their requests it was easy for me to do it this way. I wasn't like, 'oh great, that's exactly what I want to do'. It just turned out that way. It wasn't a conscious decision. The bottom line is, if my friends hadn't asked me I wouldn't have come up with the idea myself." (Jara, 36 years)

While some interviewees, like Jara, stated they never really intended to sell drugs and simply started to do so, because friends who had no connection of their own asked them to provide them with drugs (a way into selling commonly referred to as becoming a go-between; Murphy et al. 1990, see also Werse & Müller in this volume), for others it seemed to be a bit the other way around. Selling drugs appeared to be more of a possibility they were already thinking about, assuming that when buying larger amounts, others would be likely to buy from them.

> "It was because I had bought a larger amount from a friend for the first time. And then it happened that others asked me if I had some drugs. And then I started to sell with small mark-ups." (Smash, 27 years)

While reports of an unplanned, random path – a drifting into dealing (Murphy et al. 1990, Jacinto et al. 2008, Werse & Müller in this volume) – were common among the interviewees, only a few described their way into dealing as an entrepreneurial, profit-motivated choice.

> "And then my boyfriend and I started to sell drugs together. (…) Well, yes, it was a rather conscious decision. It was because of the money. I was attracted to it and realized how much money you can make when the business is going well." (Lola, 26 years)

After starting to sell drugs some women experienced a further drift, although this drift could be quite rapid. Without putting much effort into it, their circle of customers and their involvement into dealing grew rather quickly. While some enjoyed these developments others got apprehensive.

> "It started small and then it grew bigger. More people I only knew briefly got to know about it and in no time I had an established clientele. (…) I had a handful of acquaintances and word got around. If you sell good quality for reasonable prices, then, in no time… It's like in real life. If you make good prices, people come to you and there is always a demand, I think. That's the point...value for money. And since I was a decent dealer with good prices I had a large number of customers in no time. And this paid off, for me as well as for my customers." (Lola, 26 years)

> „I hadn't thought about it and hadn't planned it. Word got around among my friends and it was convenient for me. It started out that he [*supplier, C.B.*] always left me a bit more...not extreme quantities, but still...packaged sachets which I passed on to my friends. That's how it crept in. Then he was like, 'Do you wanna help me with packaging? You can have your share for free then.' And then the quantities started to get bigger and bigger and that's how it happened. (…) Then I thought, I have to scale down a little bit, because things got out of hand. Suddenly there were people I didn't know who asked me and I was like, 'Oh my god, there are too many people who know about it, this really gets around.'" (Grüner Elefant, 25 years)

3.3 Distribution practices

Of the 27 women who had ever dealt in cannabis or other illicit substances, 15 had sold drugs in the prior 12 months before the interview and 9 were still dealing at the time of the interview. Among them, 8 were dealing in cannabis and two in amphetamine (none was dealing in cocaine, ecstasy or other drugs).

13 out of the 27 women had never made any profit through selling drugs, meaning that they had only sold drugs to others at cost ("social suppliers"). An additional three interviewees had sold drugs with marginal markups, making less than 50 Euros in their most profitable month. Seven women had made up to 500 Euros in their most profitable month and two women, respectively, had made up to 2,000 Euros or more. Nearly two thirds (n=9) of the 14 interviewees who had ever sold for profit had exclusively sold cannabis in their most profitable month, whereas five women attributed their most profitable month to selling speed, ecstasy or LSD, alone or in addition to cannabis.

For none of the interviewees, dealing drugs had ever been their main source of income and only nine women reported their dealing activities to be mostly geared to make profit; among them three had sold other illicit drugs than cannabis in order to make money.

3.4 Motives and customers

The questionnaire contained a list of various motives for selling drugs and interviewees were asked to state for each motive whether they agreed or not (see Werse & Bernard in this volume). 23 out of 27 interviewees (85%) described their supplying of drugs to others as a "friendly turn". Among the 13 social suppliers, "supplying drugs to friends/friendly turn" was usually the only motive they stated. On the other hand, these women revealed various reasons, why they had never sought to increase their distribution activities and become "a real dealer".

Many said it was because of the illegality and thus the risk for prosecution and social marginalisation:

> "First of all, because it's illegal." (Lotte, 24 years)

> "Ultimately, for me the risk was too high. I thought to myself: 'Of course it would be a cool thing. You can make money easily... and super-fast.' I see it among my friends. Many people I know sell drugs. I gave it a thought but in the end, for me the risk was simply too high. Also, because I have seen it happen that things can go wrong. There were plenty of examples, also of people I have met, who had spent time in jail because of selling. And in the end, fear won over greed. And I also don't wanna do this to my parents. (…) I didn't give my parents an easy time and if they had found out that I was dealing drugs, everything would have been over. I would have had to pack up my things and move under a bridge. I had no interest in that." (Alice im Wunderland, 20 years)

> "…most of all, because it can spoil your whole life." (Miss Marple, 27 years)

> "First finishing school was too important, then studying. I stayed on path. Illegality is fascinating but only to a certain extent. I am a security fanatic. I don't want to head for the gutter and end up in jail." (Pinke Zora, 29 years)

Furthermore, the potential hassle and the expenditure of time that come with dealing were reasons not to sell for profit.

> "It is simply too time consuming. When I think back, about those guys who sold weed and there were masses of people just hanging out at their place... super annoying. (…) I am a student. I cannot start selling weed and then have all those people chilling at my place. I have to study. I don't have time for this." (Maria, 26 years)

> "I don't want to get stressed because of it. It would be too much of a hassle having to run around for someone all the time. I don't know. I am just not into that." (Josefine, 26 years)

Also, "being much sought after", which for some functioned as a motivation for dealing "proper", i.e. selling with profit (see below), worked for some as an argument against it.

> "I am simply not interested in having ten people pestering me all the time." (Calamity Jane, 33 years)

> "One reason is that many people call me up very often because they want to buy from me. That is actually the main reason (...) you feel used." (Espresso, 21 years)

In addition, some interviewees mentioned the risk of increased use when dealing drugs. In fact, this was often confirmed by the participants who had dealt drugs (see below).

> "Besides, usually the sellers smoke a lot more [weed; C.B.]. Unless they are very disciplined and do only sell, starting to sell incredibly increases their use. It's simply an automatic thing." (Espresso, 21 years)

> "Your use increases, money becomes irrelevant." (Pippi Langstrumpf, 21 years)

And some interviewees clearly expressed moral concerns.

> "I don't want to push anyone into addiction or watching them perish. That's the point: What are you doing to others? I would be less concerned about myself and more concerned about others and what could happen to them..." (Lotte, 24 years)

When compared to Werse & Müller's mixed-gender sample (in this volume), these concerns appear to be gender-driven with women being more likely than men to express moral issues as an impediment to dealing drugs (or as a reason to quit dealing as in the few cases of Werse & Müller's sample).

Others attributed their non-profit dealing practice to their good nature (pity etc.), which hindered them from making money through dealing.

> "I think I would always be like, 'Oh no, I cannot charge him that much money'... it wouldn't work." (Sweet Jane, 37 years)

> "I am too reasonable, I guess. I could organize it pretty efficiently, but on the other hand it might as well be my downfall because I would probably be too nice...with

> friends who don't have money…I would not have the heart to take their money." (Code, 26 years)

And finally, the perception of the criminal world worked as a deterrent factor.

> "I really don't have a clue how it works. Whether your suppliers put you under pressure. That's one reason. I would have to be among a circle of people I can trust." (Lotte, 24 years)

Among the 14 women who had ever sold drugs with profit, the majority (n=8) agreed (most often in addition to "doing friends a favour") to the motive "supporting own drug use". An additional three interviewees said they sold drugs in order to supplement their income and earn some extra money. Also three women agreed to the motive of "being sought after" and two women were motivated by the fact that their dealing activities brought them into contact with many different people. Other motives that were listed, such as "out of conviction" and "adventurism/thrill of the forbidden" only played a minor role, with only one woman, respectively, agreeing that this was a motive for her dealing activity. The qualitative interviews, though, revealed additional motivations.

Conversely to the aforementioned arguments *against* dealing drugs for profit, especially the risks of legal consequences as well as the strain and time investment were regarded as something interviewees wanted to be compensated for by making at least some money.

> "I charge money because I am the one who takes the risk and spends the time. I don't wanna drive around for nothing. It is time consuming and stressful. I don't want to make a loss." (Veltins, 32 years)

> "It's not to enrich myself financially. I make money, though, but it's because… I fail to see why... I mean, I take the risk... 50 grams [*of amphetamine, C.B.*], I mean it's not like carrying a weapon, though, but much more than I originally intended to buy at once." (Sina, 33 years)

Furthermore, dealing drugs was not only a method to support one's own drug use financially but also a way to secure the regular supply of good quality drugs at a low price for personal use ('connoisseur' or 'supply guarantee' motive; see Werse & Müller in this volume).

> "For me it has many advantages. For example, the drugs are of better quality and the price is great. (...) I don't have to spend all my money and do still have some stock." (Sina, 33 years)

> "Certainly it was to finance my own use. But even more than that! It was great to always have drugs at home… and a steady supply, so I didn't have to dash off every time." (Lola, 26 years)

Exceeding the motive of „supplementing own income", some interviewees stated that they were fascinated by the extravagant lifestyle of a drug dealer.

> "I think I wasn't really the one who wanted to get rich by selling drugs. I just wanted to, well... being able to buy tons of clothes, going to every party, doing whatever I wanted to do. (...) Simply having enough money to support my lifestyle which was very excessive back then." (Lilli, 34 years)

Consequently, the positive effects of selling drugs not only included "financing personal use" and "earning some extra money" but could also involve an increased sociability and social status. In addition, having drugs at hand all the time was regarded as a positive outcome. However, this positive effect could as well turn into a negative consequence when it triggered an increased use.

> "Smoking every day came along with selling. My use increased because I had my own weed at home. (…) When I bought larger amounts without knowing who to sell it to, I usually turned out to be my best customer. It never worked out. (…) It was clear: Either I sold everything within two days or I suffered a loss." (Jara, 36 years)

> "…and then my use increased enormously, because I had so much weed at home. I really smoked a lot back then." (Lola, 26 years)

Regarding the question who their customers were, it became clear that for the vast majority of interviewees it was their friends who enabled them to distribute drugs. Among the 13 women who had only sold drugs at cost, all had exclusively supplied drugs to friends or acquaintances and among the ones who had ever dealt with profits, still one third (n=5) reported only selling to friends and acquaintances. Seven women had also sold to steady customers – in five cases this was true only for cannabis and in two cases for party drugs – and two women had sold to varying customers and/or strangers (in both cases cannabis and in one case other illicit drugs as well). Thus, with regards to the whole sample of the 27 women experienced in distributing drugs, for two thirds, friends and acquaintances were their only customers.

3.5 Rules and precautions

Distributing drugs within their social network was not only convenient for the women but also functioned as a precaution against getting into legal or other trouble. All but one interviewee said that selling to friends and acquaintances was a strategy to minimize the risk of legal sanctions.

> "I only sell to friends I have known before I started to sell (...) I don't even sell to friends of friends." (Sina, 33 years)

> "In general, I only sell to friends and acquaintances, and friends of friends, but not to complete strangers. (…) I would feel very uneasy if some stranger just called me and wanted to buy some stuff... especially with me being a girl... it would give me the creeps." (K. Kinski, 27 years)

Other precautions mentioned were to limit the number of customers or to limit the amount of drugs.

> "I don't see many risks, because I don't have a wide circle of customers where someone could snitch on me. That's the point where I think, I don't have to worry... well, of course I am a bit worried but I think these thoughts are not very rational." (K. Kinski, 27 years)

> "The more drugs the higher the risk. Of course you think about it, but I usually kept the amounts within a low limit." (Veltins, 32 years)

> "I think the police know about me, but I am too unimportant for them. Ultimately, they know everything. But if they started to bust every 50 gram dealer, things would get ridiculous." (Sina, 33 years)

> "The main reason why I would never sell large quantities is because of the risk of getting caught. If I, as a mother of two children, had to face jail time – that would be pure horror." (Jara, 36 years)

Yet, some respondents had experienced situation where they had to handle larger amounts of drugs, whether that meant having a larger supply stored at home or having to pick up or drop off larger quantities – situations that were particularly stressful to them.

> "Usually I didn't worry much. The only situations I didn't like were, when we had grown our own stuff. That put me under strain, because you couldn't let it disappear so easily. But the other amounts of drugs I had at home, I didn't worry about. Larger

amounts got picked up within a short time frame and a lot of things would have had to come together to put me at risk." (Jara, 36 years)

"I always wanted to get it out of my house very quickly when it exceeded certain quantities. And usually with larger amounts, I had people who dropped them off, rather than to pick them up myself." (Veltins, 32 years).

Other protective measures included either not to talk about drugs on the phone at all or to use code words when doing so.

"I never talked on the phone about it, because there has been a situation where one of my friends was wiretapped, and our conversations got recorded. I didn't get into trouble, though, but still it was heavy." (Sonne, 26 years)

"People usually get in touch by phone and the sales talk is usually like: 'Hey I wanna throw a party and need some munchies from PX [*supermarket for the US military personal, C.B.*].' Sort of pretending I had access to PX, with munchies being the code word. Another code word was music. 'Hey could you burn a CD for me with those ten songs on it', something like that. These were the codes... or during Christmas time it was usually like: 'Hey, I've heard you made some cookies. Can I have some?'... Something like that." (Smash, 27 years)

However, it is debatable whether the use of code words is a reasonable strategy, particularly in view of the fact that many interviewees named identical code words (e.g. CDs).

The majority only sold in private or privatised settings. Whether the interviewees regarded selling in their private homes versus other places as a precaution usually depended on who their customers were, the quantities (and kind) of drugs they were selling and the profits they made. Those who only sold (Cannabis) to friends with no or a small mark-up were much more likely to regard selling at their private homes as a protective measure than women who dealt in larger quantities of cannabis and party drugs, who made higher profits and who sold to steady customers as well as strangers.

"Well, another precaution is not to meet with people somewhere in public, but always have them come to my place, since these are people I also know and meet socially." (Smash, 27 years)

"I never met with people at my place... I made appointments... and usually met them at a friend's place." (K. Kinski, 27 years)

The interviews revealed very different rules female low-level drug dealers apply to protect themselves from police intervention, with relying on the friendship with their customers appearing the most important one. Furthermore, most interviewees had a relatively low perception of their risk for legal sanctions. This was mainly attributed to the fact that they only sold to friends or people they know, mostly in private settings and usually on a non-profit or small scale. Only a few assumed that their gender played a role in decreasing the risk for legal troubles.

> "(Did you ever get into trouble?) Fortunately not, so far I have always been lucky… since I am a woman…" (K. Kinski, 27 years)

> "Just recently, I had picked up some stuff at my dealer's place and the moment I stepped out of his door, I still had the bag in my hand, there was a police car. Shock! My heart went bam bam, bam bam, bam bam. But, I look very young. I usually don't get checked by the police because I look sweet and innocent." (Code, 26 years)

The rather low level of perceived risk for criminal detection was also mirrored in the women's actual encounters with the criminal justice system. Only six women were ever charged with a drug offence – in all cases with the possession of drugs. In half of the cases the charges were dropped due to the small amount that was found. In the other half of the cases the women were convicted to pay a fine or to do community service. None had served jail time.

3.6 Perceptions of a drug dealer vs. self-perception

Most participants distanced themselves from the image of a drug dealer. Unsurprisingly, this was true for all 13 social suppliers. For those women, it was out of question that a dealer is someone who sells drugs with profit.

> "A dealer is a person that deals with drugs and gains profit from it, no matter to what extent." (Pippi Langstrumpf, 21 years)

For some, a certain regularity of purchases and sales was also relevant.

> "I would describe a dealer as someone who regularly obtains drugs and sells them to others with profit." (Alice im Wunderland, 20 years)

The social suppliers among the participants most often described their distribution activities as "a favour" or simply "a passing on".

> „It is a favour... or... well, it's difficult... of course one could say: I purchase drugs and pass them on to others and take money for it. So one could say, that's where dealing begins but um… I have never made any profit. For me, that's the difference to dealing." (Sweet Jane, 37 years)

> "(Have you ever perceived yourself as a dealer?) No. (How would you term your activities?) It's more of a passing on. If I called someone because I know he is in the city and asked him, 'hey, could you get me a bottle of wine', no one would come up with the idea saying that he is dealing in wine." (Miss Marple, 27 years)

For the 14 profit-makers, distancing themselves from the dealer image was more complicated. In order to resist the dealer identity, they had to construct more positive identities for themselves.

> "(Do you see yourself as a dealer?) No. (How do you see yourself?) As a polite disseminator. (What is a drug dealer to you?) A profiteer, who only seeks to make profit, to whom kindness and friendship are irrelevant and business is the only thing that matters." (Veltins, 32 years)

> "I am a user and... enable others to use drugs when they can't get a hold of it otherwise." (Lilli, 34 years)

In some interviews it became clear that participants occasionally struggled with their own perception of what constitutes a dealer and their self-perception of not being a dealer. This conflict is reflected in Jara's statement:

> "(What is a dealer to you?) Someone who sells illegal stuff to others with profit, in any form. (Then this definition would apply to you, wouldn't it?) No! Absolutely not! [indignantly]. Okay, then with the addition of larger amounts and a larger number of customers." (Jara, 36 years)

While for most interviewees the image of a drug dealer clearly carried a negative connotation, some rejected this negativity and offered a rather business-like description.

> "Basically, I wouldn't perceive it in a negative way. To me, a dealer is someone who sells drugs in order to make money." (Sonne, 26 years)

Others changed their self-perception when they got to a point where something significant happened that caused them to rethink their own situation and to see themselves as a dealer.

> "The moment I bought a scale, that was when it became clear to me. I said to myself, 'stop fooling yourself. You ARE a dealer'. I don't make much profit and I don't have a large business, though, but still. In the eyes of the German law and the German beak, I am a dealer. One has to admit that. I'd prefer if you could buy it in a supermarket, but that's not the case. I'm selling drugs with profit, that makes me a dealer." (Sina, 33 years)

Yet, others no longer considered themselves a dealer, because they had changed their sales practice.

> „Um... well... in the past, I guess I was a small-scale dealer. But nowadays, since I mostly do collective orders... asking people how much they want with the next purchase, I wouldn't see myself as a dealer anymore. Now I am just a middleman... yes, a provider, a transporter, so to speak. (...) I guess, I am just a kind little user who asks her friends if they wanna get something because I only do large purchases. I only feel like a dealer when someone who doesn't take part in the collective order wants to buy. Then I still feel like a dealer. But as long as it's only collective orders, I see myself as a courier, so to speak." (Smash, 27 years)

Not all women resisted the dealer identity. For some, the dealer image contained quite positive elements and they integrated this identity into their self-perception with a sense of pride. However, this was usually done retrospectively.

> "Right from the beginning... I mean, that was my goal... I wanted to do this... I sold for profit, that's what dealing is." (K. Kinski)

> "Back then I would have called myself a big dealer, but not so much anymore. Now it's more… small scale, tiny scale dealer." (Lola, 26 years)

The participants offered different justifications why they did not consider themselves a dealer. From their point of view, they were not real dealers because they only sold to people in their social network, distributing drugs was more of a social than a business activity and because they only sold on a small level with small profits. They described themselves as middlewoman, provider, transporter, enabler etc. Some interviewees however, did identify as dealers but usually applied this to their past, because they had changed their sales practice or had stopped selling at all. Still, the pathways into dealing influenced the women's self-perception as a drug dealer. In those cases, where the entrée into dealing was motivated by making money, interviewees were much more likely to identify as a dealer.

3.7 *Quitting dealing*

Only 9 out of 27 women were still dealing drugs at the time of the interview, thus two thirds had experienced a phasing-out. Typically, this took the form of a "maturing out", a phenomenon that has been widely described for drug users (see e.g. Winick 1962, Prins 1995, Kemmesies 2004, Werse & Müller in this volume). These women had reduced or quit their dealing activities due to their aging and increased social responsibilities and because dealing drugs simply no longer fit their lifestyle.

> "(Why do you sell less than you used to?) Because I go to university... my studies leave me less time... it's more strain... that's why (...) I have a different lifestyle now... different friends... everything has changed a little bit." (K. Kinski, 27 years)

Family responsibility seemed to be another relevant factor. Among the 12 interviewees with children, 6 had ever dealt in drugs. However, none of the mothers were involved in selling drugs in the month prior to the interview. Thus, responsibilities that come with children appeared to be an inhibiting factor for dealing as well as using drugs.

Lilli for example who had sold party drugs (mostly ecstasy), described how she stopped using drugs when she got pregnant. After her daughter was born she resumed smoking cannabis, though, but had considerably reduced her use of other drugs.

> "I stopped when I was pregnant with my daughter. I was 26 at this time. It's been eight years now. Well, and yes, I have used drugs within the last seven and a half years, I am honest about this, but since my daughter was born, using drugs *[other than cannabis, C.B.]* has become a rare occasion, and it has decreased systematically. And nowadays, it's only, I don't know, one or two times a year, if that's the case at all." (Lilli, 34 years)

For the majority, reducing or quitting dealing appeared to be voluntary. However, at least in Lola's case, it was a forced withdrawal motivated by external forces – in her case another drug dealer. As a novice dealer, Lola had sold drugs of good quality below the common market price. Unintentionally, she had not played by the rules and had "ripped off" competitive dealers. Her sale practice eventually triggered the attention and anger of a male drug dealer who threatened her.

> "Eventually, I stopped dealing because of the competition. Someone seriously threatened me to stop selling or otherwise I would have to suffer severe consequences. He said: 'If you don't stop selling and ruining my business because you are driving down

the prices, something bad will happen to your family. And shortly after that threat, someone broke into my car, then my house keys got stolen... and I got really paranoid, this was simply too psychotic for me. I was totally scared. And so I stopped selling." (Lola, 26 years)

Yet, Lola's phasing out was only temporary, followed by a re-entry after several years. Just weeks before the interview she had found a new connection and had started to re-establish her customer base.

"It used to be much more, but then I stopped and things drifted apart. I just recently restarted and it's building up… I want to keep it within a limit, though… first, because I don't have the time and also because I just want to support my personal use."

What is interesting about Lola's case is that she was one of the few female interviewees whose pathway into dealing drugs was clearly motivated by making money. She proudly used to identify herself as a dealer, had made larger profits and dealt on a larger scale than all other female participants. It can be assumed that she (unconsciously) ascended to a level of dealing where competition (and the use of violence) becomes more prevalent – as this is illustrated by her "bustout" (Adler & Adler 1994: 566 ff.) caused by another drug dealer. It seems that the factors "profit-oriented entry", "identifying as a drug dealer", "larger profits made" and "forced withdrawal from the drug business" contributed to her ambition to resume dealing.

4 Discussion

The researched sample consisted of 51 socially integrated recreational female drugs users. Even though this was not an inclusion criterion of the study, the vast majority was well-educated – an effect likely caused by the recruitment strategy of snowball sampling with a clear focus on students and their networks of friends. Most of the women were regular cannabis users but also used party drugs quite frequently. Twenty-seven respondents had supplied drugs at some point in their life; among them thirteen had sold drugs only at cost whereas fourteen had sold drugs with profit.

Friendship was a key feature for obtaining as well as for distributing drugs. Many interviewees often received drugs for free and shared their own drugs with others. Drugs were usually purchased in private settings and within the social network of friends. The same was true for supplying and selling drugs.

The women's pathway into distributing drugs largely followed what has been described elsewhere (e.g. Murphy et al. 1990, Jacinto et al. 2008, Werse &

Müller in this volume) as "drifting into dealing": without making a clear or conscious decision these women drifted from a user to a social supplier because they knew a seller and started to buy drugs for their friends. For only a few women, on the other hand, initiation into dealing was a profit-driven choice. These findings are well in line with other studies on recreational drug markets and drug suppliers (Murphy et al. 1990 & 2005, Jacinto et al. 2008, Coomber 2006, Taylor & Potter 2013). After their entry, some women experienced a further "drift" as their customer base and sales extended – in some cases rather rapidly.

Distributing drugs was most often claimed as helping out friends and doing them a favour. Subsidizing personal use usually motivated dealing that included making at least some profit. Additional motives contained earning extra money, but also an increased sociability and having access to drugs with a good quality-price ratio.

Interviewees who had only supplied drugs at cost stated various reasons why they did not sell with profit, with the illegality and thus the risk of prosecution being the most important one. However, legally speaking, there is little or no difference between "social supply" and a profit-oriented dealing since the (German) law generally penalises supply regardless whether it is to generate profits or not (although this factor might be taken into account when it comes to sentencing). This issue has also been discussed for other countries (Duffy et al. 2008, Potter 2009, Stevenson 2008, Taylor & Potter 2013, Lenton et al. in this volume). In this context, various scholars have suggested that social supply or minimally commercial supply should be distinguished from real dealing and should be defined separately by law (see e.g. Coomber & Turnbull 2007, Duffy et al. 2008, Potter 2009, Moyle et al. 2013).

In general, the perception of risk for detection was low among the participants, however most had some precautionary strategies for purchasing and selling drugs, with only buying from and selling to friends being the most important precautions. Others strategies included limiting the number of customers or the amount of drugs, not talking about drugs on the phone and selling in private settings.

Much like the ecstasy sellers in Jacinto et al.'s (2008) study, most interviewees distanced themselves from the identity of a drug dealer. For social suppliers this was much easier than for the profit-makers; the latter usually came up with other labels that allowed them to describe their dealing activities in positive terms. Most resisted the dealer identity because they only sold to friends and acquaintances and they only dealt on a small scale with small profits. In some cases, however, women had perceived themselves as a dealer; this was usually the case when their entry into dealing was profit-motivated.

Most women managed to maintain a non-deviant identity: Besides their drug use and distribution activities, they were not involved in other types of illegal/criminal behaviour, were holding legitimate occupations and were maintaining mainstream careers. Thus, they still had strong ties to non-deviant activities and milieus. Their non-deviant identity and their social responsibilities also seemed to play a significant role for reducing and maturing-out of dealing drugs.

There were some limitations of the study. First, since this research applied a qualitative approach and studied a small, non-representative sample of socially inconspicuous drug users and sellers, findings cannot be generalized. Nonetheless, when considered in the light of existing research on social supply and retail dealing, the findings are similar. This is especially true with regards to the meaning of friendship for acquiring and supplying recreational drugs among socially integrated drug users, pathways into dealing drugs, motives and precautions as well as the rejection of a dealer identity.

Second, gender differences were not a focus of the larger study where this subsample was drawn from. Therefore, neither the qualitative interviews nor the questionnaire contained specific questions regarding how gender structures the women's opportunities to engage in the small scale drug trade. However, since the interviews were focused but open-ended, they allowed the interviewees to express their views and experiences freely (which could also include gender specifics).

Gender was most often mentioned in the interviews as a factor in obtaining drugs, referring to women being more likely than men to receive drugs for free, a finding supported elsewhere (e.g. Rodriguez & Griffin 2005). Some also assumed that being a woman decreased their risk of police detection. In the context of supplying and selling drugs, though, gender was rarely mentioned as a factor. This might be largely attributable to the structure and organisation of recreational drug markets at the retail level that have been found to lack a hierarchical, violent and organised-crime like structure (see e.g. Taylor & Potter 2013). The friendship-based structure of this market may contribute to a subordinate significance of gender on this low level of drug distribution. Only Lola, who got into a somewhat higher distribution level, recalled a situation, where her gender had played a role. This was when she tried to re-establish her business and had to find a new supplier:

> "And when I wanted to start selling again, I asked him if I could purchase larger quantities from him. So I asked him and he said: 'Um, I'd rather not! You are a woman… and women are not supposed to have anything to do with it.' But in the end he sold it to me anyway." (Lola, 26 years).

Future research should be carried out on gender differences in retail markets, focusing not only on the gender of social suppliers and retail dealers, their gender-related sale practices, pathways into dealing etc., but also on the gender of their customers, their suppliers and so forth.

References

Adler, Patricia (1985): Wheeling and dealing: An ethnography of an upper-level dealing and smuggling community. New York: Columbia University Press.

Adler, Patricia A. & Adler, Peter (1994): Shifts and Oscillations in Deviant Careers: The Case of Upper-Level Drug Dealers and Smugglers. In: Adler, Patricia & Adler, Peter (Eds.): Constructions of Deviance. Social Power, Context, and Interaction. Belmont: Thomson Wadsworth: 560-572.

Belackova, Vendula & Vaccaro, Christian A. (2013): "A friend with weed is a friend indeed": Understanding the relationship between friendship identity and market relations among marijuana users. In: Journal of Drug Issues 43, 3: 289-313.

Bucerius, Sandra M. (2007): "What else should I do?" Cultural influences on the drug trade of migrants in Germany. In: Journal of Drug Issues 37, 3: 673-698.

Caulkins, Jonathan P. & Reuter, Peter (2006): Illicit drug markets and economic irregularities. In: Socio-Economic Planning Sciences 40: 1–14.

Coomber, Ross (2006): Pusher myths: Re-situating the drug dealer. London: Free Association Books.

Coomber, Ross & Turnbull, Paul J. (2007): Arenas of drug transactions: Adolescent cannabis transactions in England – Social Supply. In: Journal of Drug Issues 7, 4: 845-866

Denton, Barbara & O'Malley, Pat (1999) Gender, trust and business – Women drug dealers in the illicit economy. In: British Journal of Criminology 39, 4: 513–530.

Duffy, Martin, Schafer, Nadine, Coomber, Ross, O'Connell, Lauren & Turnbull, Paul J. (2008). Cannabis supply and young people: "It's a social thing." York: Joseph Rowntree Foundation.

Dunlap, Eloise, Johnson, Bruce D. & Maher, Lisa (1997): Female Crack Sellers in New York City. Who They Are and What They Do. In: Women and Criminal Justice 8, 4: 25-55.

Jacques, Scott & Allen, Andrea (2014): Bentham's Sanction Typology and Restrictive Deterrence: A Study of Young, Suburban, Middle-Class Drug Dealers. In: Journal of Drug Issues 44, 2: 212-230.

Jacinto, Camille, Duterte, Micheline, Sales, Paloma & Murphy, Sheigla (2008): I'm not a real dealer": The identity process of ecstasy sellers. In: Journal of Drug Issues 8, 2: 419-444.

Kemmesies, Uwe E. (2004): Zwischen Rausch und Realität. Drogenkonsum im bürgerlichen Milieu. Wiesbaden: VS Verlag für Sozialwissenschaften.

Maher, Lisa & Hudson, Susan L. (2007): Women in the Drug Economy. A Metasynthesis of the Qualitative Literature. In: Journal of Drug Issues 37, 4: 805-826.

Morgan, Patricia and Joe, Karen A. (1996) Citizens and outlaws: The private lives and public lifestyles of women in the illicit drug economy. In: Journal of Drug Issues 26, 1: 125–141.

Moyle, Leah, Coomber, Ross & Lowther Jason (2013), 'Crushing a walnut with a sledge hammer? Analysing the penal response to the social supply of illicit drugs'. Social & Legal Studies, 22: 553–73.

Murphy, Sheigla, Waldorf, Dan & Reinarman, Craig (1990): Drifting into Dealing: Becoming a Cocaine Seller. In: Qualitative Sociology 13, 4: 321-343.

Murphy, Sheigla, Sales, Paloma, Duterte, Micheline & Jacinto, Camille (2005): A Qualitative Study of Ecstasy Sellers in the San Francisco Bay Area. Final Report to the National Institute of Justice. San Francisco: Institute for Scientific Analysis.

Parker, Howard (2000): How young Britons obtain their drugs: Drugs transactions at the point of consumption. In: Natarajan, Mangai & Hough, Mike (Eds.): Illegal drug markets: From research to prevention policy. Crime prevention studies, Volume 11. New York: Criminal Justice Press: 59-82.

Potter, Gary R. (2009). Exploring retail-level drug distribution: Social supply, "real" dealers and the user/dealer interface. In Demetrovics, Zsolt, Fountain, Jane & Kraus, Ludwig (Eds.): Old and new policies, theories, research methods and drug users across Europe. Lengerich: Pabst Science Publishers.

Prins, Engel H. (1995): Maturing out: An empirical study of personal histories and processes in hard-drug addiction. Erasmus University Rotterdam.

Rodriguez, Nancy & Griffin, Marie L. (2005): Gender Differences in Drug Market Activities: A Comparative Assessment of Men and Women's Participation in the Drug Market. Criminal Justice and Criminology. Tempe: Arizona State University.

Steffensmeier, Darrell J. (1983): Organization Properties and Sex-segregation in the Underworld. Building a Sociological Theory of Sex Differences in Crime. In: Social Forces 61, 4: 1010-1032.

Taylor, Avril (1993): Women drug users. An ethnography of a female injecting community. Oxford: Clarendon Press.

Taylor, Matthew & Potter, Gary R. (2013): From "Social Supply" to "Real Dealing": Drift, Friendship, and Trust in Drug Dealing Careers. In: Journal of Drug Issues 43, 4: 392-406.

Topalli, Volkan, Wright, Richard & Fornango, Robert (2002): Drug Dealers, Robbery and Retaliation. Vulnerability, Deterrence and the Contagion of Violence. In: British Journal of Criminology 42, 2: 337-351.

Winick, Charles (1962): Maturing out of narcotic addiction. In: Bulletin on Narcotics 14: 1-7.

Social supply: a personal network perspective

Marieke Vlaemynck

Abstract

Social networks are key to drug markets as they are for many other types of human interaction. Rooted in both anthropology and sociology, network analysis is increasingly adopted in drug market research. Supply side studies to date mainly focus on large organised networks, and make use of police reports or telephone taps to describe the composition of these networks. The network perspective holds important opportunities to study other topics of supply, more specifically *social supply*. Already included in the name, the social aspect is deemed very important when studying supply relationships. But, at the same time, this relationship still includes an exchange of goods, which implies that a certain material or immaterial goal might be intended. This chapter discusses how a network perspective allows sketching the nuanced nature of supply relationships by placing them in a relational context. First, the way a network researcher views the world in general and drug markets in particular is discussed. Drug markets are then defined as a fluid collection of personal networks of different types of actors (e.g. users, suppliers, brokers, non-users…). It is in these particular personal networks that social supply is situated as a specific relationship between two actors that combines an aspect of exchange with an aspect of closeness.

1 Introduction

How do users and suppliers relate to each other? To what extent are they friends? To what extent do they have a consumer-client relation? This chapter puts social supply in its relational context and develops a view on supply as a tie in a wider social network in which cannabis is present. That way, we aim to unravel some of the complexity of different supply patterns.

Patterns of supply have been studied extensively in drug market research. Several studies describe retail-level suppliers as friends, acquaintances or relatives and suggest supply has an important social side (Coomber & Turnbull 2007; Duff 2005; Hough et al. 2003; Parker 2000; Potter 2009; Werse 2008).

This type of social supply is considered different from a more traditional form of *dealing*, which is associated with a commercial transaction between strangers. As a concept, social supply contributes to our understanding of the social aspect of supply. However, it is unclear what this social aspect is all about. One way of putting it is to consider suppliers as friends or friends of friends who supply cannabis. A definition of who these friends or friends of friends are is very subjective (Crossley 2010). Therefore, it is particularly difficult to compare different accounts of the social aspect of supply.

The concept is further complicated because of different interpretations of the goal of supply. There is a wide range of possible rewards that can be exchanged, ranging from cannabis, money or other material goods to even immaterial goods (Coomber & Turnbull 2007; Duff 2005; Hough et al. 2003; Parker 2000; Potter 2009; Werse 2008). This leads to different interpretations on what social supply is and what is considered commercial supply. For example, Coomber and Moyle (2014) extend social supply to *minimally commercial* supply.

This chapter argues that social network analysis can provide a more profound insight and understanding of the nature of cannabis supply. I argue that research on the structure and composition of social networks not only offers insights on various criminal organisations but can also benefit our understanding of supply. Drug market research, as well as criminology in general, increasingly uses network analysis to describe different types of organisations as well as to further nuance existing concepts. That said, several studies applied network analysis to explore the social organisation of drug markets (Morselli 2009). In recent years, the initiation and continuance of substance use is also further explored through analysis of friendship networks. For example, several studies into peer influence not only question the number of friends an individual has, but also study how structure and composition of the network influence substance use (Bauman & Ennett 1996; Michell & Pearson 2000).

Social supply seems to refer to a specific relationship between two people as a so-called user and a supplier. This chapter argues that further understanding of supply patterns should include a detailed view of the personal network that surrounds both user and supplier. As argued below, this leads to the definition of supply as a complex tie between two people. This tie combines a social relation with an exchange relation and is shaped by individual attributes as well as the relational context. A supply interaction is then characterized by a commercial as well as social motivation. However, the supply relationship can include multiple and different types of supply events with one or more network member(s). The first part of this chapter describes what is meant by a networked drug market. Second, I focus on the multiplex nature of supply ties between individuals, before thirdly exploring the embedded character of this tie. The concluding part proposes a network conceptualisation of social supply.

2 A networked drug market

Social network analysis is used to describe the composition and structure of *dark* or *covert* networks (Morselli 2009). Drug market research mainly adopts social network analysis to describe the social organisation of drug trafficking organisations. Based on mainly secondary data, network studies explore the composition and structure of these organisations. Network measures like density inform on the presence of connections between members that is actually present. On the other hand, measures of centrality can give insight in the positions of certain individuals in the network.

However, across studies the term networks is used in conceptually different ways. Dorn et al. (Dorn 2005) argue that there are three common uses of this term. First, one can see the drug market as a whole, meaning that the drug market is *one large social network* in which participants have to interact with each other (Dorn et al. 2005). In doing so, they actually construct the drug market. This perspective is in line with a traditional view of the drug market as a vertically structured supply chain. Second, drug markets can also be described as a sum of small groups of individuals, sometimes called *disorganised crime* (Paoli 2002; Reuter 1985), sometimes *networks*. In this context, some authors doubt the existence of larger criminal organisations. The concept of disorganised crime challenges the traditional hierarchical view of drug markets in exchange for a networked view (Paoli 2002). A third perspective refers to drug markets as *fluid networks*. The concept of networks is then used as a way to describe the durability of the organisation. As opposed to fixed structures which last over time, fluid networks refer to an ever-changing market. Dorn et al. (2005) argue that the first perspective is not contradicted by any author, whereas the second and third perspectives, which often co-exist, are subject to debate.

Network studies confirm the idea of flexible and dynamic organised groups, rather than strict hierarchical groupings. Criminal groups do not follow a strict hierarchy, but are flexible and organised in an informal way. McGloin and Nguyen (2013) for example point to the finding in literature on criminal networks that networks consist of varied structures, and therefore treating all groups similarly is inadequate. Drug market studies have regularly pointed out their flexible and dynamic nature (Calderoni 2012). The traditional *corporate* model, arguing that criminal organisations are centralized, with a strict division of labour and a strict hierarchy, is challenged based on the research mentioned above (Giménez-

Salinas Framis 2013). In recent years, social network analysis has focused on the nodes and links of members of these networks to provide a more profound insight and understanding of connectedness and patterns of organisation. From this point of view, some authors argue illegal networks adopt a more horizontal structure, with interchangeable roles and flexible rules (see Giménez-Salinas Framis 2013). In comparison to a more strictly organised structure, these networks are considered more resilient to external threats.

However, this does not mean that criminal groups cannot be centralized around one or two actors; for example, in an ongoing police investigation. Central individuals are tempting individuals to focus upon. Centrality is studied in terms of direct connections (i.e. degree centrality) or indirect connections (i.e. betweenness centrality). The latter expresses to what extent some people are brokers through whom other actors must go to connect with each other (McGloin & Nguyen 2013). Centrality is assumed to relate to influence and control. Morselli (2009) measured both density, the number of contacts with whom a participant is directly connected, and betweenness centrality. As such, he studied not only how many connections a person has, but also focused on individuals who have less direct contacts but hold an important intermediary position. Morselli (2009) analysed 6 Canadian cases: a terrorist network, three drug trafficking organisations and two groups that export stolen luxury vehicles. In order to visualize the network and to measure centrality, he analysed physical surveillance and electronic records as well as conversations obtained through telephone tap. The main conclusion confirms the hypothesis that criminal groups consist of loose partnerships rather than hierarchical relationships. A remarkable conclusion is the crucial position of brokers, which contrasts with the more popular view of criminal groups as a rigid organisation and supports the idea of criminal groups as fluid structures in which individuals with large brokerage capital can position themselves better than other individuals.

Social network analysis aids in exploring two aspects of collaboration in covert settings: trust and secrecy (Morselli et al. 2007). Morselli et al. describe two particular interesting studies: Erickson's (1981) study of six different covert networks[1], a network of marijuana users being one of them, and the study of Baker & Faulkner (1993) into conspiracies in a heavy electrical equipment company. Erickson (1981) stresses the importance of trust in a covert social network under risk. Organisation-wise, these networks will on the one side rely on long-existing

1 Erickson (1981) studied the following six cases: the Auschwitz underground during World War II; a rebellion group in 19th century China; a New York City Cosa Nostra family; a heroin market in San Antonio, TX; a sample of marijuana consumers from Cheltenham, England; and a Norwegian resistance group during World War II.

relationships; on the other hand the organisation will place security over efficiency when acting. In their study of conspiracies, Baker and Faulkner concluded that peripheral players are crucial to the network. These players stay at the periphery on purpose in order to protect themselves. These networks lack a clear-cut core, which has a negative effect on efficiency. Without a clear core, transmission of information takes longer. However, knowing that detection highly increases the risk of termination, this lower efficiency is a price they are willing to pay for security. Morselli et al. (2007) further argue that this security-efficiency trade-off is also influenced by the network's objective and the frequency of actions. Especially in the case of drug trafficking, peripheral actors bring security to the network (e.g. by acting as brokers between otherwise disconnected traffickers). They also insulate participants at the core (Dorn et al. 1992; Pearson et al. 2001).

Network perspectives also contribute to our understanding of the nature of organised crime. Papachristos and Smith (2012) analysed relational data of nearly 3,000 individuals connected to Al Capone's syndicate and explored the way this crime syndicate interacted with legitimate social institutions. He argues that criminal networks are *embedded*, meaning that social networks, whether criminal or non-criminal, overlap and intersect so that individuals exist in multiple social circles at the same time. Moreover, he also found ties to be *multiplex* in nature, meaning that they consist of several types of relationships simultaneously (e.g. social relation, exchange relation). Although theories accept this interdependent nature of ties, most research does not include these complexities due to data-related or methodological limitations (Papachristos & Smith 2012).

Furthermore, a growing amount of research indicates that the network perspective aids in developing guidance for law enforcement practices.

Besides the social organisation of drug trafficking organisations, social network analysis is argued to help further nuance the concept of peer influence. The relationship between peers and delinquency is one of the key themes in criminology and it is generally assumed that peers are likely to behave in similar ways as their friends. The assumption of peer influence is based on a one-dimensional concept of peer influence as *exposure to delinquent friends* (Haynie 2001; Papachristos 2011). Accordingly, peer influence is often measured by the number of delinquent friends an individual has. Social network analysts however argue that peer influence is a multi-faceted concept. The number of delinquent friends is an incomplete measure of peer influence as it fails to recognize structure and patterns within one's network. Papachristos (2011) for example argues that centrality and density of a network are important as well. In a dense network, all members are linked to each other which increases the likelihood of tendencies towards similar behaviour.

One of the key issues is the assumption that substance users mainly have substance-using friends who influence an individual's using behaviour and attitudes. Network analysts explore this issue via measures of *homophily*, the extent to which actors in a network share a pre-defined attribute (e.g. gender, age, substance use). The findings are not unanimous however some research indicates cannabis networks are formed based on prior homophily of age and gender, rather than on homophily related to substance use (Kirke 2006). Furthermore, people in a substance-using social network are more likely to start using drugs themselves (Galea et al. 2004).

Besides homophily, some studies also use measures of centrality to study the network position of users. Three positions have been most frequently identified: *members* , who belong to dense networks, *liaisons,* who are loosely connected to peers, and *isolates,* who are relatively unconnected with others (Kobus & Henry 2010). Some studies note that being a user is mostly connected with being a *member* of a dense group, while other studies argue users are predominantly rather *liaisons* who are loosely tied to the network (Kirke 2006; Kobus & Henry 2010). As Kobus and Henry suggest, a possible explanation might be that these *liaisons* have more social ties than *members* or *isolates*. Having more social ties might make it easier to obtain cannabis as well (Kobus & Henry 2010). Network studies including positional analysis point to the importance of brokers in the search for information or goods (Granovetter 1973; Burt 1992). To date, no research focuses on the position of suppliers in these networks. *Social supply* research suggests suppliers can take multiple roles, one of which being a *go-between* or *broker* (Werse 2008).

3 Supply as a tie formed by supply interactions of ego-alter and alter-alter

A network view on *social supply* discusses *social supply* in terms of a tie between users and suppliers. Previous research indicates that supply can take different forms, ranging from *dealing* to *sharing.* Therefore, I argue that *social supply* is but one variation of a broader supply tie (e.g. Coomber & Turnbull 2007; Hough et al. 2003). In order to further explore the concept, I study the complete tie between respondents (further referred to as *ego*) and members of their personal network (further referred to as *alters*). This tie combines both, a social relation and some form of exchange relation. This tie is situated within a wider personal network which encompasses all people that are involved in cannabis use or supply. The ties between these alters, besides their ties with ego, form the relational context which also influences ego's attitudes and behaviour.

3.1 Social relation

Literature suggests that not only the existence of the relation but also the strength of a social relation shapes the structure of a network. Existing research refers to suppliers in terms of *friends, family* or *acquaintances*, but remains vague on further nuancing what is meant by friends or acquaintances or even family (Potter 2009). Social network analysts suggest concepts like *friends* or *acquaintances* are far too subjective to use as they may take different meanings for different actors or even for the same actor under different circumstances (Crossley 2010). Instead, I focus on closeness indicators like intimacy and support (Mashek & Aron 2004).

3.2 Exchange relation

The exchange relation refers to the exchange of cannabis and the reward that is given. This type of relation is inherently part of the *cannabis network*, the part of the *complete network* where cannabis is used and exchanged.[2] An exchange relation is founded in complementary needs (in this case cannabis and a reward) that should be satisfied by the exchange. Literature on *social supply* indicates that this reward sometimes seems to be absent or non-monetary (Parker 2000; Harrison et al. 2007; Coomber & Turnbull 2007; Werse 2008; Hough et al. 2003; Potter 2009). Network analysts refer to these relations as *communal relations* where benefits are given in response to a need and out of concern for the welfare of the other person. In such relationships, receiving benefits does not create a specific obligation to return a comparable benefit, as it does in exchange relationships (Clark & Mills 1993). However, Batson (1993) already suggests exchange principles might be present in both exchange and communal relations. The difference between these two types of relations might be less clear-cut than anticipated (Batson 1993). However, there is a wide continuum between communal and exchange relations. In order to explore the existence of this type of relation, different

---

2 In my study, names of network members of the personal network of respondents are generated in two steps. The first name generator focuses on the complete network. Respondents name exactly 25 people who they spent leisure time with (e.g. going to pub, playing sports, family members…) during the three months prior to the interview. The second name generator focuses on the cannabis network. This particular network includes any person who was present when respondents used cannabis during the three months prior to the interview. This network includes suppliers, people as well as people who do not supply, users as well as non-users. Respondents can add any number of people. As such, cannabis networks include members of the initial complete network and/ or new people respondents mainly interact with in the context of cannabis use and supply.

types of supply patterns are examined: gift giving, receiving, selling, buying, sharing your own cannabis and sharing someone else's cannabis.

3.3 Structure

As described above, the composition of the personal network of ego is studied through individual attributes as well as through the tie between ego and alters. Network analysts argue that behaviour and attitudes are not only shaped by ties between ego and alters but also by the ties among alters, or structure (Marin & Wellman 2011). To gain further insight in this relational context of supply ties, the internal structure of both the *complete* and the *cannabis network* is studied.

Personal network studies make very limited use of structural measures due to the fact that respondents are often not able to adequately remember ties which they are not part of (Bell et al. 1998). However, studies that do integrate structural measures argue that density and centrality measures give valuable information about the social world of the network (Snijders et al. 1995; McCarty & Molina 2011; McCarty 2002). To gain some knowledge about the structure of the *complete network*, respondents are asked to indicate whether, to their knowledge, alters know each other apart from ego. Additionally, the structure of the *cannabis network* is examined by questioning whether, to the knowledge of ego, alters use cannabis together without ego being present. Besides these alter-alter relations, the position of key actors is further explored. Based on the above described research on the position of users, and the description of social suppliers as "brokers", I explore how respondents describe different roles they or other network members adopt. In doing so, these interchangeable roles are examined further.

4 Supply as a process of exchanging cannabis and reward

Social supply, as described above, is considered a specific pattern of supply. The supply tie between users and suppliers encompasses a social relation and an exchange relation. In line with Crossley (2010), we argue that this supply tie is neither absent or present, nor uniform because ties are not passive, but involve a unique history of interaction and take on different meanings for different actors (Mische & White 1998). This history of interaction created and continues to create a "social world" of shared meanings and knowledge which affects the way network members interact. This way, we explore the nature of the supply tie between users and suppliers.

4.1 *Process of exchanging cannabis*

As both the social and exchange aspects are intertwined in one tie, I opted to explore this tie through a study of supply experiences. Therefore, the actual process of exchanging is examined. This process includes the initial motivation, the different actions undertaken to exchange cannabis as well as the results of these actions. Possible results include exchanging cannabis and rewards as well as being referred to a different person. As such, social supply, or any kind of supply in that matter, can benefit from studies into network agency (Giuffre 2013) as well as Kirke's (2006) network study into the diffusion of illicit drug use in networks of teenagers.

Drug market literature as well as network studies indicate that both motivation and the process of acquiring are shaped by aspects of individual rational actions as well as a complex peer-influencing process (Aloise-Young et al. 1994; Bauman & Ennett 1996; Coggan & Mckellar 1994; Cullen 2010; Kirke 2006). My study acknowledges this, but does not aim to disentangle the extent to which peers and/or individual ratio influence the decision to obtain or to supply cannabis. In order to study social supply in depth, I focus on the actual process. I acknowledge that motivation is an important part of this process, but aim to describe the process as a whole, ranging from motivation to the resulting exchange.

The process of obtaining cannabis for example encompasses a search for information which can result in a further forwarding to other people, a positive answer or a negative answer. Although dating back to the seventies, Lee's (1969) study into the search for an abortionist is an important example of how issues of access, issues of agency, as well as issues of trust come together when looking for information about something you perceive as not accepted by the society as a whole (Giuffre 2013; Lee 1969). In case of the last option, the process is repeated until a positive outcome, in our case cannabis, is received. During this search, individuals can use information provided by other sources or take initiative themselves. For example, basic factual information and gossip is information provided by other sources (Lee 1969). In our study this entails for example all factual information about cannabis, its use and its supply. The second level refers to the shared stories about technical knowledge and sensible use (Pearson & Michell 2000; Duff 2005; Aldridge et al. 2011). It is this process that creates the network, and meanings and shared histories are further diffused. In dense networks where a lot of information on how to obtain cannabis exists, individuals are less likely to search for information outside their network. If there is little or no information present, individuals will have to find a way to enter into another network in order to find information (Giuffre 2013). As described above, I do not consider users to be purely rational actors nor completely influenced by their peers. Rather, I explore the process of being influenced by existing meanings and shared stories as well as creating further histories through interactions.

I study this process through supply experiences. In line with the discussion of the exchange tie above, this includes a discussion of possible outcomes.

From the cannabis user's point of view, the process is visualized as follows:

Figure 1 Exchange process of cannabis

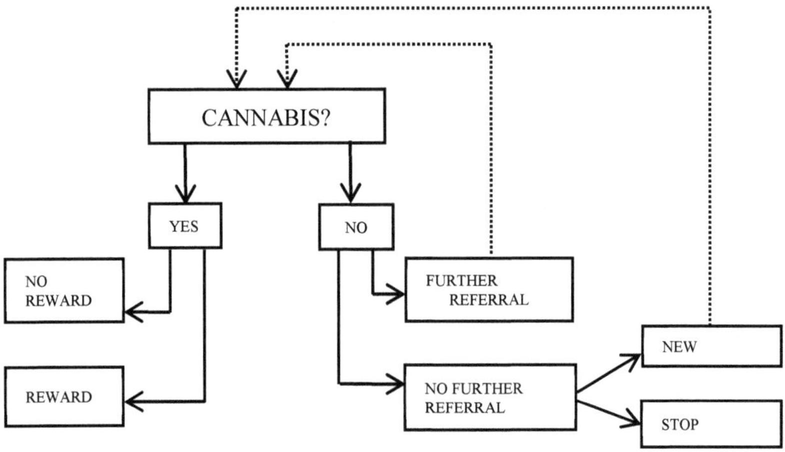

The illustration above (figure 1) depicts several outcomes. When cannabis is present, a user can either obtain cannabis or not. Not obtaining cannabis can result in a new question to another person or a *further referral*. Based on the above described research on the importance of brokers (e.g. Morselli 2009), personal experiences as a broker or go-between will shed a further light on the position of key actors in the personal network of the respondent. If respondents describe a specific alter or alters as go-between(s), we also address the reasons why certain people are contacted and why certain other people are not. This informs on the barriers of communication as well as about who respondents perceive or appoint as experts concerning supply (Lee 1969).

Obtaining cannabis can follow different patterns: dealing, swapping, gift giving, sharing or something else. Besides a description of these different patterns, I focus on the issue of *dealing*. Supply studies indicate respondents differentiate between suppliers and "real dealers" (Potter 2009; Hough et al. 2003; Coomber & Turnbull 2007; Coomber 2006). A key element in the discussion of supply patterns concerns the issue of a *reward*. This reward can be monetary or not. Coomber and Moyle (2014) studied the issue of exchanging money. According to them, a *social supply* relationship can involve a transaction of money but only to the extent this money is intended to cover the costs associated with the own procurement of the drug or the growing process (if the supplier sells home-grown cannabis). Profit therefore is defined by the intention to make money to cover other costs of living (e.g. hedonistic lifestyle, rent, food…). In this context, Coomber and Moyle extend the concept of *social supply* to *minimal commercial supply*. Personal perceptions on rewards and different types of supply can be explored through a discussion of personal experiences.

4.2 Context of supply experiences

Supply experiences are situated within the context in which they take place. In line with previous studies on the social context of smoking, the circumstances in which current supply comes into being and takes place are discussed (Amos et al. 2004; Michell & Amos 1997; Cullen 2010; Highet 2004, 2003; Bell et al. 1998). These circumstances are situated within a *social setting* as well as a *collaborative setting* where the actual exchange takes place.

Drug market research further argues that informal controls are part of the *social setting* that shapes the way how cannabis use is experienced. *Social supply* research situates supply in a *social* setting where cannabis use is considered a *social* event (Coomber and Turnbull 2007; Harrison et al. 2007; Parker 2000). One way to address this social setting in a personal network study is through a discussion of the actual physical location where cannabis is used.

Obtaining or supplying cannabis takes place in a *collaborative setting* where secrecy and security are evaluated against each other. Research also indicates that particular places can be associated with a feeling of safety or can be avoided because of fear of detection (Shewan et al. 2000). To date, little network research integrates this aspect in the study of substance use (Oliver et al. 2014). However, network research of drug markets does indicate that the trade-off between secrecy and security influences the focus of their social organisation (Morselli et al. 2007). Especially at the moment when there is activity, meaning when substances are acquired or supplied, the level of trust and secrecy will be balanced against efficiency in what Morselli et al. (2007) describe as "*risky collaborative settings*".

5 Conclusion

Social supply contributes to our understanding of the social aspect of different patterns of supply. However, to date there remains room for debate on what this social aspect is actually about. One way of putting it, is to consider suppliers as *friends* or *friends of friends* who supply cannabis. A definition of who these friends or friends of friends are is very subjective (Crossley 2010). Therefore, it is particularly difficult to compare different accounts of the social aspect of supply.

Aiming at understanding and clarifying the grey area that still surrounds *social supply*, I argue that supply research could benefit from the network perspective. This network perspective implies a particular view on drug markets in general, but also on more specific supply patterns.

Network studies on drug markets argue networks in drug markets exist in multiple forms (Dorn et al. 2005). Some consider networks as a specific form of social organisation within the traditional upper, middle and lower level of drug markets. Others argue drug markets also can take the form of one large network, which combines loose partnerships. Network studies on the position of go-betweens or brokers confirm that drug markets rather exist of loose partnerships than as a strict vertical organisation. One characteristic of such an organisation is the interchangeability of roles (Giménez-Salinas Framis 2013). Accordingly, we situate supply in an ever changing, dynamic market where suppliers not only take the role of supplier at one moment, but take on one or more different other social roles (e.g. user, 'not being a user', friend, family member, colleague) at a different moment or even simultaneously (e.g. a friend who is also a supplier takes on both of these roles at the moment cannabis is exchanged).

A network view of the nature of supply is further completed by an understanding of networks as embedded and multiplex (Papachristos 2012). In line with the two sides of social supply –the social and commercial aspect– we argue that a supply relationship is multiplex in nature. Furthermore, the mere presence of a social aspect supports the argument that supply ties are embedded in more than one social circle at the same time. For instance, suppliers are, besides being in an exchange relation, sometimes also family members who participate in other social activities. That way, supply ties overlap within private surroundings as well as in what Papachristos (2012) refers to as *criminal* social circles. Furthermore, the tie between these egos is multiplex as the exchange and social relations exist simultaneously.

Studies of users' networks also deepen our theoretical understanding of the composition of networks in which cannabis is present (Haynie 2001; Papachristos

2012). Research into the multi-faceted nature of peer influence indicates that networks are composed based on prior homophily of age and gender, rather than substance use (Kirke 2006). Studies into the position of suppliers and users, again, point to the importance of brokers or go-betweens in the process of exchanging cannabis (Werse 2008; Burt 1992; see also Werse & Müller and Werse & Bernard in this issue).

Based on the above considerations, I propose a conceptualisation of supply as part of a broader multiplex tie:

> Supply is a *transaction moment* which is the result of an *exchanging process* and can take *multiple forms*. Supply is part of *multiplex ties* between *two individuals, embedded* in multiple social circles, part of a *collaborative setting* and shaped by the wider *relational context*.

- *It is a moment*: Supply basically is the moment where a "commodity" (e.g. cannabis) is transferred from person A to person B. The roles of person A and B are interchangeable, at one time person A is the supplier, at another moment person B is the supplier.
- Which is the result of an *exchange process*: Supply is the result of a process, which can be instigated by person A asking person B for cannabis or person B offering cannabis to person A. In both cases the answer of the other person can be either yes or no. If the answer is no, one can be referred further, start a new search or decide not to use or supply.
- Which *can take multiple forms*: This moment can take different forms. Each of these forms is described in terms of motivation, location and people involved. As a result, a reward might be exchanged. This reward can be monetary or non-monetary.
- This moment *is part of multiplex ties*: The relation between those involved is characterized by a relation that has a certain level of closeness and is to a certain level goal-oriented. The social relation can exist outside of the transaction. Sometimes this "relation outside of the transaction" barely exists.
- Between *two individuals*, at that time user and supplier. However, these are not the only roles these individuals occupy as they often are friends, colleagues or family at the same time. Sometimes this relation takes place through a referral. These intermediary people are often users who happen to know somebody in a different network and arrange for other users.
- *Embedded*: Supplier and user are part of different social circles at the same time.

- Part of a *collaborative setting*: At the time when cannabis is exchanged, the perceived level of trust and secrecy can be balanced against efficiency and influence the process of exchanging cannabis.
- *In a wider relational context*: It is part of a wider context which consists of existing stories about how to use, how to get or grow, which amount should be bought and what is an acceptable price. Actors in the network have relations among each other. Sometimes these are also supplier-user relations.

To conclude, I would like to emphasize that this concept is the result of an elaborate literature study. At the time of the publishing of this chapter, the author has developed a computer-assisted personal interview to examine the composition and structure of personal networks in which cannabis is present. A group of 50 respondents created together with the researcher their network in a software programme. Simultaneously, the meaning of supply ties was explored.

References

Aldridge, J., Measham, F., & Williams, L. (2011). Illegal leisure revisited. Changing patterns of alcohol and drug use in adolescents and young adults. (Adolescence and Society). London: Routledge.

Aloise-Young, P. A., Graham, J. W., & Hansen, W. B. (1994). Peer influence on smoking initiation during early adolescence: a comparison of group members and group outsiders. Journal of Applied Psychology, 79(2), 281-287.

Amos, A., Wiltshire, S., Bostock, Y., Haw, S., & McNeill, A. (2004). 'You can't go without a fag...you need it for your hash' - a qualitative exploration of smoking, cannabis and young people. Addiction, 99(1), 77-81, doi:10.1111/j.1360-0443.2004.00531.x.

Baker, W. E., & Faulkner, R. R. (1993). The social organization of conspiracy: Illegal networks in the heavy electrical equipment industry. American Sociological Review, 58(6), 837-860.

Batson, D. (1993). Communal and Exchange Relationships: What is the Difference? Personality and social psychology bulletin, 16(3), 677-683, doi:10.1177/0146167293196002.

Bauman, K. E., & Ennett, S. T. (1996). On the importance of peer influence for adolescent drug use: Commonly neglected considerations. Addiction, 91(2), 185-198.

Bell, R., Pavis, S., Cunningham-Burley, S., & Amos, A. (1998). Young men's use of cannabis: Exploring changes in meaning and context over time. Drugs; Education, Prevention and Policy, 5(2), 141.

Burt, R. (1992). Structural holes: the social structure of competition. Cambridge: Harvard University Press.

Calderoni, F. (2012). The structure of drug trafficking mafias: the 'Ndrangheta and cocaine. Crime Law and Social Change, 58(3), 321-349, doi:10.1007/s10611-012-9387-9.

Clark, M. S., & Mills, J. (1993). The difference between communal and exchange relationships: What it is and is not. Personality and Social Psychology Bulletin, 19, 684-691.
Coggan, N., & Mckellar, S. (1994). Drug-Use Amongst Peers - Peer Pressure or Peer Preference. Drugs-Education Prevention and Policy, 1(1), 15-26.
Coomber, R. (2006). Pusher myths: Re-situating the drug dealer. London: Free Associatin Books.
Coomber, R., & Moyle, L. (2014). Beyond drug dealing: Developing and extending the concept of 'social supply'of illicit drugs to 'minimally commercial supply'. Drugs: education, prevention and policy, 21(2).
Coomber, R., & Turnbull, P. (2007). Arenas of drug transactions: Adolescent cannabis transactions in England - Social supply. Journal of Drug Issues, 37(4), 845-865.
Crossley, N. (2010). The social world of the network. Combining qualitative and quantitative elements in social network analysis. Sociologica, 1, 1-34.
Cullen, F. (2010). 'Two's up and poncing fags': young women' smoking practices, reciprocity and friendship. Gender and Education, 22(5), 491-504.
Dorn, N., Levi, M., & King, L. (2005). Literature review on upper level drug trafficking. Home Office Online Report 22/05. London: Home Office.
Dorn, N., Murji, K., & South, N. (1992). Traffickers: Drug markets and law enforcement: Psychology Press.
Duff, C. (2005). Party drugs and party people: examining the 'normalization' of recreational drug use in Melbourne, Australia. International Journal of Drug Policy, 16(3), 161-170, doi:DOI 10.1016/j.drugpo.2005.02.001.
Erickson, B. H. (1981). Secret societies and social structure. Social Forces, 60(1), 188-210.
Galea, S., Nandi, A., & Vlahov, D. (2004). The social epidemiology of substance use. Epidemiologic reviews, 26(1), 36-52.
Giménez-Salinas Framis, A. (2013). Illegal Networks or Criminal Organizations: Structure, Power and Facilitators in Cocaine Trafficking Structures. In C. Morselli (Ed.), Crime and Networks. New York: Routledge.
Giuffre, K. (2013). Communities and networks: using social network analysis to rethink urban and community studies. Cambridge: Polity Press.
Granovetter, M. (1973). The strength of weak ties. American journal of sociology, 78(6), 1360-1380.
Harrison, L. D., Erickson, P. G., Korf, D. J., Brochu, S., & Benschop, A. (2007). How much for a dime bag? An exploration of youth drug markets. Drug and Alcohol Dependence, 90, S27-S39, doi:10.1016/j.drugalcdep.2006.09.009.
Haynie, D. L. (2001). Delinquent peers revisited: Does network structure matter? 1. American journal of sociology, 106(4), 1013-1057.
Highet, G. (2003). Cannabis and smoking research: interviewing young people in self-selected friendship pairs. Health Education Research, 18(1), 108-118.
Highet, G. (2004). The role of cannabis in supporting young people's cigarette smoking: a qualitative approach. Health Education Research, 19(6), 635-643, doi:10.1093/her/cyg089.

Hough, M., Warburton, H., Few, B., May, T., Man, L., Witton, J., et al. (2003). A growing market: The domestic cultivation of cannabis. York: Joseph Rowntree Foundation.

Kirke, D. M. (2006). Teenagers and Substance Use: Social Networks and Peer Influence. Basingstoke and New York: Palgrave Macmillan.

Kobus, K., & Henry, D. B. (2010). Interplay of network position and peer substance use in early adolescent cigarette, alcohol, and marijuana use. The journal of early adolescence., 30(2), 225-245.

Lee, N. H. (1969). Search for an Abortionist. Chicago, IL: University of Chicago Press.

Marin, A., & Wellman, B. (2011). Social network analysis: an introduction. In J. Scott, & P. J. Carrington (Eds.), The SAGE handbook of social network analysis (pp. 11-25). London: Sage.

Mashek, D. J., & Aron, A. (2004). Handbook of closeness and intimacy: Psychology Press.

McCarty, C. (2002). Structure in personal networks. Journal of Social Structure, 3(1), Online.

McCarty, C., & Molina, J. L (2011). Personal networks. Research and applications. Draft, Online: http://grupsderecerca.uab.cat/egolab/sites/grupsderecerca.uab.cat.egolab/files/pna.pdf

McGloin, J. M., & Nguyen, H. (2013). The importance of studying co-offending networks for criminological theory and policy. In C. Morselli (Ed.), Crime and Networks (pp. 13-27). New York: Routledge.

Michell, L., & Amos, A. (1997). Girls, pecking order and smoking. Social Science & Medicine, 44(12), 1861-1869.

Michell, M., & Pearson, L. (2000). Smoke rings: social network analysis of friendship groups, smoking and drug-taking. Drugs: education, prevention and policy, 7(1), 21-37.

Mische, A., & White, H. C. (1998). Between conversation and situation: public switching dynamics across network-domains. Social Research, 65(3), 295-324.

Morselli, C. (2009). Inside criminal networks: Springer.

Morselli, C., Giguère, C., & Petit, K. (2007). The efficiency/security trade-off in criminal networks. Social Networks, 29(1), 143-153, doi:http://dx.doi.org/10.1016/j.socnet.2006.05.001.

Oliver, K., Crossley, N., Edwards, G., Koskinen, J., Everett, M., & Broccatelli, C. (2014). Covert networks: structures, processes and types. Working paper of the Mitchell Centre for Network Analysis.

Paoli, L. (2002). The paradoxes of organized crime. Crime, Law & Social Change, 37, 51-97.

Papachristos, A. V. (2011). The coming of a networked criminology. Measuring Crime & Criminality: Advances in Criminological Theory, 17, 101-140.

Papachristos, A. V., & Smith, C. M. (2012). The Small World of Al Capone: The Embedded Nature of Criminal and Legitimate Social Networks. Available at SSRN: http://dx.doi.org/10.2139/ssrn.2159899.

Parker, H. (2000). How young Britons obtain their drugs: Drugs transactions at the point of consumption. Crime Prevention Studies, 11, 59-82.

Pearson, G., Hobbs, R., Jones, S., Tierney, J., & Ward, J. (2001). Middle market drug distribution.

Pearson, M., & Michell, L. (2000). Smoke Rings: social network analysis of friendship groups, smoking and drug-taking. Drugs: Education, Prevention & Policy, 7(1), 21-37.

Potter, G. (2009). Exploring retail-level drug distribution: Social supply, 'real' dealers and the user/dealer interface. In Z. Demetrovics, J. Fountain, & K. Kraus (Eds.), Old & new policies, theories, research methods and drug users across Europe (pp. 50-74, ESSD Series). Lengerich: Pabst Science Publishers.

Reuter, P. (1985). The organization of illegal markets: and economic analysis. Washington: National Institute of Justice.

Shewan, D., Dalgarno, P., & Reith, G. (2000). Perceived risk and risk reduction among ecstasy users: the role of drug, set, and setting. International Journal of Drug Policy, 10(6), 431-453.

Snijders, T., Spreen, M., & Zwaagstra, R. (1995). The use of mulitlevel modeling for analysing personal networks: networks of cocaine users in an urban area. Journal of Quantitative Anthropology, 5, 85-105.

Werse, B. (2008). Retail markets for cannabis—users, sharers, go-betweens and stash dealers. Cannabis in Europe: Dynamics in perception, policy and markets, 106-123.

Global patterns of domestic cannabis cultivation: sample characteristics and patterns of growing across eleven countries[1]

Gary R. Potter, Monica J. Barratt, Aili Malm, Martin Bouchard, Thomas Blok, Anne-Sofie Christensen, Tom Decorte, Vibeke Asmussen Frank, Pekka Hakkarainen, Axel Klein, Simon Lenton, Jussi Perälä, Bernd Werse and Marije Wouters
(The Global Cannabis Cultivation Research Consortium)

Abstract

Aims: To provide an overview of: demographic characteristics; experiences with growing cannabis; methods and scale of growing operations; reasons for growing; personal use of cannabis and other drugs; participation in cannabis and other drug markets; contacts with the criminal justice system for respondents to an online survey about cannabis cultivation drawn from eleven countries (N=6530). Important similarities and differences between the national samples recruited will be discussed.

Method: This paper utilizes data from the online web survey of predominantly 'small-scale' cannabis cultivators in eleven countries conducted by the Global Cannabis Cultivation Research Consortium (GCCRC). Here we focus primarily on descriptive statistics to highlight key similarities and differences across the different national samples.

Findings: Overall there was a great deal of similarity across countries in terms of: demographic characteristics; experiences with growing cannabis; methods and scale of growing operations; reasons for growing; use of cannabis and other drugs; participation in cannabis and other drug markets, and contacts with the criminal justice system. In particular, we can recognise that a clear majority of those small-scale cannabis cultivators who responded to our survey is primarily motivated for reasons other than making money from cannabis supply and have

---

1 Reprinted from The International Journal of Drug Policy, Vol. 26, no. 3 (March 2015), pp. 226-237, Copyright 2015, with kind permission from Elsevier. Minor formal changes have been made regarding (cross) references.

minimal involvement in drug dealing or other criminal activities. These growers generally come from 'normal' rather than 'deviant' backgrounds. Some differences do exist between the samples drawn from different countries suggesting that local factors (political, geographical, cultural etc.) may have some influence on how small-scale cultivators operate, although differences in recruitment strategies in different countries may also account for some differences observed.

1 Introduction

The traditional view of a global cannabis market consisting of production in developing countries for export to consumers in the developed world is increasingly outdated. Large scale outdoor cultivation has been long established in countries like Australia, Canada, the USA and New Zealand. With the advent of indoor cultivation techniques and the wide dissemination of both technical expertise and growing technologies, cannabis is now produced on a significant level across most of the industrialised world (Potter et al. 2011). With 'traditional' producer countries in the developing world continuing to cultivate, the UN confirms cannabis production to be a truly global phenomenon with 172 countries and territories reporting cultivation in the 2008 World Drug Report (a year where particular attention was given to the phenomenon of cannabis cultivation; UNODC 2008). This globalisation of cannabis cultivation continues to be a significant feature in global drug markets, and also a particular problem for researchers: "Providing a global picture of levels of cannabis cultivation and production remains a difficult task: although cannabis is produced in practically every country in the world, its cultivation is largely localized and, more often than not, feeds local markets. (UNODC 2013: xi)

Research into cannabis cultivation in the developed world to date has largely consisted of nationally focused work generating typologies of cannabis growers (e.g. Nguyen & Bouchard 2010; Potter & Dann 2005; Weisheit 1991), or national studies focusing on specific aspects of cultivation in individual countries (e.g. Bouchard 2007; Bouchard et al. 2009; Decorte 2010; Douglas & Sullivan 2013; Hakkarainen et al. 2011a; Hakkarainen et al. 2011b; Hammersvik et al. 2012; Malm 2006; Plecas et al. 2005; Potter 2010a; Weisheit 1992). Whilst there is some work that discusses cultivation in neighbouring states (Hakkarainen et al. 2011a on Finland and Denmark; Athey et al. 2013 on Belgium, Finland and Denmark; Jansen 2002 on Switzerland and the Netherlands), and a compendium that draws on studies from a dozen different countries and regions around the world (Decorte et al. 2011), there has been an absence of any significant internationally comparative research. However, such a global phenomenon would clearly benefit from some coordinated international research, a point also recognised by the United Nations Commission on Narcotic Drugs in a recent report calling specifically for further "research on the different methods of cannabis cultivation and the role of cannabis seeds therein (INCB 2013, para. 69).

Internationally comparative approaches to research provide many benefits, particularly around providing insights into how national legal and cultural variations impact on both patterns of (specific types of) crime and on assessing policy responses to (specific) crime(s) (e.g. Heidensohn 2008). Indeed, Hardie-Bick et al. (2005: 1) assert that "[a]ny criminology worthy of the name should contain a comparative dimension. The contents of cultural meanings that are loaded into the subject of criminology are too variable for it to be otherwise. It is fair to say that most of the important points made by leading scholars of criminology are comparative in nature." In the example of cannabis cultivation, we can begin to see how patterns of cultivation, both common and similar in terms of global trends, may or may not differ between different countries and regions. The research reported here aims to explore both similarities and differences in small-scale cannabis cultivation in eleven different countries. The potential to inform future policy responses is obvious.

This paper reports on the preliminary general findings of the (semi-) standardised International Cannabis Cultivation Questionnaire (ICCQ) (Decorte et al. 2012), developed by the Global Cannabis Cultivation Research Consortium (GCCRC) and conducted in eleven countries to date. We begin with a brief overview of our methodology before outlining some interesting general findings. Although we accept that sampling and other methodological issues necessitate some caution in generalising from these findings (see Barratt et al. 2015, and Barratt & Lenton 2015), we believe we can make a number of interesting and valid comparisons between the national and international patterns of domestic cannabis cultivation in our data set of respondents from this limited number of developed nations, at least for those that we might loosely think of as 'small-scale cannabis growers'. In particular, we provide some comparative commentary on who grows cannabis, reasons for growing, methods of growing, market involvement ('dealing'), and contact with the police and other criminal activities of growers. As well as presenting some findings that are of interest in their own right, a key aim of this paper is also to provide some background for a series of papers (some in the special edition of the IJDP in which this paper was published first, others in more recent issues, e.g. Werse 2015, or under preparation) that will explore particular aspects of national and international patterns of cannabis cultivation in greater depth.

2 Methods

Our methodology has been described in some detail elsewhere (Barratt et al. 2012; Barratt et al. 2015), so a brief overview will suffice for current purposes. Following on from successful online surveys into cannabis cultivation in Belgium (Decorte 2010) and Denmark and Finland (Hakkarainen et al. 2011a; see also Hakkarainen & Perälä in this volume), the GCCRC sought to develop a standardised online survey to allow for the collection of meaningfully comparative data in all participating countries: the ICCQ (Decorte et al. 2012).

The 35 item core ICCQ includes modules on: experiences with growing cannabis; methods and scale of growing operations; reasons for growing; personal use of cannabis and other drugs; participation in cannabis and other drug markets; contact with the criminal justice system; involvement in other (non-drug related) illegal activities, and; demographic characteristics. Other modules were added by sub-sets of participating countries to reflect the differing research interests of those involved (see e.g. Hakkarainen et al. 2015, Lenton et al. 2015, Nguyen et al. 2015, and Paoli & Decorte 2015). The ICCQ also includes items to test eligibility and recruitment source.

We implemented a broad-based recruitment strategy and techniques to maximise the breadth of recruitment coverage mindful of the different conditions within each of the countries studies. Promotion strategies included: an international project website and blog hosted at a .nl address to highlight our association with a model of cannabis control supported by many in our target population (i.e. the Dutch 'coffee-shop' model); Twitter recruitment involving following prominent cannabis Twitter accounts and engaging with cannabis users; discussions hosted on cannabis related online forums where the researchers continue to engage with respondents while answering questions about the study; posting to and engaging with Facebook groups associated with cannabis culture; mainstream media coverage (television, radio, newspaper); alternative media coverage through provision of flyers to alternative music shops, head shops, street press, festivals etc.; distribution of flyers to grow shops; online and hard-copy advertising in cannabis-related magazines and websites; providing social media sharing buttons so respondents can easily share the survey with their social networks; and providing a link to printable flyers so respondents who wished to pass details of the survey to their friends could do so more privately. The mix of strategies varied from country to country (see Barratt et al. 2015 for a fuller discussion); however many of these strategies were international, leading people to the project website (www.worldwideweed.nl) where they could then choose the survey associated with their country of residence.

It is important to acknowledge the limitations of the internet-based research methods used here. Most importantly, samples of cannabis cultivators were volunteers, and not all cultivators had an equal chance of being included in the sample, resulting in coverage error. Our findings, therefore, cannot be said to represent all cannabis growers, and it is difficult to precisely estimate the importance of bias in our samples. Nevertheless there are various strategies we have taken to minimise sampling limitations. For example, we have used a wide variety of recruitment and promotion strategies and by removing any financial incentive to respond to the survey, we have reduced the likelihood of fraudulent responding.

As well as the particular problems of recruiting samples to online surveys we must also concede that different national contexts and different recruitment strategies in each country also lead to the problem of how comparable the samples we recruited from each country are to each other. Straus (2009) notes that it is common for cross-national comparisons to be made using convenience or purposive sampling, and argues that the overall context effects associated with living in a specific nation may still be discernible in comparative analyses, even though the representativeness of the resultant samples from each country is unknown. Further, it is also important to note that many of the limitations faced by online purposive sampling are broadly similar to 'traditional' face-to-face methods of studying hidden populations. Representative sampling methodology, as used in household surveys, is also prohibitively expensive to administer to the general population in ways that would access large numbers of cannabis cultivators. Additionally, most existing national and international data on cannabis cultivation is based on detections and arrests by law enforcement which obviously has its own biases. It is hoped that the results of the current research with self-selected samples of cannabis cultivators completing an online questionnaire will produce a useful counterpoint to the available law enforcement data. Fuller discussions of these issues can be found in Barratt et al. 2015.

Findings presented in the current paper are based on the data acquired through eight of the ICCQ surveys covering eleven countries: North America (covering Canada and the US), Belgium (covering both major language groups found in the country), Denmark, Finland, Germany (covering also Austria and German-speaking Switzerland), the Netherlands, the UK, and Australia. These eight datasets were merged for the ICCQ questions – this involved ensuring different datasets used the same coding structures, e.g. recoding questions from imperial into metric measurements as well as translation into English. Questions with 'other please specify' string variables were recoded where possible into existing categories, and some new recoded categories were created.

3 Selecting eligible samples

Not all respondents to our surveys have been included in the data presented here. Three rules were used to determine eligible samples for analysis in this paper:

1. Respondents answered 3 eligibility questions at the beginning of the questionnaire. These were: (a) aged 18 years or over, (b) resided in the country of the survey, (c) reported that they had grown cannabis at least once. Respondents who did not meet these criteria were not presented with the remaining questionnaire.
2. Q3 of the ICCQ asked 'how long ago did you last grow cannabis?' In order to reflect only recent trends in growing, we have excluded the participants who reported last growing cannabis more than 5 years ago and those who did not know, refused or skipped this question.
3. The samples reported here completed at least half of the core ICCQ questions. There were 35 questions in the ICCQ (excluding 3 eligibility questions). 27 questions were asked of all participants, 1 was used for criterion 2, so 26 were included in missing data analysis. Dichotomous indicators of completeness were calculated for each question, where 1 = any response recorded including a 'don't know' or 'refused' response, and 0 = 'no response' recorded including missing or skipped. Respondents were retained in the sample if they had completed 14 or more of the 26 core ICCQ questions.

After applying these rules, we were left with a final sample of 6530 across the eleven countries (see Table 1 for a breakdown of the final sample; see Barratt et al. 2015 for a more detailed discussion of eligibility and inclusion criteria).

Table 1: Final sample size per country

	Belgium (BE)	USA (US)	Canada (CN)	Australia (AU)	Finland (FI)	Denmark (DK)	Nether-lands (NL)	Germany (DE)	Austria (AT)	Switzer-land (CH)	UK	*Total*
Sample size	1065	645	63	491	1179	814	277	1348	129	101	418	*6530*

Table 2: Gender and age

	BE	US	CN	AU	FI	DK	NL	DE	AT	CH	UK	*Total*
Gender (%)												
Male	91	88	93	88	90	91	90	95	91	93	95	*92*
Female	9	12	7	12	10	9	10	5	9	7	5	*8*
Total N	*988*	*572*	*58*	*489*	*1147*	*810*	*261*	*1266*	*117*	*95*	*397*	*6200*
Age												
Median	26	26	25	35	26	31	32	26	25	25	33	*27*
IQR	22-34	21-36	21-36	27-47	23-31	23-43	23-44	22-33	22-31	21-33	25-41	*22-36*
Range	18-81	18-86	18-65	18-71	18-71	18-70	18-70	18-74	18-55	18-53	18-63	*18-86*
Total N	*986*	*645*	*63*	*485*	*1152*	*810*	*252*	*1243*	*117*	*94*	*381*	*6228*

4 Analysis

Results are presented for a selection of comparable core ICCQ items for the eleven countries included. For this paper, we have concentrated primarily on descriptive statistics to give a general overview of our findings with emphasis on both key commonalities and notable differences across different countries. Categorical or ordinal responses are presented as percentages of valid cases (rounded to the nearest whole number). Medians and interquartile ranges (IQRs) are presented for continuous 'count' variables, such as age, number of plants, yield and surface area, as these are less-biased descriptors than means/standard deviations. A dash (-) in a table indicates the item was not asked in that country. Deeper analysis of the relationships between different variables and across different countries will follow in subsequent papers.

5 Findings

5.1 Demographics characteristics

There is some broad commonality across our samples, which suggests this cross-national comparison can give some useful insights into differences and similarities in growing experiences across the different country samples, even if questions remain as to how representative each sample is of its parent (national) population of cannabis growers. Gender ratios (Table 2) are similar across the surveys with male respondents outnumbering female respondents by a ratio of just over 9:1. Ages (Table 2) were similar for most countries with the majority of respondents in their early-20s to mid-30s, but the median age of respondents was notably higher for the Australian, Danish, Dutch and British samples. Patterns of employment status (Table 3) were not dissimilar, although Belgium and the German language survey (Germany, Austria and Switzerland) recruited a notably larger proportion of students, and the US more unemployed people. The UK recruited a higher proportion of people claiming benefits and/or pensions than the other countries. Overall, respondents were far more likely to report some form of employment: those reporting various forms of non-employment (aside from being students) were small minorities in all countries.

Table 3: Employment status

	BE	US	CN	AU	FI[a]	DK	NL[a]	DE	AT	CH	UK	*Total*
Employment status (%[b])												
Full-time work	40	33	51	44	-	38	-	43[c]	39[c]	47[c]	41	*41*
Part-time or casual work	10	20	16	13	-	11	-	12	13	18	8	*12*
Self-employed	8	21	18	17	-	9	-	10	13	14	17	*12*
Student (any type)	38	17	22	12	-	27	-	33	35	33	12	*27*
Unemployed – looking for work	7	13	9	5	-	8	-	6	9	4	9	*7*
Benefits/ pension/ disability	3	5	2	9	-	9	-	3	3	1	16	*6*
Home duties	1	5	0	2	-	2	-	2	0	1	8	*2*
Retired	1	4	4	4	-	8	-	0	0	0	1	*3*
Not seeking work	1	2	4	9	-	3	-	2	3	1	1	*3*
Total N	*989*	*451*	*45*	*488*	-	*811*	-	*1282*	*118*	*97*	*398*	*4679*

[a] Question not asked in a comparable way in Finland and the Netherlands.

[b] Respondents invited to tick more than one option; columns can total more than 100%.

[c] In the German language version of the survey (Germany, Austria and Switzerland) 'Apprenticeship' was also an option. Full-time work and apprenticeship categories have been merged into 'Full-time work' for this table.

Household arrangements (Table 4) varied across the countries. Belgium and Switzerland had a notably higher proportion of respondents living with their parents, and Finland and Denmark had higher rates of respondents living alone – with Belgium and the US having notably lower proportions in this category. Those living alone were a sizable minority in all countries; respondents tended to report some kind of shared living arrangements (most commonly with partners, but also commonly with other family members). Although the surveys also asked about educational level and ethnicity, categories were not comparable between countries and are therefore not reported in this paper.

5.2 Cannabis and other drug use

Over two-thirds of respondents across all surveys reported that they first used cannabis (Table 5) before the age of 18, with less than 5% reporting initiation after the age of 25. Americans, followed by Austrians and then British respondents reported the youngest age of first use, on average, with the Finnish respondents notably reporting an older age of first use. The patterns found here are broadly reflective of other research looking at initiation into drug use in these countries. Clearly most respondents in all surveys were regular or heavy users of cannabis (e.g. use today or in last week; Table 5), but those from the US and UK were most likely to have smoked 'today', with Finns the least. For all countries other than Denmark, over half of respondents reported also using cannabis that was not homegrown, and for most countries a majority also reported using hash (resin), with Australians (at 27%) standing out here as the least likely to also have used hash.

For all countries except Switzerland (which was one of the smallest samples), the majority of respondents had not used drugs other than cannabis (in various forms, including synthetic cannabinoids), alcohol and tobacco in the last year (Table 6), although for Finland and Austria, and (to a lesser extent) Canada and Germany, nearly half of respondents did report taking other illicit drugs in the last 12 months. In most other countries (Denmark being the notable exception) around one-third or more respondents reported taking other illicit drugs in the last year. In general, magic mushrooms and ecstasy were those other illicit drugs most likely to have been consumed, and those reporting use of any particular drug were generally a small minority.

Table 4: Household

	BE	US	CN	AU	FI	DK	NL[a]	DE	AT	CH	UK	*Total*
I live with: (%)												
My spouse/ partner/ boyfriend/ girlfriend	37	47	33	59	39	42	-	25	26	21	47	*38*
My child/ren[b]	17	20	11	29	12	22	-	11	10	14	24	*17*
My parents[b]	31	21	19	10	4	9	-	23	14	32	12	*17*
My grandparents	0	3	0	0	0	1	-	2	1	0	1	*1*
My siblings or other family members	3	0	0	3	4	2	-	4	4	3	5	*3*
My friends	5	7	6	4	5	5	-	11	11	7	5	*7*
My housemates	9	11	14	12	7	4	-	13	18	11	9	*9*
No-one, I live alone	17	18	31	14	39	32	-	27	29	23	21	*27*
Total N	*989*	*348*	*36*	*488*	*1174*	*811*	-	*1283*	*118*	*97*	*398*	*5742*

[a] Question not asked in the Netherlands in a comparable way.
[b] Includes step children and step parents.

Table 5: Cannabis use

	BE	US	CN	AU	FI	DK	NL	DE	AT	CH	UK	*Total*
How old were you when you first used cannabis? (%)												
I have never used cannabis	2	1	3	0	0	1	0	0	0	2	0	*1*
Less than 16 years old	35	50	43	35	22	42	34	37	49	44	46	*36*
16-17 years old	40	24	22	35	29	31	32	36	30	37	25	*32*
18-25 years old	21	22	22	26	44	23	24	23	18	15	25	*27*
More than 25 years old	3	3	10	4	5	3	10	4	2	1	4	*4*
Total N	*1056*	*643*	*63*	*490*	*1179*	*812*	*269*	*1312*	*125*	*99*	*404*	*6452*
When was the last time you used cannabis? (%)												
Today	43	66	57	57	27	43	46	39	50	42	66	*44*
Not today, but in the last week	36	20	28	22	42	34	39	38	32	41	24	*34*
Not in the last week, but in the last 30 days	11	5	8	7	17	11	7	13	10	5	4	*11*
Not in the last 30 days, but in the last 12 months	7	6	3	11	11	9	6	7	7	7	6	*8*
I have not used cannabis in the last 12 months	3	2	0	3	3	3	2	3	2	3	1	*3*
Never used cannabis	2	1	3	0	0	1	0	1	0	2	0	*1*
Total N	*1052*	*635*	*60*	*478*	*1174*	*804*	*270*	*1305*	*124*	*98*	*397*	*6397*

Table 6: Other drug use

	BE	US	CN	AU	FI	DK	NL	DE	AT	CH	UK	*Total*
In the last 12 months, have you used any of the following drugs? (%[a])												
Alcohol	88	68	76	75	90	74	76	76	83	75	72	*79*
Cigarettes	71	53	50	57	80	68	71	71	74	61	67	*69*
Cannabis that is not home-grown	78	58	62	58	79	46	64	64	73	68	63	*66*
Hash (resin)	60	52	59	27	49	58	57	38	34	50	47	*48*
Magic Mushrooms	13	20	26	16	34	10	14	15	24	15	12	*18*
Ecstasy (MDMA)	18	11	19	18	15	6	20	15	20	28	16	*15*
Amphetamine (speed)	8	6	10	12	15	6	12	14	17	14	5	*11*
Cocaine (includes crack cocaine)	13	6	10	7	5	8	11	6	12	13	13	*8*
LSD	7	10	14	14	12	3	8	7	12	15	7	*8*
Other opioids	1	9	10	8	12	2	1	4	5	8	7	*6*
Benzodiazepines and sedatives	2	7	5	8	15	2	4	3	5	9	8	*6*
Synthetic cannabinoids (Spice, Kronic, etc)	1	8	0	13	5	1	1	5	2	1	6	*5*
Other pharmaceutical drugs	2	5	5	1	5	1	1	1	0	1	2	*3*
Methamphetamine (meth, crystal, ice)	1	3	3	7	4	0	1	2	3	2	2	*2*
Ketamine	1	0	2	0	0	1	2	0	1	0	6	*1*
Heroin	0	2	0	1	1	1	0	0	2	6	1	*1*
Illicit drugs other than cannabis[b]	32	34	41	39	48	21	33	41	47	52	34	*37*
Total N	*1049*	*601*	*58*	*488*	*1178*	*811*	*276*	*1309*	*125*	*99*	*404*	*6398*

[a] Respondents invited to tick more than one option; columns total more than 100%.

[b] Report of use of any drug other than Cannabis that is not home-grown, Hash (resin), Synthetic Cannabinoids, Alcohol and Cigarettes.

5.3 Growing experiences

Both the median and range of 'age of first grow' was broadly similar in all samples (Table 7). The vast majority of respondents started growing in their late teens and early twenties, but all countries included respondents who started growing at a much younger age (as young as 10 in seven of the countries) and those who started much later in life (including some in their 60s and 70s).

In general, growers responding to our survey were quite inexperienced (Table 7) with roughly two-thirds (64%) of the whole sample reporting growing 5 crops or fewer. Only three countries (the UK, Australia and Denmark) had a majority of respondents who reported having grown six crops or more – and these were three of the four countries (the Netherlands being the other) where the median age of respondents was in the 30s instead of the mid-20s. Clearly older respondents have had more time to build experience, but it is hard to infer anything more than this: more experienced growers may have been less likely to respond to the survey in the first place, or lack of experience may reflect the fact that domestic cultivation as a wide-spread phenomenon is still relatively new in many countries, for example. In total, 67% of respondents 'succeeded first time' and 83% had at most only one failed attempt before their first successful crop (ranging from 70% in the US to 90% in Denmark and 92% in Austria; Table 7).

5.4 Growing method and scale

Respondents from the US, the UK, Canada and Finland were all more likely to grow indoors than out (Table 8) which may reflect climate (especially in Finland), opportunity (outdoor growing being less likely for those who live in densely populated areas) or concerns over detection (with these last two being related to each other). Although these options were not available in the North American survey, a large proportion of respondents in each country reported some kind of combination of indoor and outdoor growing. It is interesting to note that Potter (2010a) previously found in the UK that although most growers grew indoors, many cited a *preference* for growing outdoors – but often didn't have access to suitable outdoor growing sites and/or expressed concerns over having their crops detected or stolen.

Table 7: Age of first grow, no. of crops grown, attempts before first successful grow

	BE	US	CN	AU	FI	DK	NL	DE	AT	CH	UK	*Total*
Age of first grow												
Median age in years	20	20	20	20	21	21	21	20	19	18	22	*20*
IQR	18-25	17-24	18-24	17-25	19-24	18-26	18-30	17-24	17-23	16-20	18-30	*18-25*
Range	12-71	10-65	12-52	10-65	10-64	10-66	10-66	10-74	14-53	12-46	10-59	*10-74*
Total N	*993*	*602*	*59*	*456*	*1175*	*661*	*277*	*1346*	*129*	*101*	*408*	*6207*
How many crops ever grown? (%)[a]												
Not yet harvested my first crop	10	13	11	3	7	1	8	6	2	2	2	*7*
1 crop	20	12	16	12	14	11	15	18	18	14	10	*15*
2 to 5 crops	46	36	33	33	45	37	42	47	41	52	36	*42*
6 to 10 crops	14	14	16	19	18	21	15	14	25	16	20	*17*
11 to 20 crops	5	11	6	17	9	14	9	8	9	8	13	*10*
21 to 50 crops	4	8	13	11	5	11	6	4	4	6	8	*6*
More than 50 crops	2	6	5	5	2	5	6	3	2	2	10	*4*
Total N	*1038*	*640*	*63*	*478*	*1124*	*796*	*256*	*1260*	*122*	*96*	*398*	*6271*
How many times did you fail before you succeeded in getting a crop? (%)[a]												
Succeeded first time	60	65	68	59	66	77	70	69	74	69	66	*67*
1 attempt	19	5	5	18	19	13	13	18	18	18	20	*16*
2 attempts	7	10	13	11	6	7	5	5	4	7	6	*7*
3 attempts	3	4	2	4	1	1	3	2	1	3	4	*2*
4 attempts	1	2	2	2	0	0	2	1	0	1	1	*1*
5 or more attempts	1	2	0	3	1	1	1	0	1	0	1	*1*
I have not yet harvested my first crop	10	13	11	3	7	1	7	7	2	2	2	*7*
Total N	*1042*	*639*	*63*	*473*	*1155*	*788*	*271*	*1248*	*121*	*96*	*407*	*6303*

[a] Columns can total more than 100% due to rounding.

Table 8: Location and size of set-up

	BE	US	CN	AU	FI	DK	NL	DE	AT	CH	UK	*Total*
Do you typically grow indoors or outdoors? (%[a])												
Indoors	34	80	68	27	62	39	33	47	44	32	76	*49*
Outdoors	36	20	32	41	3	29	34	10	11	25	5	*20*
Both indoor and outdoor in the same growing period	12	-	-	26	32	20	22	27	35	29	15	*21*
Seedlings grown indoors, then planted outdoors	18	-	-	6	4	13	11	16	10	14	4	*10*
Total N	*929*	*558*	*56*	*462*	*1041*	*764*	*232*	*1170*	*120*	*93*	*386*	*5811*
Number of mature plants per crop[b]												
Median	3	6	5.5	4	4	6	5	6	9	9	4	*5*
IQR	2-6	3-12	4-21.5	2-6	2-6	4-12	3-5	4-12	5-12	5-20	2-6	*3-9*
Range	1-100+	1-100+	1-100+	1-100+	1-100+	1-100+	1-100+	1-100+	1-100+	2-100+	1-100+	*1-100+*
Total N	*814*	*535*	*52*	*426*	*1000*	*702*	*211*	*1004*	*91*	*82*	*358*	*5275*
Space typically used to cultivate cannabis (in square metres)[b]												
Median	2	1.9	3.15	3.3	2	4	2	2	2	3	2	*2*
IQR	1-5	0.9-9.3	0.7-9.075	1-8	1-3	1-9	1-5	1-5	1-5	1-7.5	1-4	*1-5*
Range	1-100+	<0.1-100+	0.2-100+	0.1-100+	0.5-21	1-100+	1-21	1-100+	1-81	1-100	0.2-100+	*<0.1-100+*
Total N	*802*	*519*	*52*	*399*	*978*	*676*	*205*	*676*	*66*	*65*	*337*	*4775*

Note: This table only shows those respondents who have harvested at least one crop

[a] %s may not total 100 due to rounding.

[b] Only respondents who have harvested at least one crop and reported growing one or more mature plants per crop were included in this analysis.

The number of mature plants grown per crop (Table 8) varied across the countries although in all countries the majority of respondents stuck to relatively low numbers of plants. The median across the whole sample was 5, ranging from 3 in Belgium to 9 in Austria and Switzerland (both of which were particularly small samples). In some countries it seems likely that growers were influenced by official or semi-official policies of tolerance to small-scale cultivation. Exploration of the impact of cannabis cultivation laws on self-reported growing practices in this sample will be the focus of subsequent papers from the GCCRC (with a first one already published: Werse 2015). Although the median number of plants grown was in single figures in all countries, and the IQR only reached 20 plants in two countries, all countries included some respondents who reported growing 100 or more plants. The space typically given over to cultivation (Table 8) was broadly similar across all countries, and it was not necessarily the case that those countries where respondents reported higher numbers of plants also reported larger space used for growing.

Yield (in terms of 'usable dried cannabis'; Table 9) per plant was similar across all samples, although Australian and, to a lesser extent, Dutch respondents reported notably higher results here. Both of these countries have particularly well established traditions of domestic cultivation, which may suggest that expertise (and/or established strains commonly used) developed within national growing communities has contributed to this pattern, alternatively, the result for Australia may be due to climate and geography which are conducive to outdoor growing. In general, outdoor growers produce larger plants with the median yield per plant being significantly higher for respondents who grew outdoors (median = 1.8 ounces, IQR 0.7–3.5, $n = 1431$) compared with those who grew indoors (median = 1.2 ounces, IQR 0.7–2.5, $n = 2339$; Wilcoxon signed-rank test: $z = -8.46$, $p < .001$).

Although the IQR for the sample as a whole was 0.7-3 ounces per plant, peaking to an upper limit of 4.4 ounces in the Netherlands and 5.4 in Australia, a number of countries included respondents reporting very large quantities of cannabis per plant. Although this may partly be a result of respondent error in completing this question (e.g. through mis-understanding weights, or through mis-typing entries) many of us who have conducted empirical work with cannabis growers have seen some very large plants indeed – and a trawl of the internet shows that 'monster' plants can and do exist.

Table 9: Yield

	BE	US	CN	AU	FI	DK	NL	DE	AT	CH	UK	*Total*
Typical yield (i.e. usable dried cannabis) per plant (ounces[a])												
Median	1.4	1.1	1.1	3	1.6	1.3	2.1	0.9	1.0	1.2	2	*1.4*
IQR	0.6-3.5	0.4-2.6	0.5-3.2	1.4-5.4	0.8-3.1	0.7-2.6	0.9-4.4	0.6-1.8	0.7-1.8	0.7-3.2	1-3.9	*0.7-3*
Range	<0.1-92.59	<0.1-58.8	<0.1-7.1	<0.1-70.6	<0.1-52.9	<0.1-24.7	<0.1-52.9	<0.1-69.9	<0.1-10.6	<0.1-28.2	<0.1-36	*<0.1-92.59*
Total N	*638*	*326*	*34*	*389*	*526*	*649*	*179*	*982*	*89*	*81*	*281*	*4174*
Typical yield (i.e. usable dried cannabis) per crop (ounces[a])												
Median	3.6	7.1	3.5	10	7.1	10.6	10.6	7.1	8.8	10.6	8	*7.1*
IQR	1.8-10.6	2.1-19.8	1.5-23.5	4-25	2.5-12.3	3.5-21.2	3.5-28.2	3.5-14.1	4.4-16.8	7.1-27.3	4-18	*3.2-17.6*
Range	0.1-740.8	<0.1-3527.4	0.6-705.5	<0.1-352.7	<0.1-352.7	0.9-1763.7	<0.1-740.8	<0.1-7054.8	0.2-225.8	0.4-811.3	0.1-360	*<0.1-7054.8*
Total N	*731*	*339*	*36*	*415*	*540*	*700*	*201*	*1114*	*113*	*89*	*294*	*4572*

Note: only those who had completed at least one crop were included in the analyses for this table.
[a] All figures rounded to 1 decimal place.

Yield per crop (Table 9) varied quite dramatically across the different countries, peaking at 10.6 ounces in Denmark, the Netherlands and Switzerland, but particularly low in Canada (3.5) and Belgium (3.6). It is not necessarily the case that those who grow more plants get higher yields per crop, nor that those utilising a larger growing area necessarily produce more cannabis: this supports observations in previous research that some growers simply prefer to grow a number of small plants while others prefer to grow a smaller number of larger plants (e.g., Potter, 2010a).

5.5 Reasons for growing

When respondents reported their reasons for growing cannabis (Table 10), we again find some strong similarities across the different countries but also some striking differences. Cost, provision for personal use, and pleasure were amongst the top reasons for growing across all countries. In the German language survey (reaching Germany, Austria and also German speakers in Switzerland) 'The cannabis I grow will never contain adulterants' was also offered as an option which proved to be particularly important (the most cited reason for cultivation in Germany and Austria, and third most cited reason in Switzerland) – clearly it would have been interesting to include this option in the other surveys and future sweeps of the ICCQ will include this as standard. Overall, the top five reasons for growing cannabis were, in order, 'It provides me with cannabis for personal use' (84%), 'I get pleasure from growing cannabis' (83%), 'It's cheaper than buying cannabis' (75%), 'To avoid contact with the illegal circuit (e.g. street dealers, criminals)' (72%) 'The cannabis I grow is healthier than the cannabis I buy' (68%). The sixth most popular response altogether was 'Because the plant is beautiful' – chosen by 48% of respondents overall, but not available in the Dutch or Belgian surveys. For those countries where this option was available, only Finland (49%) had fewer than half choosing this response.

Notably, only 11% of respondents overall chose 'so I can sell it' as a reason to grow cannabis, although this rose to 28% in the US and 33% in Canada, showing North American respondents to be much more likely to be motivated by the possibility of financial returns than their European or Australian counterparts. Within Europe, the Finns and the Dutch (both at 14%) were more likely to choose this option than any other countries: it may be that for the Dutch this represents the possibility of selling cannabis directly to coffee-shops, whereas for the Finns this may reflect the relatively under-developed cannabis market in 'remote' Northern Europe compared to the other European countries covered by the survey.

Table 10: Reasons for growing cannabis

	BE	US	CN	AU	FI	DK	NL	DE	AT	CH	UK	*Total*
It provides me with cannabis for personal use	79	76	76	89	90	86	76	84	90	87	93	*84*
I get pleasure from growing cannabis	84	76	78	78	84	80	85	86	87	94	82	*83*
Cheaper than buying cannabis	79	90	92	72	73	60	64	74	80	71	84	*75*
To avoid contact with criminals	66	57	54	66	81	80	36	77	85	63	83	*72*
The cannabis I grow is healthier than the cannabis I buy	67	60	56	67	62	68	63	82	76	77	75	*68*
Because the plant is beautiful	-	70	68	56	49	58	-	64	68	70	65	*48*
To provide myself with cannabis for medical reasons	19	81	56	54	53	43	42	35	41	26	53	*44*
I wanted to see whether I could grow it	39	64	67	35	37	39	43	44	34	43	55	*43*
The cannabis I grow is a more consistent product	15	60	56	45	49	29	24	45	41	42	66	*41*
So I can share it / give it to my friends and acquaintances	41	59	70	37	41	44	44	30	35	37	26	*40*
For activist reasons (e.g. ecological ideology, fair trade)	40	35	29	28	44	34	32	43	41	41	31	*38*
I can flush the cannabis I grow to remove chemical residue	21	57	64	41	-	26	25	50	56	49	61	*33*
Because the plant is easy to take care of	37	45	54	26	31	32	27	26	28	30	37	*32*
Growing your own cannabis is not as risky as buying it	36	41	44	35	23	30	8	26	28	22	40	*30*
Because it is easier to grow than to buy	45	35	38	26	46	12	14	15	23	8	27	*29*
The cann. I can grow is stronger than the cann. I can buy	10	55	49	20	17	26	12	21	15	18	28	*23*
To provide others with cannabis for medical reasons	8	49	38	20	17	18	15	13	14	16	18	*18*
The cann. I can grow is milder than the cann. I can buy	24	9	10	12	5	11	16	10	8	16	12	*12*
So I can sell it	8	28	33	9	14	5	14	7	7	8	9	*11*
The cannabis I grow will never contain adulterants	-	-	-	-	-	-	-	94	91	85	-	-
The cann. I can grow tastes better than the cann. I can buy	35	-	-	-	-	-	44	-	-	-	-	-
Legally cultivating medical marijuana	-	12	3	-	-	-	-	-	-	-	-	-

Note: Values cited are % of respondents choosing each reason. The question asked respondents to tick all options that applied to them.

Notable differences between countries include wide variations in those reporting cultivating for their own or somebody else's medical use (much more likely in the US; least likely in Belgium). We might speculate that in the US, where (in some states) there is legal provision for medical cannabis use, claiming medical use reduces some of the stigma associated with being a cannabis user, akin to a sophisticated 'neutralisation' technique (cf. Sykes & Matza 1957). Similarly, other countries (such as Canada) allow for some legal medical cultivation – however, a full discussion of the different policies relating to medical-use cultivation and how these may relate to our findings is beyond the scope of the current paper (but see Hakkarainen et al. 2015, for further discussion on growing for medical reasons). The desire to grow cannabis that was weaker, rather than stronger, than that available on the black-market was peculiar to Belgium, whereas the desire to grow cannabis that was stronger than available on the market was particularly important in America. At the same time, Belgians, followed by the Dutch, were least concerned with wanting to ensure consistency of product when compared to what they could buy. Both these and other factors may point to the role that features of the domestic market have in motivating growers: in Belgium and the Netherlands, there is easy access to the de-criminalised Dutch 'coffee-shop' market, dominated by a wide selection of generally strong varieties of cannabis (Niesink & Rigter 2013). More traditional black-markets, however, are not known for consistency of product and, indeed, are often associated (correctly or not, cf. Coomber 2006) with concerns around adultery and general inconsistency of standards (e.g. strength and purity). North Americans in general seemed less concerned about avoiding 'contact with the illegal circuit' than European respondents, although the Dutch sample were notably less concerned with this than any other group (which may again reflect the coffee-shop system). Curiosity was more important in North America than elsewhere, and more important in the UK than elsewhere in Europe.

5.6 Market participation

Although there were some clear differences in growers' involvement in the distribution of cannabis (Table 11), overall profiles were broadly similar in this area. Unsurprisingly, the vast majority of growers reported consuming at least part of their crops for personal cannabis use (although very small minorities in each sample did not report using any of their crop for personal consumption). Roughly a quarter of the entire sample reported swapping some of their harvest with other growers, varying from 15% in the UK and Denmark to 30% or more in Belgium, Switzerland and Austria, and 73% in the Netherlands. In all countries except the

Netherlands over half of all respondents reported giving away some of the cannabis they produced. Although the precise reasons for the variation in responses here is unclear, the overall picture supports the idea of cannabis use – and even cannabis growing – as a social experience (cf. Weisheit, 1991, 1992; Potter, 2010a, 2010b) and are involved in what is often termed in the literature as 'social supply', a key element of non-commercial cannabis cultivation noted by both Potter, 2010a and Hough et al., 2003 in the UK context and also observed in studies of growers in Finland and Denmark, for example (Hakkarainen et al. 2011a, Frank et al. 2011). Perhaps more significantly from a criminal justice perspective, a sizable minority (around one-third of all respondents) reported selling cannabis to others. Although the distinction was not made in the North American survey, in nearly all countries selling to cover the cost of growing was more common than selling for profit, although well over 10% of respondents did report the latter. It is interesting to note that the proportions reporting actually selling cannabis (for profit or otherwise) were higher than the proportions reporting 'so I can sell it' as a reason why they grow cannabis (Table 10) in the first place – this supports the observation made by Potter (2010a) that getting a financial return on cannabis cultivation may be something that develops after growers discover there is a market for their produce (often, in Potter's work, among friends and acquaintances along the model of social supply). It is also interesting to note that the North American respondents were much more likely to cite 'so I can sell it' as a reason to grow cannabis, but only slightly more likely to actually sell some of their cannabis than most of the European samples.

Selling (either for profit or to cover costs) was associated with higher total crop yield (Wilcoxon signed-rank test: $z = -12.64$, $p < .001$). Sellers reported a median crop yield of 10.6 ounces (IQR 5.3–24.7; n = 1014) while non-sellers reported a median crop yield of 6.3 ounces (IQR 2.6–114.1; n = 2142). For those respondents who did report selling some of their last crop, the majority in all countries reported that their income from cannabis cultivation contributed to less than 10% of their total income (Table 11), but with sizeable minorities reporting much higher proportions of their income coming through selling cannabis, particularly in the US, Canada and the UK. The North American respondents were also the most likely to report selling drugs other than cannabis, although this activity was reported only by a small minority (less than 10% of respondents in most countries other than the US and Canada; 7% in the sample as a whole).

Table 11: Market participation

	BE	US	CN	AU	FI	DK	NL	DE	AT	CH	UK	*Total*
What did you do with the cannabis you grew in the last 12 months? (%)												
Consume for personal use	96	98	94	97	98	97	92	97	96	96	99	*97*
Swap with other growers	30	28	25	18	28	15	73	20	35	32	15	*26*
Give away (or share)	81	69	75	65	84	64	15	78	76	79	54	*71*
Sell (incl. both to cover costs and for profit)	33	38	34	24	32	17	23	34	32	39	22	*29*
Sell to cover costs of growing	25	-	-	19	26	15	15	30	25	33	20	*23*
Sell for profit	18	-	-	12	14	6	15	14	17	18	11	*13*
Keep in your possession	59	-	-	18	26	23	46	46	49	53	17	*36*
Total N	*634*	*364*	*32*	*314*	*681*	*614*	*199*	*781*	*72*	*66*	*257*	*4014*
What percentage of total income came from cultivation activities? (%)[a]												
0-10%	77	54	70	68	70	77	61	64	78	77	58	*68*
11-50%	11	26	0	18	23	18	26	25	17	19	23	*21*
51-100%	12	20	30	14	7	5	13	11	4	4	19	*12*
Total N	*152*	*131*	*10*	*56*	*175*	*94*	*31*	*264*	*23*	*26*	*43*	*1005*
Have you sold any drugs other than cannabis or cannabis products in the last 12 months? (%)												
No	96	82	72	93	92	99	94	96	97	91	96	*93*
Yes	4	18	28	7	8	1	6	4	3	10	4	*7*
Total N	*735*	*489*	*43*	*338*	*799*	*141*	*206*	*932*	*78*	*74*	*270*	*4105*

[a] Only those respondents reporting selling 1% or more of their crop (whether for profit or for covering costs) were included in this analysis.

5.7 Police contact and other illegal activity

Generally respondents thought that 'the risk of getting caught by police for growing cannabis' (Table 12) was 'low' or 'very low' compared to 'high' or 'very high' by a ratio of nearly 4:1, but this varied quite widely across the samples. Germans (42%), followed by Austrians (36%) and Canadians (30%) were most likely to see the risk as 'high' or 'very high' compared to 21% of the whole sample. Conversely, Belgians (52%), Americans (51%) and the Dutch (45%) were most likely to report the risk as 'very low': this may reflect (perceived or actual) official tolerance to small-scale cultivation in these countries (although in America this varies considerably by state). However, these perceptions of risk were not always matched by experience (Table 13): Finns (25%), Austrians (21%) and Australians (20%) were the most likely, with Americans (6%) and Belgians (9%) the least likely, to report that they had actually come into contact with the police through their cultivation activity. In total, only 15% of our respondents across all surveys had had such police contact.

About three-quarters of respondents overall (ranging from 62% in Finland to 87% in Belgium and 95% in Canada – although the Canadian sample for this question was small) reported that they had never been convicted of a criminal offence (Table 13), and minor violations aside, only very small proportions of respondents reported involvement in any criminal activity (other than drug-related) in the last 12 months (this peaked in Finland where 5% reported involvement in property crimes and 2% in violent crimes). The picture here is of a largely law-abiding sample, aside from participation in cannabis cultivation and other drug-related crimes. (Although 15% – peaking at 29% in Belgium and dropping to 0% for both North American countries – reported lesser 'violations' such as fare evasion or traffic violations; those citing non-criminal violations varied widely across the different cohorts although this is probably as much a reflection on the different legal codes in each country as actual participation in particular activities.)

Table 12: Police contact related to cannabis cultivation

	BE	US	CN	AU	FI	DK	NL	DE	AT	CH	UK	*Total*
What do you estimate is the risk of you getting caught by police for growing cannabis? (%[a])												
Very high	1	1	2	4	2	2	4	8	1	0	4	*3*
High	8	15	28	17	12	13	12	34	35	23	24	*18*
Low	39	33	42	53	57	49	38	49	51	57	47	*47*
Total N	925	616	60	447	1094	735	229	1171	106	93	346	*5822*
Have you ever come into contact with the police because of your cannabis growing? (%[a])												
No	92	94	90	80	75	91	89	86	79	85	82	*86*
Yes	9	6	10	20	25	10	12	14	21	15	18	*15*
Total N	*1004*	*620*	*60*	*481*	*1169*	*803*	*260*	*1289*	*119*	*96*	*396*	*6297*

[a] Only those respondents reporting selling 1% or more of their crop (whether for profit or for covering costs) were included in this analysis.

Table 13: Criminal convictions and criminality beyond cultivation

	BE	US	CN	AU	FI	DK	NL	DE	AT	CH	UK	*Total*
What do you estimate is the risk of you getting caught by police for growing cannabis? (%[a])												
No	87	83	95	74	62	71	85	73	64	71	71	*74*
Yes	13	17	5	26	38	29	15	27	36	29	29	*26*
Total N	999	618	60	490	1172	806	264	1282	120	97	398	*6306*
Have you engaged in any illegal activity in the last 12 months, excluding all cannabis and illicit drug use, cultivation, selling? (%)												
Violation (e.g. fare evasion, traffic violation) [non-criminal offence]	29	-[a]	-[a]	6	10	15	20	22	25	26	6	*15*
Property offences (e.g. burglary, fraud, theft, robbery, blackmail)	3	2	0	1	5	2	2	2	1	2	2	*3*
Violent offences (e.g. assault, stabbing, shooting, rape)	1	1	0	0	2	1	1	1	0	1	1	*1*
None	69	97	100	91	84	82	77	75	75	71	91	*81*
Total N	*956*	*617*	*60*	*483*	*970*	*796*	*249*	*1290*	*118*	*97*	*398*	*6034*

[a] Question asked in a different format in North American survey.

6 Discussion

We must remind the reader of some important caveats to our results. We cannot claim that our samples are representative of broader populations of cannabis growers in any of the participating countries. At the very least, we expect a bias towards smaller-scale cannabis growers who are less involved in drug markets and/or other types of crime: those with greater criminal involvement would probably be less likely to respond to our survey as they are likely to have greater concerns about possible criminal justice repercussions resulting from reporting their activities. The fact the survey is online also suggests a bias to those demographic groups more likely to both have access to and regularly use the internet – particularly for those countries where recruitment strategies were predominantly online (see Barratt et al. 2015). As such we are keen to emphasise that results discussed are for our samples and not necessarily generalisable to broader growing populations. Nevertheless, we feel that the patterns identified point us towards some useful conclusions and have something to say about our understanding of cannabis-growing populations in the countries researched, with implications for both future policy and future research considerations.

Firstly, small-scale cannabis cultivation (at least) is clearly quite wide-spread across Europe, North America and Australia, with large numbers of those involved willing to participate in research of the kind reported on here. Although growers responding to our survey were predominantly male and younger adults, our findings suggest some involvement in cultivation across both genders and all age groups. Most of our respondents had jobs (or were students) and a majority had shared living arrangements. Likewise, the majority of our respondents were largely law-abiding (aside, of course, from their cannabis cultivation and other drug-related activities): these are people who live more-or-less normal lives rather than some deviant or anti-social sub-group.

Somewhat unsurprisingly, our growers tended to be frequent users of cannabis. Although a key reason for growing cannabis was to supply their own consumption, they also reported getting cannabis from sources other than their own cultivation: personal cultivation does not usually satisfy an individual's consumption requirements (although this may be as much through users' desires to consume a variety of cannabis products as any inability to produce as much as they consume). Although many did use other drugs, the majority did not, and very few suggested what might be seen as particularly problematic patterns of drug use (e.g. use of heroin, or extreme poly-drug use).

Our growers tended to start cultivating in their late teens and early twenties (i.e. young adulthood) although some started much younger and others much later in life. Growing was something that respondents turned to later in life than they started using cannabis: they seem to have become regular users before they turned to cultivation. Generally they hadn't grown cannabis that often, although significant numbers reported high levels of experience. Mostly they found cannabis cultivation easy (in that they reported success after one or two attempts): clearly this criminal activity is not one that is difficult to become either involved or successful in, at least for those motivated to participate (and at least for those who have access to the internet – a necessary feature for those who responded to our online survey, and a key source of information about cannabis growing noted in other research; Potter 2010a; Bouchard et al. 2011; Decorte 2010).

Across our developed-world samples, indoor cultivation is more common than outdoor cultivation, although this varied quite dramatically across the participating countries. It seems likely that method of cultivation chosen is influenced by a number of factors that are likely to include physical-geographical (climatic and agronomic conditions), social-geographical (e.g. access to outdoor growing opportunities and population densities), political (law and policy) and also cultural (national and local traditions of cannabis use and cultivation as well as broader cultural mores around, for example, rural/urban lifestyles) aspects. This is an area where further analysis of our data – and further research – should shed more light.

Regardless of preferred cultivation methods, most of our respondents operate on a small scale preferring low numbers of plants and small areas given over to cultivation, although this did vary between countries (and may in part be due to growers' recognition of national or local policy around some lenience towards growing a certain number of plants, as well as individual preferences). Of course, our methodology was geared more towards small-scale growers than large commercial operations. Nevertheless, some growers in our survey reported much larger growing operations: growing more than 100 plants at a time was reported by at least some respondents from all countries.

Yield, both per-plant and per-crop, also varies across countries. This is undoubtedly partly related to growing methods, particularly the choice to grow indoors or outside, but also growers' preferences. Importantly, it is not always the case that greater numbers of plants led to greater yields. Very large yields were claimed by some respondents in most countries: limited number of plants does not necessarily effectively limit yields. A key policy related point here is that a small number of plants can produce a large quantity of cannabis and growers who choose to cultivate only small numbers of plants, possibly in response to national law or policy factors, can still generate very large yields. Restrictions on number of plants, such as has been the case in Australia, the Netherlands or Belgium (for example) (Room et al. 2010), and will be the case under the new proposed models in Colorado and Uruguay (Room 2014), may prove to be a relatively blunt instrument if the idea is to reduce individual growers' productivity. However, one regulatory option is to give police discretion to put evidence before the court if, in their view, the yield from a small number of plants seems greater than a personal use amount (see Lenton 2011).

One of our most important findings is that most of the small-scale growers in our sample are motivated more by practical and ideological concerns than a desire to make money. Taken together, these and other features of the data support the repeated observation in the literature that cannabis cultivation is often a rational choice for some cannabis users who wish to minimise the harm associated with buying cannabis (cost, criminal involvement associated with buying cannabis, uncertainty or undesirability of quality of cannabis available on the black-market), whist also being an aesthetic and/or 'ideological' choice (Potter 2010a; Decorte 2010). Cultivating for medical purposes is also important to a number of growers (see Hakkarainen et al. 2015 for further discussion here).

While only one-third of our respondents reported actually selling (with more reported selling to cover costs than selling to make money, and with most of those who did sell reporting that this was not a major part of their income), most of our respondents did report some level of involvement in cannabis supply. Interestingly, North American respondents were most likely to sell cannabis, most likely to cite selling as a reason for growing, and most likely to get involved in selling other drugs. A key point to take here is that while a majority of our cannabis growers are involved in the *supply* of cannabis, they are not generally drug *dealers*. Instead, a vast majority of the respondents give away some part of their product for free, by sharing, swapping and gift giving. These observations show the importance of 'social supply' among cannabis-using networks with its blurred lines between selling and sharing drugs (see all other chapters in this volume). *Intent* to make money is, notably, *not* a major driver for many of the cultivators who participated in our surveys (although it is, of course, very likely that those who are driven by profits were also less likely to participate in an online survey), but higher proportions of growers reported that they did sell some of their cannabis than reported being able to sell cannabis as a reason for growing: for some (a small minority), cultivation may act as a way into drug dealing even if this wasn't the original intention. Potter (2010a) has previously described this phenomenon as the 'slippery slope', and this pattern fits the concept of 'drift' reported both in those who escalate from 'social supply' to 'real dealing' (Taylor and Potter, 2013, Werse & Müller in this volume) and in escalation of criminality more generally (Matza, 1964).

Finally, cannabis cultivation was generally not seen as risky, although higher numbers reported police contact than perceived the likelihood of getting caught as high or very high. Some quite major intra-country differences in both perceptions of risk and actual experiences with the police (although these didn't correlate: countries with high perceived risk were not the ones with the highest levels of police contact). This is another area where further analysis of our data will be important.

7 Conclusions

This paper reports some initial findings from work that is very much on-going. In particular, we intend future papers that develop analyses of the relationship between variables in the ICCQ and political and cultural contexts of different countries, and multivariate analyses to tease out the relationships between growers' methods, motives and market participation. In particular we wish to explore the differences between 'small' and 'large' scale, or 'commercial' and 'non-commercial' cultivation. We also intend, in collaboration with local researchers, to launch the survey in a number of other countries in both the developed and developing world (current plans to run the survey in Uruguay are especially interesting given the recent developments effectively legalising small-scale cultivation in that country) and to repeat the survey in the near future (with more rigorous standardisation of both the survey questions and recruitment and promotion methods). A repeat sweep will be particularly interesting in countries like the US and Belgium where significant policy changes are taking place.

Future research aside, we can draw attention to some key points that can be made from the findings presented here, and that have clear relevance not just to our academic understanding of cannabis cultivation in developed-world countries but also to policy considerations. Significantly, there should be no assumption that most small-scale cannabis growers are criminally or socially deviant: instead, most tend to come from more-or-less normal socio-economic backgrounds with minimal involvement in drug dealing (as opposed to social supply) or other types of crime. Indeed, a commonly-cited reason for growing cannabis is actually to *avoid* involvement with criminals (in the form of traditional dealers and the black-market). Equally, it should not be assumed that involvement in cannabis cultivation comes about from a desire to make money (although saving money may be an important factor). Having said this, the observation that involvement in cultivation may lead a small minority of individuals to drift into dealing, albeit usually on a small scale, is important.

Acknowledgments

We would like to thank the thousands of cannabis cultivators who completed our questionnaire. Our research would not be possible without your efforts. Thank you to all the people and organisations who supported and promoted our research, including but not limited to: A-clinic Foundation, Bluelight.org, Cannabis Consumer organisation "WeSmoke", Cannabis Festival 420 Smoke Out, cannabismyter.dk, Chris Bovey, Deutscher Hanfverband, drugsforum.nl, eve-rave.ch, Finnish Cannabis Association, grasscity.com, grower.ch, hampepartiet.dk, Hamppu Forum, hanfburg.de, Hanfjournal, jointjedraaien.nl, land-der-traeume.de, Nimbin Hemp Embassy, NORML-UK, Österreichischer Hanfverband, OZStoners.com, partyflock.nl, psychedelia.dk, rollitup.org, Royal Queen Seeds, shaman-australis.com, thctalk.com, Vereniging voor Opheffing Cannabisverbod (VOC), wietforum.nl, wiet-zaden.nl, and all the coffeeshops, growshops and headshops that helped us. The German team would like to thank Anton-Proksch-Insitut, Dr Alfred Uhl (Vienna, Austria), and infodrog.ch, Marcel Krebs (Bern, Switzerland), who gave consent to address Austrian and Swiss respondents and assisted their team with recruitment of Swiss and Austrians. We would like to acknowledge the Nordic Centre for Welfare and Social Issues (NVC) for funding our project meetings. SL and MJB through their employment at the National Drug Research Institute at Curtin University were supported by funding from the Australian Government under the Substance Misuse Prevention and Service Improvement Grants Fund. MJB is now funded through a National Health & Medical Research Council Early Career Researcher Fellowship (APP1070140). The Belgian study was funded through the Belgian Science Policy Office, under the Federal Research Programme on Drugs (grant no. DR/00/063). The US/Canada study received funding from the College of Health and Human Services at California State University, Long Beach. The German study received refunding from a prior project funded by the Deutsche Forschungsgemeinschaft (DFG, German Research Association).

References

Barratt, M.J. & Lenton, S. (2015): Representativeness of online purposive sampling with Australian cannabis cultivators. International Journal of Drug Policy, 26 (3): 323-326.

Barratt, M.J., Bouchard, M., Decorte, T., Asmussen F.V., Hakkarainen, P., Lenton, S., Malm, A., Nguyen, H. & Potter, G. (2012): Understanding global patterns of domestic cannabis cultivation. Drugs and Alcohol Today, 12(4): 213-221.

Barratt, M.J., Potter, G., Wouters, M., Wilkins, C., Werse, B., Perälä, J., Mulbjerg Pederson M., Nguyen H., Malm A., Lenton S., Korf, D., Klein A., Heyde J., Hakkarainen P., Frank V.A., Decorte T., Bouchard M. & Blok T. (2015): Lessons from conducting trans-national internet-mediated participatory research with hidden populations of cannabis cultivators. International Journal of Drug Policy, 26 (3): 238-249.

Bouchard, M. (2007): A capture-recapture model to estimate the size of criminal populations and the risks of detection in a marijuana cultivation industry. Journal of Quantitative Criminology, 23, (3) 221-241.

Bouchard, M., Alain, M. & Nguyen, H. (2009): Convenient labour: the prevalence and nature of youth involvement in the cannabis cultivation industry. International Journal of Drug Policy, 20 (6): 467-474.

Bouchard, M., Potter, G. & Decorte, T. (2011): Emerging Trends in Cannabis Cultivation – and the Way Forward. In: T. Decorte T, G. Potter, M. Bouchard (eds.): World Wide Weed: global trends in cannabis cultivation and its control. Ashgate: Aldershot.

Coomber, R. (2006): Pusher myths: Re-situating the drug dealer. London: Free Association Books.

Decorte, T. (2010): Small scale domestic cannabis cultivation: an anonymous web survey among 659 cultivators in Belgium. Contemporary Drug Problems, 37 (2): 341-370.

Decorte, T., Potter, G. & Bouchard, M. (2011): World Wide Weed: global trends in cannabis cultivation and control. Ashgate: Aldershot.

Decorte, T., Barratt, M.J., Nguyen, H., Bouchard, M., Malm, A. & Lenton, S. (2012): International Cannabis Cultivation Questionnaire (ICCQ) (Version 1.1). Global Cannabis Cultivation Research Consortium, Belgium.

Douglas, J. & Sullivan, R. (2013): The role of child protection in cannabis grow-operations. International Journal of Drug Policy, 24 (5): 445-448.

Frank, V.A., Christense, A.S., Villumsen, S. & Dahl, H.V. (2011): Cannabis dyrkning i Danmark [Cannabis growing in Denmark]. In: V.A. Frank, H.V. Dahl (eds.): Cannabis- Forbrug, interventioner og marked i Danmark [Cannabis – Consumption, interventions and markets in Denmark]. Aarhus: Aarhsu University Press, 147-171.

Hakkarainen, P., Frank V.A., Barratt, M.J., Dahl, H.V., Decorte, T., Karjalainen, K., Lenton, S., Potter, G., Werse B. (2015): Growing medicine: Small-scale cannabis cultivation for medicalpurposes in six different countries. International Journal of Drug Policy, 26 (3): 250-256.

Hakkarainen, P., Frank, V.A., Perälä, J. & Dahl, H.V. (2011a): Small-scale cannabis growers in Denmark and Finland. European Addiction Research, 17 (3): 119–128.

Hakkarainen, P., Perälä, J. & Metso, L. (2011b): Kukkaa pukkaa – Kannabiksen kotikasvatus Suomessa [Bud, bud, bud – Home growing of cannabis in Finland]. Yhteiskuntapolitiikka, 76 (2): 148–168.

Hammersvik, E., Sandberg, S. & Pedersen, W. (2012): Why small-scale cannabis growers stay small: Five mechanisms that prevent small-scale growers from going large scale. International Journal of Drug Policy, 23 (6): 458-464.

Hardie-Bick, J., Sheptycki, J. & Wardak, A. (2005): Transnational and Comparative Criminology in a Global Perspective. In: J. Sheptycki, A. Wardak (eds.): Transnational and Comparative Criminology. London: GlassHouse Press.

Heidensohn, F. (2008): International Comparative Research in Criminology. In: R.D. King, E. Wincup (eds.): Doing Research on Crime and Justice. Oxford: Oxford University Press.

Hough, M., Warburton, H., Few, B., May, T., Man, L-H., Witton, J. & Turnbull, P.J. (2003): A growing market: The domestic cultivation of cannabis. York: Joseph Rowntree Foundation.

INCB (2013): The use of cannabis seeds for illicit cultivation: report of secretariat Commission on Narcotic Drugs, 56th session, Vienna 11-15 March 2013.

Jansen, A. (2002): The economics of cannabis-cultivation in Europe. Paper presented at the 2nd European Conference on Drug Trafficking and Law Enforcement. Paris, 26th and 27th September, 2002. Available at http://www.cedro-uva.org/lib/jansen.economics.html. [accessed: 15th April 2014].

Lenton, S. (2011): Changing cannabis laws to facilitate a shift to domestic cannabis production as a harm reduction strategy – a case study. In: T. Decorte, G. Potter, M. Bouchard (eds.): World Wide Weed: the globalisation and localisation of cannabis cultivation. Farnham: Ashgate.

Lenton, S., Frank, V.A., Barratt, M., Dahl, H.V. & Potter, G. (2015): Attitudes of cannabis growers to regulation of cannabis cultivation under a non-prohibition cannabis model. International Journal of Drug Policy, 26 (3): 257-266.

Malm, A. (2006): Marihuana Cultivation in British Columbia: Utilizing spatial and social network analysis to inform evidence-based policy and planning. Unpublished PhD. Dissertation. Simon Fraser University.

Matza, D. (1964): Delinquency and Drift. New York: John Wiley and Sons, Inc.

Nguyen, H. & Bouchard, M. (2010): Patterns of youth participation in cannabis cultivation. Journal of Drug Issues, 40 (2): 263–294.

Nguyen, H., Malm, A. & Bouchard, M. (2015): Production, perceptions, and punishment: Restrictive deterrence in the context of cannabis cultivation. International Journal of Drug Policy, 26 (3): 267-276.

Niesink, R. & Rigter, S. (2013): THC-concentraties in wiet, nederwiet en hasj in Nederlandse coffeeshops [THC concentrations in weed, nederweed and hash in Dutch coffeeshops]. Utrecht: Trimbos Instituut.

Paoli, L. & Decorte, T. (2015): Assessing the harms of cannabis cultivation in Belgium. International Journal of Drug Policy, 26 (3): 277-289.

Plecas, D., Malm, A.E. & Kinney, B. (2005): Marihuana Grow Operations Revisited: 1997-2003. Ottawa, Canada: Royal Canadian Mounted Police.

Potter, G.R. (2010a): Weed, Need and Greed: a study of domestic cannabis cultivation. Free Association Books: London.

Potter, G.R. (2010b): You Reap What You Sow: the profit, pleasure and pain in domestic cannabis cultivation. In: T. Decorte, J. Fountain (eds.): Pleasure, pain and profit. European perspectives on drugs. Pabst: Lengerich.

Potter, G.R. & Dann, S. (2005): Urban Crop Circles: Urban Cannabis Growers in the North of England. In: W. Palacios (ed.): Cocktails and Dreams: Perspectives on Drug and Alcohol Use. Pearson Prentice Hall: Upper Saddle River, New Jersey.

Potter, G., Bouchard, M. & Decorte, T. (2011): The Globalization of Cannabis Cultivation. In: T. Decorte, G.R. Potter, M. Bouchard (eds.): World Wide Weed: global trends in cannabis cultivation and its control. Ashgate: Aldershot.

Room, R. (2014): Legalising a market for cannabis for pleasure: Colorado, Washington, Uruguay and beyond. Addiction 109(3): 345-351.

Room, R., Fischer, B., Hall, W., Lenton, S., & Reuter, P. (2010): Cannabis Policy: Moving Beyond Stalemate. Oxford University Press: Oxford.

Straus, M.A. (2009): The national context effect. Cross-Cultural Research, 43 (3): 183–205.

Sykes, G. & Matza, D. (1957): Techniques of neutralization: A theory of delinquency. American Sociological Review, 22 (6): 664-670.

Taylor, M. & Potter, G. (2013): Drug dealers and friendship networks: Drift, friendship and trust in drug dealing careers. Journal of Drug Issues, 43(4): 392-406.

United Nations Office on Drugs and Crime (2008): 2008 World Drug Report. Vienna: United Nations.

United Nations Office on Drugs and Crime (2013): 2013 World Drug Report. Vienna: United Nations.

Weisheit, R.A. (1991): The intangible rewards from crime: the case of domestic marijuana cultivation. Crime and Delinquency, 37 (4): 506–527.

Weisheit, R.A. (1992): Domestic Marijuana: A Neglected Industry. New York: Greenwood Press.

Werse, B. (2015): Legal issues for German-speaking cannabis growers. Results from an online survey. International Journal of Drug Policy, November 2015, DOI: 10.1016/j.drugpo.2015.10.007

Green, green grass of home – Small-scale cannabis cultivation and social supply in Finland

Pekka Hakkarainen and Jussi Perälä

Abstract

Three different datasets are used to study the home growing of cannabis and social supply connected to it in Finland. Data from a representative population survey (N=2,023) traces the prevalence of home growing. Data from an online questionnaire among cannabis growers (N=1,298) in spring 2009 and interviews with home growers (N=38) are used to draw a portrait of growers and to describe their thinking: What does home growing involve in practice? Who are the growers? What is the purpose of growing, and what happens to the crop?

The study reveals that, in line with European and international trends, the cannabis market in Finland is very much herbalised. According to the population survey, some 40,000–60,000 people in Finland have at least sometimes tried growing cannabis, and there are thousands of active growers. Around one in ten Finns indicated that they personally knew a cannabis grower.

The home growing of cannabis is related to local drug markets. Home growing allows people to overcome the problem of limited supply and, at a lower cost, to produce better quality cannabis than is available in the street markets. Apart from enjoying it for personal use, small-scale growers share their harvest with friends and acquaintances. Some home-grown cannabis is sold, but most of it goes to a limited circle of friends. Participants in the study describe themselves as "ideological" cannabis growers. Cannabis is not grown for money or for profit, but for personal enjoyment and for sharing with friends. Typically, home growers have 1–5 plants in limited indoor space at home.

1 Introduction

Hashish smuggled from North Africa dominated the European cannabis markets for a long time, but the situation changed in the 2000s. In some countries, such as the Netherlands and Great Britain, the majority of cannabis is domestically grown (Potter et al. 2011). There has been a significant increase in the small-scale home growing of cannabis (Decorte 2010a). There are a number of contributing factors. New varieties of cannabis have been developed that are suitable for a range of growing conditions, and at the same time, technology enabling indoor growing has advanced rapidly. Detailed instructions on how to grow marijuana are available on the Internet, and there are numerous online forums for exchanging experiences and information with other growers. Shortly said, cannabis cultivation has become much easier, and the quality of the final product has improved dramatically.

Domestic growing of cannabis represents a challenge to drug control policies, which are largely based on the prevention of import and smuggling. Furthermore, it questions approaches that focus on central supply and markets controlled by organised crime.

This paper provides a summary of the results of a research project launched in Finland in 2008 on the home growing of cannabis. The research involved conducting personal interviews with Finnish cannabis growers and an Internet-based survey. Based on this material, we were able to build a description of Finnish small-scale growers, their activities and their mindset. We also included questions regarding the home growing of cannabis in population-based studies to allow us to make the first scientific assessments of its prevalence in Finland. We have previously published some results of our work in international forums (Hakkarainen & Perälä 2011; Hakkarainen et al. 2011a). This article addresses the following topics:

- How common is the home growing of cannabis in Finland?
- What does home growing involve in practice?
- Who are the home growers?
- What is the purpose of growing, and what happens to the crop?

2 Research material

(1) Interviews with growers. For research purposes, interviews were conducted with 38 Finnish home growers of cannabis. Material was collected in 2008 (June–December). To recruit interviewees, the study was advertised on related websites (particularly on www.hamppu.net). The interviewees were guaranteed full anonymity. The response was very positive, and more people offered to take part in the study than we were able to interview. The final study material included 36 men and 2 women. The interviewees were aged from 18 to 58 but the majority (N=23) were young adults aged 25–34. The majority of the interviewees had a job (N=21) or were students (N=14). Only three people were unemployed at the

time the interview was conducted. More than half were married or were living with a partner (N=20). One fourth had children. The interviewees had very dissimilar backgrounds in terms of experience in cultivation. Some were working on their first crop while others had experimented with several crops, different technological solutions and hybrid varieties. The sizes of cannabis plantations typically varied between one and ten plants, which means home cultivation is a very small-scale operation. The largest plantation reported in the interviews was 40–50 plants. The interviews were conducted in different parts of Finland.

The interviews were face-to-face interviews, which were recorded. The subjects were asked to describe their experiences and cultivation practices, to discuss their motives and goals, to assess their relationships with other people and the authorities, and their views on Finland's drug policy. The duration of the interviews was from 1.5 to 3 hours. The subjects often showed the interviewer their plants and equipment, as well as photos of previous crops and plants. The interviewees gave the impression that they wanted to talk openly about their farming operations in order to bring their views into the public discussion, which, they felt, was lacking the growers' perspective almost entirely. The interviews were conducted by researcher Jussi Perälä.

(2) Online survey. For research purposes, an anonymous online survey for Finnish home growers of cannabis was conducted in 2009. A *Webropol* survey form was available on the website of the National Institute for Health and Welfare (THL) at www.thl.fi/kukka for one month, from May to June. Since the survey dealt with criminal activity, full confidentiality of information was required. Protection of the interviewees was thoroughly discussed by the THL research ethics committee. For instance, the IP addresses of the respondents were not recorded in any form. The survey was advertised on three different sites (www.paihdelinkki.fi, www.kannabisuutiset.worldpress.com and www.hamppu.net) with the objective of reaching the target group.

The questionnaire was based on a similar survey conducted originally in Belgium in 2006 (Decorte 2008 and 2010b). Danish researchers then modified the questionnaire for a survey they conducted in 2008, and a dozen new questions on some cultivation-related details were added to the Danish version in Finland (Hakkarainen et al. 2011a). These questions addressed issues such as motivation for growing, experiences and methods of growing (indoor/outdoor, soil/hydroponics etc.), use of crops and potential distribution, the pros and cons of home growing, and the risks and experiences of being subject to control. Only fully completed questionnaires were accepted for inclusion in the study. Some questionnaires contained obvious inconsistencies and were excluded from the study. All in all, responses were very matter-of-fact, and the number of rejected questionnaires was very small.

Considering the privacy and confidentiality of the information requested, the final number of respondents is high: a total of 1,298 of whom 1,054 were current growers (= had grown cannabis during the past year). Response to the survey was positive, as evidenced by the fact that around one third of the respondents wrote open comments in the space provided at the end of the questionnaire. In the comments section, the respondents assessed the questions, offered detailed information on specific questions, suggested some improvements, but a large number simply expressed their satisfaction with the issue being addressed scientifically.

One of the problems of the survey was that we had no way of controlling whether one person filled in the survey more than once. Considering that the questionnaire had 65 questions, it is, however, unlikely that anyone would have been tempted to answer more than once. A more serious problem is the weakness associated with web surveys: we do not know the population, therefore we are unable to assess the representativeness of the sample (Couper 2000). However, one of the strengths of a web survey is its ability to reach special groups (Sills and Song 2002). In population studies based on random sampling, it is very difficult to reach a sufficient number of respondents required for more detailed analyses of a relatively rare phenomenon such as the home growing of cannabis. It would require a huge sample for which, in real life, sufficient financial resources are simply not available. Even though the results of our web survey are not generalizable to the entire population or even the entire subgroup of cannabis home growers, the data obtained from these little over one thousand respondents allow us to create a more precise and detailed description of the main features of cannabis home growing in Finland than a representative population-based survey would permit[1]. However, we must recognise that large-scale growers striving to gain financial benefit from their operations are not likely to be interested in responding to these types of surveys. Consequently, surveys and interviews primarily target home growers operating on a fairly small scale.

(3) Population survey materials. In addition to material obtained through interviews and the web survey, this article draws on THL's population surveys. A drug survey conducted in 2010 on the basis of random sampling of the Finnish population aged 15–69 addressed the use of hashish and marijuana separately, providing a basis for comparing the consumption of these substances. The respondents were also asked if they had ever grown cannabis, or if they knew anyone who had. The material was collected by Statistics Finland through a postal survey, but respondents were also able to reply on the Internet. To an additional

---

1 This online survey was one of the headstones of the international GCCRC survey that also included Finland (see Potter et al. in this volume).

sample, replying online was offered as the first choice. The total number of approved responses was 2,023, and the response rate was 48%.

3 How much?

In Finland, as in other European countries, hashish has traditionally been the most popular cannabis product (Salasuo 2006). Finnish Cannabis Association's activists Timo Larmela and Ilkka Laine (1992: 104) described the situation in the early 1990s as follows:

> "There was very little marijuana in the markets. The reason is that marijuana is much more difficult to smuggle than hashish. High-quality marijuana is usually domestically grown, but it is rarely sold in the markets. The marijuana that is being sold has a bad reputation, as it primarily consists of the bottom leaves with low THC content. The growers usually keep the trim leaves with the highest THC content for themselves."

Confiscation statistics (e.g. Kontula 1986) and user studies (Hakkarainen 1987) confirm the dominance of hashish in the Finnish drug markets. In fact, the use of marijuana has been considered so insignificant that previous drug surveys addressed the use of cannabis generally.

However, confiscation data indicates that the situation changed in the 2000s (Perälä 2009). Back in the 1980s, only a few dozen cannabis plants were confiscated by the police annually, and in the 1990s the number had grown to a few hundred plants. But since 2001, several thousands of plants have been confiscated annually. For example, in 2008, the police confiscated 14,000 plants, in 2009 12,500 plants, and in 2010 15,000 plants (Kainulainen 2011).

In 2010, ten per cent of Finns (20% of men and 13% of women) reported having used cannabis at some point in their lives (LT). Of the total population, 4.5 per cent had used cannabis in the past 12 months (LY) and 1.5 per cent in the past 30 days (LM). There has been a notable change in the consumption patterns of hashish and marijuana. Marijuana (LT = 13%, LY = 4%, LM = 1%) has caught up with hashish (LT = 12%, LY = 2%, LM = 1%) and even outperformed it in terms of popularity. Marijuana is more commonly used than hashish among under 35-year-olds. The herbalisation of the cannabis markets is likely to be a result of the home growing of cannabis, even though the volume of smuggled marijuana may have grown in response to increased demand.

Table 1 shows the results of the drug survey conducted in 2010 regarding cannabis cultivation and home growing. In the survey, the respondents were asked

(a) if they personally knew anyone who grew cannabis and (b) if they personally had grown cannabis at some point or within the past 12 months.

Table 1: Cannabis growing and knowing growers by gender and age 2010 (%)

	Knows a grower	**Has grown cannabis**	
		Ever	Past 12 months
All	10	1,4	0,2
Men	11	2,3	0,5
Women	9	0,5	0
15–24	16	1,7	0,6
25–34	21	4,2	0,2
35–44	10	1,4	0
45–69	3	0,3	0,2

In autumn 2010, one of ten Finnish people said they personally knew someone who grew cannabis. This proportion is surprisingly high, and in the younger age groups it was even more common to know someone who grew cannabis. According to the survey, one fifth of those aged under 35 personally knew a grower. This connection directly affected the person's own use. Half (52%) of those who knew a cannabis grower reported having used marijuana at some point in their lives while only nine per cent of those who did not know a grower had used marijuana. The difference between those who knew growers and those who did not was even more striking when asked about recent use (LY: 25% vs 2%; LM: 9% vs 0%). One third of male respondents under the age of 35 said they had smoked a joint in the past year.

More than one per cent of the respondents said they had grown cannabis at some point. Cannabis growing was clearly more common among men than women. In the group of respondents aged 25–34, four per cent had some experience in growing cannabis. However, a considerably smaller percentage had grown cannabis within the past year.

It is impossible to say how reliable the answers to questions regarding personal experience of cannabis cultivation were. Considering the fact that the manufacture of drugs is a more serious offence than use, the reported numbers for manufacture may be intentionally smaller than those for simple use. On the other hand, considering the current popularity of growing, the figures may be excessive due to the fact that cannabis growers have been more active in responding than other population. This is entirely possible, as less than half of the selected sample responded to the survey.

In any event, the numbers provide the first population-level assessment of the extent of cannabis cultivation based on a statistically significant sample. A proportionate assessment of the percentages of cannabis growers against the total population suggests that roughly 40,000 – 60,000 Finns have, at some point in their lives, grown cannabis. The percentage of people who had grown cannabis in the past year is so small that any population assessment made on that basis would be highly random. It is likely that the number of active growers is slightly less than 10,000. This is in line with the assessment of the National Bureau of Investigation (10,000 households) in 2007 (Perälä 2009). If our estimate is correct, the 1,298 respondents of the web survey would represent approximately 15 per cent of all Finnish cannabis home growers. This indicates the survey has successfully reached the target group of the study.

Figure 1 shows the cultivation popularity growth trend on the basis of the age at which the respondents reported having grown their first crop. One of the two curves in the diagram was based on the results of the 2010 population survey, the other one on the results of the web survey. Based on the year of birth, the person's age at the time of first-time growing was converted into a cultivation year. Since pre-classified alternatives were used in the web survey, averages were applied in the figure. Cumulative distributions indicate the proportion of growers who had produced their first crop by a certain time.

Figure 1: Trend of small-scale cannabis cultivation in Finland (extrapolation from survey data; %)

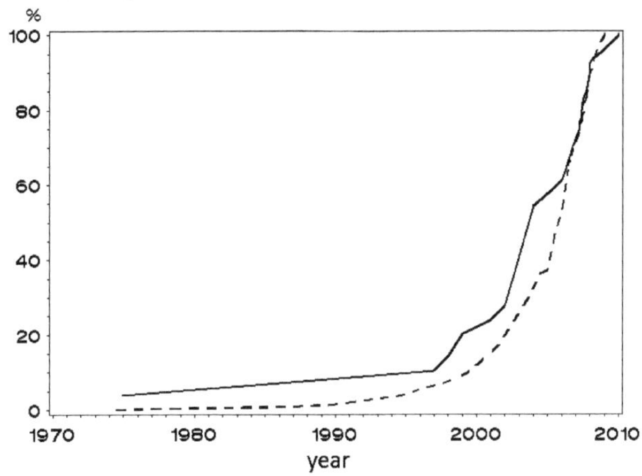

Dashed line= Web survey, continuous line = Drug survey 2010

The curves draw a very similar picture of the development. Home growing of cannabis took a sharp upward turn in the early 2000s, and almost all survey respondents had produced their first crops after that. This confirms the insignificance of domestic marijuana in the early 1990s, as evidenced by Larmela and Laine (1992) and the confiscation statistics. Since the 2000s, new growers have been emerging each decade.

4 How?

Chapter 50 of the Finnish Criminal Code prohibits the selling and buying of cannabis seeds for use as a narcotic substance. Consequently, there are no shops in Finland that supply cannabis seeds. So, how to get started? Researcher Jussi Perälä (2009: 126) offers the following description of cannabis home cultivation in Finland:

> “People buy seeds on the Internet. You can also receive or buy seeds from other growers, or exchange them. (...) Sometimes growers use plant cuttings instead of seeds. The equipment required for growing is easy to buy and relatively inexpensive. A well-informed grower can safely build a fairly inconspicuous cannabis farm. (...) Typical locations for growing cannabis plants at home include a wardrobe, a closet or another similar small space large enough for a dozen or so plants.“

Perälä has obtained this information from official sources, through his own ethnographic research, and from a cursory review of the material collected for this study. A more detailed description will be provided based on the results of the online survey and interviews with growers. The distribution of responses to the online survey is assessed on the basis of the number of plants the respondents reported they were growing at a time. The vast majority (72%) of the respondents grew 1–5 plants at a time. The second largest group (18%) was those growing 6–10 plants whereas the remaining respondents (7%) were pooled in a single category of “more than ten plants”. Consequently, the results of the survey are, by and large, representative of small-scale growing of cannabis. Only little over two per cent of the respondents said they had grown more than 20 plants at a time, with three respondents reporting to have cultivated several hundreds of plants at a time. Some respondents (2%) refused to answer questions regarding the number of plants; they are only included in the total counts.

Since the cannabis plant is not indigenous to the Finnish flora, cultivation requires some skills and special knowledge of horticulture, for instance on lighting conditions and fertiliser use. Table 2 indicates that the most important sources of information are the Internet[2] and other growers. A similar social network is also vital for seed procurement: the Internet and other growers were the primary sources while cannabis dealers were the least significant. Those growing more than five plants also benefited from their previous crops.

Table 2: Growers' information sources and seed procurement methods (%)

	Number of plants per crop			
	1-5 plants (n=935)	6-10 plants (n=237)	11+ plants (n=97)	Total (n=1298)
The meaning of a source as essential				
Internet	94	90	85	92
Other growers	79	80	80	80
Friends	62	63	66	62
Literature	40	45	46	42
A cannabis dealer	4	5	9	5
Obtaining seeds and cuttings				
From Internet	64	76	64	65
From other growers	49	62	63	52
From previous crops	35	47	66	39
From a shop abroad	4	7	12	5
From a cannabis dealer	5	6	4	5
Other	15	14	21	15

It is easy to get started with the help of the Internet and friends, but it takes patience, effort and regular care to produce a high-quality crop. Simply putting some seeds and soil in a jar on the window sill will not produce results. Almost all respondents of the web survey said they tended to their plants every day, or more than once a week. In face-to-face interviews, growers emphasised that cultivation had become a pastime and a passion for them (Hakkarainen & Perälä 2011). Growers enjoyed taking care of the plants, learning more about cultivation, developing their equipment and having peer discussions. As a pastime, it was compared to gardening, growing chilies or making wine.

The respondents mainly grew the main varieties of cannabis: Indica and Sativa. One of ten respondents grew exclusively one or the other, but it was more

2 The Internet contains a large number of websites dedicated to cannabis cultivation. The first Finnish-language guide to growing cannabis has been available for downloading since 1996.

common to grow both either at the same time or alternately. One of four respondents grew hybrids (such as White Widow, Skunk No. 1 and Jack Herer). Little more than half of the respondents only grew plants indoors. A third had grown plants outdoors and indoors, but just a few only outdoors. Indoor growing was most typical when the size of the cultivation was small. This is understandable, as growing just one plant or a few plants requires very little space. One third of growers with 1–5 plants needed less than one square metre of space for growing. More than half of all growers were able to fit their plants into a space of two square metres. However, according to ethnographic observations, outdoor growing may have increased in popularity recently with strains that survive in the Nordic climate and because of the tightened control of indoor cultivation.

An observation has been made worldwide that the growing systems used by home growers for small-scale cultivation can be surprisingly sophisticated, and that the police easily interprets this as a sign of professional activity even though it may simply be an indication of the growers' passion for their hobby (Decorte 2010a). In the following extract from an interview, the interviewee explains the technological applications he uses in a hydroponics system:

> "I can put everything on the computer, the electronic meter monitors and records everything once an hour, the digital timer looks after everything, the irrigation works as a steady flow." (Male, 26 years)

Most of the growers who responded to the web survey said they took care of their plants alone, but there were also a few joint projects. The smallest cultivations were most predominantly tended to by just one person. In families where both spouses were growers, cultivations may still be separate.

> "We both grow cannabis and basically we have our own places for growing and in practice I take care of my own plants and then I help my husband with the nutrients and so on. (…) My surplus goes to my husband and my motive is to produce for both of us (…)." (Female, 25 years)

Table 3 shows the quantity of marijuana growers reported to obtain from one plant. The quantities range from 25 to more than 100 grams. According to international literature, one plant grown indoors produces approximately 25–28 grams of cannabis (e.g. Bouchard 2007). Compared to these numbers, the Finnish growers appear to have produced good crops. The possibility of achieving high crops per plant makes the growing more interesting.

Table 3: Production and investments (%)

	Number of plants per crop			
	1 - 5 plants	6-10 plants	11+ plants	Total
	(n=935)	(n=237)	(n=97)	(n=1298)
Yield (i.e. usable dry cannabis) per plant typically in grams				
Less than 25 g	22	14	23	21
25–50 g	21	18	25	21
51–100 g	18	23	15	19
More than 100 g	9	12	9	9
Don't weigh the crop	15	20	16	16
Not yet harvested the crop/ don't want to answer	14	14	11	15
Estimated potency of cannabis in last crop				
Very strong	38	49	63	42
Mid-range	38	34	21	35
Mild/very mild	10	5	6	9
Not yet harvested the first crop/ don't know/ don't want to answer	14	12	10	14
Investment in last crop				
Less than 20 euros	17	8	14	15
20–50 euros	28	24	22	26
50–100 euros	21	21	10	20
100–250 euros	17	21	24	18
250–500 euros	6	14	10	7
More than 500 euros	2	4	9	3
Not yet harvested the crop/ don't know/ don't want to answer	9	8	10	10
How many crops of cannabis so far				
Not yet harvested the first crop	14	8	13	13
One crop	19	12	6	16
2–5 crops	43	38	22	40
6–10 crops	12	18	21	14
11–20 crops	4	10	14	6
More than 20 crops	3	6	14	4
Don't know/don't want to answer	5	7	9	7

The same applies to the opportunity of affecting the quality of one's own crop. More than 40 per cent of the respondents estimated that the marijuana they obtained from their plants was strong or very strong, and only nine per cent felt their product was mild or very mild. The objective of achieving a high THC content often came up in interviews. As the following quotation shows, the end seems to justify the means.

> "How to get the highest possible THC content? (...) One good tip is that one week before harvest you poke a nail through the plant's roots. Somehow the plant foresees that it's going to die and it makes one final push. When it does so, more visible crystal resin forms. There's a notable difference in crystal resin if you torture the plants the last week before harvest and keep them in the dark for three days compared to if you don't. These tips are half based on my own growing experience and half based on what I've heard from other growers." (Male, 26 years)

The sums invested prove that home growing is very inexpensive. More than two thirds of the respondents reported that they had invested no more than 100 euros in their most recent crop. If an investment of 100 euros in four plants yields 25 grams of marijuana per plant, the price per gram of the home-grown product is one euro. Typical market prices are between 10–15 euros per gram (Perälä 2009). However, this calculation fails to take into account all related costs (such as time and effort invested in looking after the plants and concealing the operations, as well as the risk of being caught). Another contributing factor is whether a person is a first-time grower or whether an infrastructure already exists. As Table 3 shows, 40 per cent of the respondents were already growing their 2nd–5th crops, and some had grown at least 20 crops. Growers who had invested large sums in their most recent crop estimated the yield and the quality of their plants higher than those who had invested smaller sums.

5 Who?

The population survey revealed that home growing experiments were much more common among men than women (Table 1). It is therefore not surprising that the majority of web survey respondents were also men. In addition, Table 4 shows that more than half of the web survey respondents were aged under 25. The proportion is larger than the results of the population survey gave reason to expect. It is probable that young people and men were more active in participating in the online survey than others.

Table 4: Social characteristics of cannabis growers, part I (%)

	Number of plants per crop			
	1-5 plants (n=935)	6-10 plants (n=237)	11+ plants (n=97)	Total (n=1298)
Gender				
Man	93	92	91	93
Woman	7	8	9	7
Age				
15–24	57	53	51	56
25–34	38	36	27	37
35–44	4	11	13	5
45–60	1	1	9	2
Marital status/ partnership				
Single	60	56	48	58
Married	7	9	22	8
Cohabitation	27	30	25	27
Divorced/widowed	2	2	2	2
Don't want to answer	4	3	3	5
Children				
Yes, living at home	8	12	22	10
Yes, not living at home	1	3	6	2
No	88	81	68	85
Don't want to answer	3	4	4	3
Housing				
Living with parents	10	11	13	10
Living alone	41	41	28	39
With a spouse or partner	34	38	45	35
With friends or others	13	8	12	12
Don't want to answer	3	3	1	3
Professional education				
Vocational school	29	29	30	29
Vocational high school	21	22	26	22
University	13	11	11	13
None of these	30	34	32	31
Don't want to answer	6	4	1	5

Table 4: Social characteristics of cannabis growers, part II (%)

	Number of plants per crop			
	1-5 plants (n=935)	6-10 plants (n=237)	11+ plants (n=97)	Total (n=1298)
Occupational status				
Employed	39	31	36	37
Entrepreneur	5	9	11	6
Unemployed	13	20	23	16
Student	31	26	18	29
Other	9	13	11	10
Don't want to answer	2	1	1	2
Income (pre-tax)				
Less than 500 euros	29	34	21	30
500–999	20	21	30	20
1000–1999	23	18	15	22
2000–2999	14	15	19	14
3000 or more	7	6	7	7
Don't want to answer	7	6	8	7

A third were married or living with a partner. One out of ten had children living in the same household. Almost 40 per cent lived alone. More than 40 per cent had completed upper secondary school, and more than every tenth had a university degree or a similar degree of higher education. Almost one third had completed vocational educational, and a fifth had completed intermediate vocational education or had a degree from a university of applied sciences. 43 per cent of the respondents had a job, 16 per cent were unemployed and 29 per cent were students. Many respondents reported a rather low gross income, which, to some extent, can be attributed to the large number of young people and students. An examination of the respondents by the size of cannabis cultivation shows that those growing more than ten plants were older, more often married, had more often children living in the same household, had a lower level education, and were more likely to be unemployed than the other respondents.

Since the respondents in the web survey were predominantly male and represented the two youngest age groups, we compared males aged 15–34 with the same male age groups of the population survey of 2010. This examination showed that cannabis growers were not a deviant or a marginalised group. There were, however, some differences compared with the standard population. Cannabis is typically grown by male adolescents and young adults who are more likely than other members of their age group to live alone and are less settled in terms of family or children. There are no major differences in terms of basic and vocational education, but compared to the standard population, many were unemployed at the time of the survey, and their income level was lower than in the reference group. What is discernible about the youngest age group of growers is that they seem to move out of their childhood home and get a job earlier than others in their age group.

Table 5: Personal use of cannabis, %

	Number of plants per crop			
	1-5 plants (n=935)	6-10 plants (n=237)	11+ plants (n=97)	Total (n=1298)
Frequency of use from own crop				
More than once a day	13	22	28	16
Daily/nearly daily	31	40	34	33
1–2 times per week	32	22	18	29
A couple of times per month	17	11	7	15
Less frequently	4	3	7	4
Don't want to answer	3	2	5	4
Estimated consumption in grams per week				
Less than 1 g	21	15	12	19
1,0–2,99	34	18	18	30
3,0–6,99	30	26	36	29
7,0–13,99	11	24	16	13
14,0 g or more	5	18	18	9
Does provide enough for personal use				
Yes	66	59	62	64
Depends on harvest	20	31	23	22
No	7	3	9	6
Don't know	6	5	4	6
Don't want to answer	1	1	1	2

Table 5 contains figures illustrating the personal cannabis use of home growers. A comparison of these figures against the data from the population survey shows that the number of daily users among home growers is considerably large while the number of those using cannabis less than 1-2 times a week is considerably small. Only six per cent of the Finnish cannabis users (last year prevalence in the population survey) are daily users, and approximately 80 per cent use cannabis less frequently than once a week (Hakkarainen et al. 2008). This suggests that the web survey respondents are very active users of cannabis. The weekly consumption in grams confirms this: the 22% who used more than 7 grams a week (1 gram per day) could perhaps be categorised as heavy users of cannabis. These users largely relied on their own crop to fulfil their needs. They were also relatively experienced users. More than half (63%) had started using cannabis no later than at the age of 17 and almost half (46%) had been using cannabis for more than five years.

6 Why?

Finland's Criminal Code prohibits the cultivation of cannabis plants. Sowing, planting or simply being in possession of seeds is a punishable narcotics offence (Kainulainen 2009: 174f.). According to the recommendation of the Office of the Prosecutor General (2010) a prosecutor can demand imprisonment for growing more than 10 plants and a fine if there are fewer plants. According to Finnish legislation, cannabis growing is a punishable offence, and the legislation is strictly enforced. Getting caught growing cannabis at home may have serious legal implications and, consequently, cause problems in everyday life. Why do people who are no different from any law-abiding citizens take this risk?

Results of the web survey suggest that securing a supply for personal use (87%) is a key motivation for growing cannabis. The second most important motivating factor is the pleasure growers derive from the growing itself (87%), which suggests cultivation is considered a hobby-like activity. A third important motivating factor is to stay away from the illegal drug market and to avoid the related crime (88%). Many respondents (49%) also felt that growing cannabis themselves is less risky than buying it on the street. Respondents also claimed home-grown cannabis was cheaper (75%), stronger (41%) and healthier (75%). The health claims probably have to do with the users' beliefs that hashish or marijuana sold on the streets contains weight-increasing additives or impurities. The poor quality of cannabis available on the Finnish drug markets was often repeated in interviews with growers.

> "Well, the availability of soap bar hash went down and the quality went lower and lower (…) I wouldn't put that same 'shoe sole' in my pipe ever again." (Male, 29 years)

Similarly, nearly all respondents said they wanted to avoid dealing with criminals.

> "I noticed that I would rather use cannabis than alcohol. I didn't want to get involved in any crime and since it's a natural product, I thought why not grow it myself. (...) I'm a regular and decent citizen and I grow hemp in my closet." (Male, 29 years)

The web survey also asked growers what they considered the downsides of cannabis growing. The biggest downside was the risk of being caught by the police and getting arrested and convicted. The interviews revealed that one common way of addressing this fear was to keep the size of the cultivation small, or at least sufficiently limited to ensure the cultivation does not constitute an aggravated narcotics offence. Growers had accurate knowledge regarding judicial practice and the criteria for aggravated narcotics offence. Many growers considered the smell of the plants a major problem in terms of the risk of getting caught. Particularly in the final stages of growing cannabis in confined spaces, the smell can easily spread outside the home, and may attract attention. This is how many cannabis farms are exposed (Perälä 2009). One fifth of the respondents considered friends visiting their home, hoping to get a sample, a disruptive element. Frequent visits also increase the risk of exposure. Interestingly, one fifth of the respondents considered it a downside that producing their own crops made them smoke more than they needed to. Factors limiting the use of cannabis include availability and small one-time purchases (Kinnunen 1992). Home growing changes the situation since a large supply of cannabis is available for long periods of time.

Almost one fifth (19%) of the web survey respondents had been caught by the police, and 14 per cent said they had been sentenced for growing cannabis. These numbers were smaller for growers whose farms were limited to 1–5 plants. Similarly, almost a fifth (18%) of the respondents felt that the risk of being exposed was high or very high. One out of four growers with a cultivation of more than ten plants felt this way.

Even though the risk of being exposed was reported as the most significant downside of home growing, the majority of respondents (66%) still considered the risk of getting caught small or very small. Producing a supply for personal needs, avoiding crime and other risks involved with street dealers, and other criteria in favour of home growing outweighed the risks of getting caught. Many respondents also referred to ideological aspects of home growing. In interviews, home growers expressed a great deal of criticism against the controls society imposes on cannabis and on the general attitudes. Many criticised the fact that society is prepared to tolerate the harms caused by alcohol but adopts a very rigid approach to cannabis (Hakkarainen & Perälä 2011). As an intoxicating substance, cannabis was considered relatively harmless, and to some it was an alternative to alcohol.

It is interesting to see how the attitudes among the Finnish population have changed in this respect. In 1992, only one of ten respondents said they did not think growing cannabis should be a punishable offence whereas in 2010, one fifth (19%) of the respondents felt this way. As many as 43 per cent of male respondents under the age of 35, and 24 per cent of females shared this view. In conclusion, home growing of cannabis and attitudes towards it seems to be linked not only to gender but to age and generation, too (Hakkarainen 2005).

7 Distribution

Next, we will discuss the purposes for which the respondents grew cannabis. Results are shown in Table 6. The results show that by far the most common motive was the pleasure derived from the use of cannabis. Another interesting observation was that as many as 58 per cent of the respondents said they grew cannabis for medicinal purposes. Two thirds of growers with a farm of more than ten plants indicated medicinal use as their growing purpose, which makes sense as the consumption is likely to be more regular and require larger quantities than use as an intoxicant (Dahl & Frank 2011).

Table 6: The purpose of cannabis growing (%)

	Number of plants per crop			
	1-5 plants	6-10 plants	11+ plants	Total
	(n=935)	(n=237)	(n=97)	(n=1298)
For pleasure from personal use	96	92	88	94
For medical purposes	56	63	68	58
For selling to other	13	22	26	15
For giving or sharing with others	56	70	66	59

In 2010, only a few dozen people were using legally obtained cannabis for medicinal purposes in Finland. It seems that self-prescribed medicinal use is far more common. The following extract from an interview with a person who was using cannabis to alleviate back pain and neuralgia caused by an accident illustrates the difficulty of the situation:

> "My situation is that none of my friends know I'm using. Only my wife knows, and my parents. That's all the people who know. It makes it really unpleasant, having to keep it a secret, especially the growing. If friends come over, there's all the fuss with

> hiding the plants and getting rid of the smell and so on. What annoys me most is that I feel like I'm doing something bad all the time." (Male, 26 years)

Popular opinion is not entirely against the medicinal use of cannabis. In a drug survey conducted in 2010, 40 per cent of Finnish people were in favour of allowing the legal procurement of cannabis for medicinal purposes. The majority thought pharmacy distribution was the most suitable procurement method, but in age groups 15–24 and 25–34, home growing was also considered an acceptable alternative (21% and 28%).

It is possible that in a country with very strict drug control policies, growers feel pressured to justify their growing activities and claim they do so for medicinal (i.e. acceptable) purposes. If the material is filtered to identify only those who said they grew cannabis exclusively for medicinal purposes, the proportion is only three per cent. Meanwhile, 16 per cent grew cannabis purely for pleasure. This situation is aptly described by a Finnish reggae artist Jukka Poika in his song *Siviiliuhrit (Civilian casualties):* "For some it's a drug, for some it's medicine, for most it's both of these."

There is a demarcation line in domestic cannabis cultivation, which separates "ideological" growing purely for own pleasure and commercially motivated growing (Weisheit 1992; Potter 2007; Decorte 2010a). Even though it is customary for ideological growers to offer samples to their friends and they may occasionally sell their surplus crops, this demarcation line is significant. It separates two distinctly different production methods and two different types of markets (Potter 2009). As Table 6 indicates, 15 per cent of the respondents reported selling as one of the reasons for growing cannabis. However, sharing the product with friends was clearly a more important objective (59%) than selling. Table 7 provides more detailed information on the selling and sharing of cannabis.

A considerably large part of the respondents said they had never sold or exchanged any of their home-grown cannabis. Meanwhile, most said they often gave or offered part of their crops to friends for free. As pointed out in international research literature, sharing and enjoying cannabis together in the users' social networks is a characteristic of the cannabis culture, unlike other drug subcultures (Room et al. 2010, 60ff.).

Table 7: Selling, giving and sharing home-grown cannabis (%)

All respondents	Number of plants per crop			
	1 - 5 plants	6-10 plants	11+ plants	Total
	(n=935)	(n=237)	(n=97)	(n=1298)
Selling				
Ever sold	32	49	54	36
Ever swapped with somebody	21	20	11	20
Never sold nor swapped	44	28	32	40
Don't know/don't want to answer	3	3	3	4
Giving for free				
To friends and acquaintances	86	87	81	85
To everybody who wants	3	3	5	3
To nobody	10	6	11	9
Don't want to answer	2	4	2	3
Those who have ever sold	Number of plants per crop			
	1 - 5 plants	6-10 plants	11+ plants	Total
	(n=299)	(n=115)	(n=52)	(n=471)
Earnings from last crop				
Less than 100 euros	47	30	33	41
100–200 euros	18	24	12	19
200–1000 euros	20	20	31	21
More than 1000 euros	4	10	21	7
Don't know/don't want to answer	11	16	4	12
To how many people sold from last crop				
1–3 people	61	54	58	59
4–10 people	29	33	29	30
More than 10 people	4	9	8	6
Don't know/don't want to answer	7	4	5	6
Sold to whom				
To people who are personally known	94	93	88	93
To people who use for medical purposes	1	2	6	2
To everybody who wants to buy	3	2	4	3
Don't want to answer	2	3	2	2

A fifth of the respondents reported having exchanged cannabis flowers. More than one third reported having sold cannabis occasionally; the proportion grew with the size of the cannabis farm. However, the financial benefit from selling seems to be rather modest. The majority (81%) of those who reported any sales had earned less than 1,000 euros, and even lower earnings of less than 200 euros were very common (60%). Not selling could also be construed as a means of reducing the risk of getting caught and mitigating the legal implications. As a rule, cannabis was sold to a small number of people, and mostly to the grower's personal friends of acquaintances. The following extract from an interview illustrates the line between sharing and selling.

> "Whenever I go visit someone, I share for free (...), but on occasion I have 'disposed of' some surplus for a small amount of money. I'm willing to share my supply, but if someone wants to buy for their personal use or to take home, I have made some exceptions. But that's just exceptions, and for good friends only." (Male, 33 years)

Finnish small-scale growers had very similar attitudes towards the commercial use of their crops as those reported in a Danish study, although the Danish home growers were even more reluctant to sell (Hakkarainen et al. 2011a). Small-scale home cultivation of cannabis is primarily for personal use. Despite having sold cannabis on occasion, the respondents of the survey were, as a rule, ideological cannabis growers. People do not grow cannabis for the money, or to make profit, but for the pleasure of growing, enjoying and sharing it with friends.

8 Conclusions

Material from various sources was used in our study, allowing us to examine the home growing of cannabis in Finland from different perspectives.[3] Population surveys offered information on the consumption of various cannabis products, the prevalence of home growing, and the popular opinion on cannabis. A web survey and interviews with growers helped us formulate a description of the growers and of their mindset.

Even though the number of respondents to the web survey was large, the results should be interpreted bearing in mind that the respondents mainly consist of small-scale cannabis growers. The study does not include large-scale growers driven by commercial motivation. Similarly, it is likely that experimental growers

3 We would like to thank everyone who participated in the study and especially those who had the courage to talk about their experiences and express their views on an issue that is forbidden and carries sanctions.

who rarely, if at all, visit drug-related websites, are not very well represented in the sample. The majority of the respondents are active growers who are long-term heavy users of cannabis. Undoubtedly, the respondents also include several pro-cannabis activists (see Kekoni 2007) who are active participants in related discussions in online forums, and who are most probably well represented in the survey. The tendency of respondents to "bend the truth" (as it is always the case with drug and alcohol related surveys) must be taken into account, but on the whole the overall information should be considered reasonably reliable.

The results indicate that the Finnish cannabis market development follows international and European trends. Marijuana is now a more popular cannabis product than hashish. This is a significant change in any market and accentuates the importance of domestic production. According to the results of the population survey, 40,000–60,000 Finns have at some point experimented with cannabis growing, and there are thousands of active growers. In addition to personal use, many share their crops with friends. Some home-grown cannabis is also sold, but according to Perälä (2009) its role in the drug market is quite insignificant. However, the growing demand for marijuana is likely to make commercial production more attractive. Actually, there are signals of an increased number of new small-scale and middle-scale producers and dealers in the markets, especially in Helsinki metropolitan area.

The cannabis home growing culture in Finland is characterised by social supply and sharing of information, seeds and bud. Home growing is also a popular trend in the global drug subcultures. It is easy to participate over the Internet regardless of geographic location. In fact, Finland's remote location off the main international drug routes may well contribute to home growing. Home growing removes the barriers of limited supply, and provides the user with better-quality cannabis than is generally available on the street market and at a much lower cost. Therefore, there is a connection between home growing and the local and global drug markets. This could be one of the reasons why home growing of cannabis is a more powerful trend in Finland than in Denmark, where it is easy to buy high-quality cannabis on the streets (Hakkarainen et al. 2011a). Home growing is also an alternative to buying cannabis on the street. In fact, small scale growers specifically stressed they wanted to avoid the criminal activity associated with street dealing.

Finnish home growers use cannabis both as a recreational drug and for medicinal purposes. It is interesting that such a large proportion of respondents claim to use cannabis for medicinal purposes. Medicinal use of cannabis has attracted a great deal of international attention, and its acceptability is likely to have affected the respondents' opinions. Interestingly, a significantly large proportion of Finnish people are willing to accept the legal procurement of medicinal cannabis. In younger age groups, home growing of cannabis as a legally permitted way of supplying medicinal cannabis is widely supported. All in all, the results of the drug survey of 2010 indicate that an increasing number of Finns think home growing of cannabis should not be a punishable offence. This is the popular view among the younger age groups and particularly among young men. In other words, not only has the volume of home growing changed, but attitudes have changed, too. Increased tolerance can also be seen in the number of grow shops which seem to be on rise.

In Finland, the use of cannabis has increased especially among young men (Hakkarainen et al. 2011b). Home growing of cannabis was also most common in this group, indicating that home growing was seen as a way of securing the supply of one's favourite drug. Growers were prepared to invest time and effort into growing, and many described it as their hobby. It seems that gardening has become a popular pastime for many young Finnish men.

References

Bouchard, M. (2007): A capture-recapture model to estimate the size of criminal populations and the risks of detection in a marijuana cultivation industry. Journal of Quantitative Criminology, 23: 221–241.

Dahl, H. & Asmussen Frank, V. (2011): Medical marijuana – exploring the concept in relation to small scale cannabis growers in Denmark. T. Decorte, M. Bouchard, G. Potter (eds.), World wide weed – Global trends in cannabis cultivation and its control (pp 116–141). Farnham: Ashgate.

Couper, M. P. (2000): Web surveys – A review of issues and approaches. Public Opinion Quarterly, 64: 465–494.

Decorte, T. (2008): Domestic cannabis cultivation in Belgium: on (un)intended effects of drug policy on the cannabis market. D. Korf (ed.), Cannabis in Europe: Dynamics in perception, policy and markets (pp 69–86). Lengerich: Pabst.

Decorte, T. (2010a): The case for small-scale domestic cannabis cultivation. International Journal of Drug Policy, 21: 271–275.

Decorte, T. (2010b): Small scale domestic cannabis cultivation: An anonymous Web survey among 659 cannabis cultivators in Belgium. Contemporary Drug Problems, 37: 341–370.

Decorte, T., Bouchard, M. & Potter, G. (eds.) (2011): World wide weed – Global trends in cannabis cultivation and its control. Farnham: Ashgate.

Dementrovics, Z., Fountain J. & Kraus L. (eds.) (2009): Old and new policies, theories, research methods and drug users across Europe. Lengerich: Pabst.

Hakkarainen, P. (1987): Huumausainekulttuuri ja käyttötavat Suomessa [Drug culture and drug taking habits in Finland]. Turku: University of Turku.

Hakkarainen, P. (2005): Drug use as a generational phenomenon. L. Kraus & D. Korf (eds.), Research on drugs and drug policy from a European perspective (pp 48–61). Lengerich: Pabst.

Hakkarainen P. & Perälä J. (2011): With a little help from my friends—Justifications of small-scale cannabis growers. T. Decorte, M. Bouchard & G. Potter (eds.), World wide weed – Global trends in cannabis cultivation and its control (pp 143–166). Farnham: Ashgate.

Hakkarainen, P., Kainulainen, H. & Perälä, J. (2008): Measuring the cannabis market in Finland – A consumption-based estimate. Contemporary Drug Problems, 35: 321–345.

Hakkarainen, P., Asmussen Frank, V., Perälä, J. & Dahl, H. (2011a): Small-scale cannabis growing in Denmark and Finland. European Addiction Research, 17: 119–128.

Hakkarainen P., Metso L. & Salasuo M. (2011b): Hamppuikäpolvi, sekakäyttö ja doping – Vuoden 2010 huumekyselyn tulokset. [The hemp generation, mixed use and doping – Results from the 2010 Drug Survey.] Yhteiskuntapolitiikka, 76: 396–413.

Kainulainen, H. (2006): Seuraamuskäytäntö huumausaineen käyttörikoksissa [Sanction practices in drug offences]. Helsinki: The National Research Institute of Legal Policy. Reports 219.

Kainulainen, H. (2009): Huumeiden käyttäjien rikosoikeudellinen kontrolli [Criminal control of drug users]. Helsinki: The National Research Institute of Legal Policy. Reports 245.

Kainulainen, H. (2010): Huumausaine, alkoholi- ja dopingrikokset [Crimes on drugs, alchol and doping]. Rikollisuustilanne 2010 [Crime trends in Finland]. Helsinki: The National Research Institute of Legal Policy. Reports 250: 209–222.

Kekoni, T. (2007): Kannabiksen käyttö, yhteiskunnallinen reagointi ja siihen vastaaminen: Kannabisaktivistien näkökulma [The use of cannabis, societal reaction and response to it: The perspective of cannabis activists].Tampere: Acta Universitatis Tamperensis.

Kinnunen, A. (1992): Hallittu huumeiden käyttö on mahdollista [Controlled use of cannabis is possible]. Alkoholipolitiikka, 57: 38–44.

Kontula, O. (1986): Huumausainerikokset ja niiden kontrolli: Tilanne Suomessa 1960-luvulta 1980-luvulle [Drug crimes and control: Situation from the 1960s to the 1980s in Finland]. Helsinki: The National Research Institute of Legal Policy. Reports 76.

Kontula, O. (ed.) (1992): Huumeiden käyttäjät Suomessa [Drug users in Finland]. Hämeenlinna: Kirjayhtymä.

Korf, D. (ed.) (2008): Cannabis in Europe: Dynamics in perception, policy and markets. Lengerich: Pabst.

Kouvonen, P., Stretting, A. & Rosenqvist, P. (eds.) (2006): Drugs in the Nordic and Baltic countries. Helsinki: Nordic Council for Alcohol and Drug Research.

Kraus, L. & Korf, D. (eds.) (2005): Research on drugs and drug policy from a European perspective. Lengerich: Pabst.

Larmela, T. & Laine, I. (1992): Kannabiksen käyttäjänä Suomessa [Being cannabis user in Finland]. O. Kontula (ed.), Huumeiden käyttäjät Suomessa [Drug users in Finland] (pp 68–118). Hämeenlinna: Kirjayhtymä.

Perälä, J. (2009): Kannabismarkkinat ja –tuotanto [Cannabis markets]. S. Rönkä, & A. Virtanen (eds.), Huumetilanne Suomessa 2009 [Drug situation in Finand] (pp 124–128). Helsinki: National Institute for Health and Welfare (THL). Reports 40/2009

Potter, G. (2007): Weed, need and greed. Domestic marijuana production and the UK cannabis market. Ph.D. thesis. University of Sheffield.

Potter, G. (2009): Exploring retail-level drug distribution: Social supply, 'real' dealers and the user/dealer interface. Z. Demetrovics, J. Fountain & L. Kraus (eds.), Old and new policies, theories, research methods and drug users across Europe (pp 50–74). Lengerich: Pabst.

Potter, G. & Bouchard, M. & Decorte, T. (2011): The globalization of cannabis cultivation. T. Decorte, M. Bouchard, G. Potter (eds.), World wide weed – Global trends in cannabis cultivation and its control (pp 27–60). Farnham: Ashgate.

Room, R., Fisher, B., Hall, W., Lenton, S. & Reuter, P. (2010): Cannabis policy – Moving beyond stalemate. Oxford: Oxford University Press.

Rönkä, S. & Virtanen, A. (eds.) (2009): Huumetilanne Suomessa 2009 [Drug situation in Finand]. Helsinki: National Institute for Health and Welfare (THL). Reports 40/2009.

Salasuo, M. (2006): Drug supply and seizures. P. Kouvonen, A. Stretting & P. Rosenqvist (eds.), Drugs in the Nordic and Baltic countries (pp 127–154). Helsinki: Nordic Council for Alcohol and Drug Research.

Sills, S. J. & Song, C. (2002): Innovations in survey research: An application of Web-based surveys. Social Science Computer Review, 20: 22–30.

The Office of the Prosecutor General (2010): Suositus syyttäjän seuraamuskannanotoksi kannabiskasvien sisäkasvatustapauksissa [Guidelines for prosecutors in the cases of indoor cannabis cultivation]. Helsinki: The Office of the Prosecutor General 10.6.2010.

Weisheit, R. (1992): Domestic marijuana. A neglected industry. New York: Greenwood Press.

Building trust and using violence within a drug dealing network in Austria

Meropi Tzanetakis

Abstract

This chapter explores how a network of upper-level drug dealers in Austria is organised with regard to the role of trust and violence. For approaching the subject matter, an in-depth qualitative case study was applied. On the one hand, the analysis focuses on mechanisms used for building trust and loyalty, on the other hand the role of using violence for settling disputes and for resolving conflicts was taken into account. Interestingly, physical violence was used only in one case, whereas several cases of threats against individuals from the network and from competitors were mentioned. Furthermore, I conclude that trust and loyalty seem to be required skills for successful drug dealing. Building trust and loyalty helped avoiding conflicts, and each actor involved in the network benefited from long-lasting business relationships. For example, as soon as the couriers (people who were recruited for transporting hashish) proved themselves to be trustworthy, they were introduced to the source of supply and allowed to perform a complete drug transport independently. The couriers were also provided with higher compensation for their commitment. This research is one of the few empirical studies in the field of upper-level drug dealing for German speaking countries.

1 Introduction

Drug distribution is a highly profitable global business. Neither law enforcement, drug seizures nor the war on drugs led to a verifiable reduction of the global drug problem on the supply and demand side during a period of 1998 to 2007 (Reuter & Trautmann 2009). Despite the fact that law enforcement efforts are increasing, drug retail prices have declined in Western countries as Reuter and Trautmann conclude. To sum up, drug dealing is highly effective and efforts to control or eradicate it have been fruitless so far.

Some studies have been conducted for the US and Latin American countries, analysing organisational dynamics of upper-level drug dealing networks and groups (e.g. Kenney 2007; Desroches 2007; Marez 2004; Natarajan 2000; Krauthausen 1997, Adler 1993; Reuter & Haaga 1989). Nevertheless, equivalent empirical research on higher levels of drug distribution is almost entirely missing for European countries (Zaitch 2002; Pearson & Hobbs 2001; Paoli 2000; Dorn et al. 1992). There is a lack of empirical data on upper-level drug dealing networks, plus a lack of theoretical concepts explaining organisational dynamics of high-level drug distribution. Moreover, there are different definitions on upper-level drug dealing, each capturing certain aspects (Wehinger 2011; Matrix Knowledge Group 2007; Ritter 2006; Dorn et al. 2005; Pearson & Hobbs 2001; Dorn et al. 1992). Most research literature focuses on retail drug markets and less on higher levels (Reuter 2014; Wehinger 2011). The reasons for the limited empirical research on upper-level drug dealing include the fact that gaining access to the research field itself is limited (Besozzi 2001). On the one hand, there are covert and secretive law enforcement agencies and on the other hand, there are covert and secretive high-level drug dealers – none of them like to offer a glance behind the scenes.

In order to address the outlined research gap, the present chapter is based on an empirical analysis of a higher-level cannabis dealing network in the European Union. This research applies a working definition of upper-level drug dealing for the European context, which takes current literature on higher levels of the illicit drug trade into account (Desroches 2007; Dorn et al. 2005; Matrix Knowledge Group 2007). For this purpose, high-level drug trafficking is defined as a cross-border activity, within which the illicit goods are purchased in one country, smuggled to a different one and are being resold with profit in a third country. The activities happen on a regular basis, although the group or network might not persist for a long time. Furthermore, the peculiar way of trading shows a professional manner and involves sophisticated logistics. Finally, we suggest that the quantity and purity of illicit drugs should not be used as an indicator for the wholesale level in Europe, because the differences between the countries and networks/groups involved are too big.

Individuals, groups or networks involved in illicit drug trading cannot rely on judiciary, law enforcement agencies or a penal system in case of conflict (Reuter 2009). Hence, the use or the threat of violence can be applied to manage the risk that comes along with illicit activities (Goldstein 1985). As Reuter (2009) and Thoumi (2003) point out, evidence suggests that illegality per se does not automatically lead to high levels of violence. Nevertheless, there are specific drug markets that are very violent, e.g. the Mexican drug markets (Reuter 2009; Thoumi 2003). In general, the degree of violence being used in illicit drug markets is controversially discussed among researchers (Reuter & Trautmann 2009; Gambetta 2009; Thoumi 2003; Zaitch 2002; Pearson & Hobbs 2001; Adler 1993; Dorn et al. 1992; Arlacchi 1986; Reuter 1983). Moreover, there are diverse purposes for the use of violence. It may evolve due to competition among drug traffickers, inside a network or group of drug dealers or between sellers and law enforcement agencies (Reuter 2009). In any case, violence is prone to attract the attention of law enforcement authorities to the illicit activities and therefore to discourage business (Zaitch 2002; Reuter 1983).

Other mechanisms of preventing or resolving conflicts or strengthening internal cohesion in drug trading networks can be, for example, the development of trustworthiness, loyalty, dependence, or the termination of the business relationship (Tzanetakis 2013; Zaitch 2005; Paoli 2003; Gambetta 1990; Reuter & Haaga 1989). Although trust is based on a social relation, which is often used to either describe how dealers cooperate in regard to risks associated with illicit activities or to explain networks of kinship or ethnic ties, it "lacks a comprehensive theoretical and empirical underpinning" (von Lampe & Johansen 2004: 160). Closely connected to trust is uncertainty, distrust, suspicion, paranoid anxiety and misunderstanding (Gambetta 1996). There are a large number of definitions of trust, which are based on the particular disciplinary perspective and research interest. In our research we used the definition offered by Gambetta (1990: 217): "Trust (or, symmetrically, distrust) is a particular level of the subjective probability with which an agent assesses that another agent or group of agents will perform a particular action, both before he can monitor such action (or independently of his capacity ever to be able to monitor it) and in a context in which it affects his own action."

In contrast to many other chapters of this anthology, this chapter focuses on a profit-motivated type of drug dealing. By using an in-depth qualitative case study approach, we will analyse the role of using violence for settling disputes and for resolving conflicts on the one hand and, on the other hand, how building trust and loyalty evolved over time.

2 In-depth case study analysis

An explorative case study (Yin 2009) was conducted on an Austrian-based network of 55 drug dealers, who were involved in buying, smuggling and reselling tons of hashish not only in Austria, but also in Spain, the Netherlands, Sweden and Hungary.

The case selection of a single network was based on a purposeful random sampling strategy (Patton 1990). The purpose of a random sample is credibility, not representativeness and it was chosen according to the explorative and in-depth research question. Additionally, purposeful random sampling allows selecting information-rich cases for in-depth study. Therefore, the central selection criteria were both information content and composition of sample. The selection procedure was the following: file numbers were requested from the Austrian Ministry of Justice for drug dealing offences involving large quantities (Narcotic Substances Act, §28 Abs.4 SMG), decided at the Criminal Court Vienna; a list with 106 file numbers was divided into sub-populations and finally reduced to 30, according to purposeful random sampling. The 30 court files were examined separately and further restricted according to the following criteria: cross-border activity, poly-drug dealing, money laundering, corruption and use of violence. Moreover, subsequent information on the involvement of a single person or a group, the number of people prosecuted, the form of trading (street level, retail, middle market, and upper level), previous convictions, export/ import activities etc. was recorded. Finally, one court file including about 2,000 pages of investigation records, phone-tapping protocols, accusations, trial protocols and verdicts met most of the criteria and was chosen for an in-depth analysis.

The data for the qualitative case study was collected in three ways. First, semi structured interviews were conducted with one imprisoned man convicted for drug-dealing offences at three points in time (over a period of one year). Second, three semi-structured interviews with experts from the Austrian Federal Criminal Agency – Department of Anti-Money Laundering, Drug-Related Crime and International Police Cooperation – were conducted. Third, we gained insight into all court files generated during criminal proceedings on one higher-level drug-dealing network. The interviews were transcribed and all data were analysed with qualitative content analysis (QCA) (Schreier 2012), a method suitable for systematically describing the meaning of qualitative material. Furthermore, the software program MAXQDA 10 (Verbi GmbH 2011) was used as a tool to organise all data sets.

While building a coding frame for this analysis, a combination of deductive and inductive strategies was applied to interpret the data gained. According to the deductive approach, the categories were built on previous research on upper-level drug dealing namely on Dorn et al. (1992), Reuter & Trautmann (2009), Wilson & Stevens (2008), Pearson & Hobbs (2001), Dorn et al. (2005), Desroches (2003), Adler (1993), and Reuter & Haaga (1989). The inductive approach used categories, which were derived from the interviews and the court file. Mayring's subsumption technique was used to generate and build the data driven part of the coding frame (Mayring 2008). Therefore, each relevant segment was either subsumed under an already existing subcategory or a new subcategory was generated. This procedure was repeated until the point of saturation.

The coding frame for the present study meets the quality standards for QCA (Schreier 2012). It can be considered reliable (error-free) to the extent that two independent coders agreed on assigning the units of coding during the pilot phase. Hence, during an extensive discussion between the coders, problematic items were identified and agreement was achieved where units of coding were interpreted differently. Moreover, for assessing the validity of the coding frame (does it capture what it sets out to?), face validity (used for the inductive coding frame) and content validity (used for the deductively built coding frame) were selected. Face validity is given for the coding frame due to the fact that not many units of coding were assigned to residual categories. The coding frame's content validity is related to the consistency of the coding frame. In this way, content validity corresponds with reliability. To sum up, the coding frame shows high validity due to inductively and deductively generated categories, it was tested on part of the material, and only few units of coding were assigned to the residual categories. This analysis is one of the very few qualitative and at the same time empirical research in the field of upper-level drug dealing for German-speaking countries; among the few exceptions is Paoli (2000).

3 Findings and discussion

A quick overview of the activities of the network analysed gives a first idea on the dimensions of trading activities the dealers were involved in. About 55 people operated continuously for a duration of two years. The vast majority of these individuals were male and Austrian citizens, 12 out of 55 were women. They were involved in buying tons of hashish and kilos of cocaine from different sources in Spain and the Netherlands. For this purpose, drugs were hidden in prepared vans and up to 12 people were hired to ride these transporters from Austria to either Spain or the Netherlands and back (and sometimes they were smuggling to Sweden, too). Meanwhile, other actors of the network took a plane to travel to those countries, in order to test the quality of the drugs and then to pay the source. Back in Austria, the drugs were stored in apartments, garages and open-air storage places. On the one hand, the drugs were resold at eight special bars, which were rented by other actors of the network, directly to users or indirectly through an intermediary. On the other hand, the illicit drugs were resold to seven smaller customers (less than 10 kg) and five bulk buyers (more than 10 kg per transaction). Finally, the money was invested to buy new transporters and cars. Some of the actors also ran a real estate business in a neighbouring state of Austria. Furthermore, the people involved ran several bank accounts in Austria and in a neighbouring state. However, the roles of almost all participating actors changed over time. The network of high-level dealers can be regarded as 'business criminals' who dealt for their personal enrichment in the first place (Dorn et al. 2005). This type of dealing can be regarded as the antithesis or opposite pole to the concepts of social supply (see most other chapters in this volume) or minimally commercial supply (Coomber & Moyle 2013).

This chapter focuses particularly on findings concerning organisational characteristics and interpersonal relationships of high-level drug dealers with special regard to the use of violence and mechanisms of trust applied.

3.1 Role of violence in business relationships

An initial finding of the case study analysis was that the network analysed would not use violence as a primary means of solving conflicts. Thus, the thesis that violence plays a subordinate role on the wholesale level of drug markets (Reuter & Haaga 1989; Adler 1993; Pearson & Hobbs 2001; Desroches 2003 2007; Dorn et al. 2005; Wehinger 2011) could be confirmed.

For analytical purposes, violence as a category was divided into the use of violence among the network and using violence as a means to solving conflicts against/ from competitors or customers. While violence inside the network was mentioned 38 times, violence from or against other individuals was only mentioned five times across all data analysed. The numbers indicate that the use of violence, either as force or as threat, was more frequent internally.

3.1.1 The use of violence within the network

The analysis indicates that only one particular incident of physical violence occurred during the period of at least one year. In this case, one actor of the network shot another player in the thigh. This was stated in the court file as following:

> "Because ZTR[1] did not pay off his debts, he was shot in his left thigh by the 'bodyguard' of CES, who then was hit on the head with an object by CES. The 'bodyguard' himself died in the meantime under mysterious circumstances." (G-AK 1.1, §989)[2]

1 An acronym was used to provide anonymity of the subjects involved.

2 Different acronyms were used for each of the three data sets: court files, transcriptions of drug-dealer interviews, and transcriptions of interviews with Austrian Federal Police. The numbers indicate the exact position in each document.

The interviewee, however, put the readiness to use violence into perspective as he explained that the actor would have been limitless in principle, by stating:

> "Of course he would have done it if I had asked him to do it. He would have killed his mother if someone had asked to do that. But it was not just for me, he would have done it for anybody, no matter who." (I-D 2.3, §74)

More frequently mentioned and much more important than the exercise of violence was the threat of violence. Having a violent reputation seemed to be sufficient in most cases of fraud or rip-offs.

> "I: What happened if someone stole money from you? D: Well, he would have had to consider it carefully. It happened once that a guy stole a car. My colleagues were looking for him. I was told that he allegedly went to Russia or so. He would not have dared to do that with me, 'cause he probably would not have survived it." (I-D 2.2, §236)

Additionally to using a threatening rhetoric, possessing and carrying weapons was common for the drug distribution network. Hence, the Austrian police had confiscated two firearms and one rifle. The interviewed drug dealer explained that carrying a gun was meant for self-protection in the first place.

> "I just bought the gun, nothing more. I took it with me sometimes, but not in a way that I would use it to shoot someone. It was just for protecting myself." (I-D 2.3, §47)

Secondly, carrying a gun was regarded as a means to do business more efficiently.

> "It was important for me to do business. For me it was like any other business, like running a pizzeria or a grocery. There are also grocers that carry weapons. However, it was not my aim to drift into violence. I just did solid business, back then business was going well. For sure, sometimes someone attempts to defraud you, but...well, you can't do anything in such a case. It happens from time to time" (I-D 2.3, §50).

According to the material analysed, the guns were not used except for the one instance mentioned above.

Some other time, another player was prohibited from entering one of the special bars where the illicit drugs were re-sold because he was carrying a gun.

According to the self-assessment of the interviewed drug dealer, theory and practice seem to be worlds apart regarding the use of violence. Although, from his point of view, sometimes it would be appropriate to use force, it also attracts the attention of the police, which would disrupt the business.

> "It isn't like in a movie. Yes, it can happen, but...I know it, I thought about it ten years ago, but in real life, it's different. It's always easy to talk. Actually, it isn't that

> easy to tell someone, go there and beat him up. If it would be that easy, there would be murderers instead of burglars here in prison. Everybody knows, if they get him, he will talk to the police. I was aware of that, too." (I-D 2.3, §350)

3.1.2 Violence against or from outsiders of the network

Acts of physical or mental violence were mentioned in two ways in the analysed material: On the one hand, actors from the network sometimes carried a gun for security reasons when selling hashish in bulk (i.e. more than 10 kilos per transaction). This is expressed in the following example, which is an extract of a legal file:

> "(…) during that point of time, HFG was positioned on the other side of the street in order to guard the delivery of the goods while being armed with a gun." (G-AK 1.1, §2021)

On the other hand, the network was threatened by a competing one in the greater area of Vienna. Some actors had previously worked with the other network, but switched sides at a later point. However, according to the material analysed, these threats did not lead to other forms of violence. One dealer talked about the threatening situation during an interview:

> "Already in those days they told me 'look out, 'cause we are physically stronger than you. Don't forget that if we won't pay you off.' After a while, I told him 'well in that case you'll see what the outcome will be'. Sure, they threaten people…but they also know, with me it's different: they have to put it into practice and not just threaten me. Once I am dead, they don't need to pay anymore, but as long as I am alive they will have to." (I-D 2.3, §46)

3.2 Ambiguity of trust and distrust

As outlined in the previous section, a main finding of the case study analysis suggests that the network rarely used violence as a means of settling disputes. On the contrary, building relationships of trust and loyalty were strategies to avoid problems arising in the first place, which is also supported by research conducted by Reuter & Haaga (1989), Pearson & Hobbs (2001), Desroches (2005), and Dorn et al. (2005). Moreover, long-lasting business relationships are mutually beneficial for all members of the network. However, this very rational business approach (Reuter & Haaga 1989) was simultaneously accompanied by distrust and betrayal within the network (Gambetta 1996). Business relationships were also terminated due to internal conflicts.

In the following, some examples from the data analysed are used to illustrate the ambiguity of trust and distrust that occurred at the same time. The category of trust, reliability and secrecy was mentioned 22 times and the category of distrust, betrayal and fraud 23 times.

3.2.1 Building trust, reliability and secrecy over time

Our data suggest that trust is a mechanism of social interaction, which evolved over time and helped to establish a professional operation. With regard to the source of supply, exchange of currencies, knowledge of couriers about the transported goods and the access to the storage places, trust and reliability grew over the course of the relationships. However, trust and secrecy also shaped the social relation of most actors of the network.

The source of supply from which hashish was bought in the Netherlands or Spain, was chosen randomly when the network started their illicit activities. Due to high purchasing prices, later on the network contacted former business partners through which new sources were established that offered hashish at lower prices. Over time, a long lasting and trustworthy business relationship was formed with one source of supply. One drug dealer mentioned that stable prices and a reliable counterpart – in the sense of: 'you get what you pay for' – were important elements of this relationship of trust.

> "The guys from the Netherlands were random acquaintances, but we became friends since they were reliable. Most of them were not reliable. You have to be lucky to meet people you can trust. With them, I could be sure, if I put money in the van everything will run as agreed before. They put the goods in the van in exchange for the money and then they returned the van" (I-D 2.1, §133)

The network participants bought large quantities of hashish on a regular basis from the source of supply mentioned above. According to the data, the amount of drugs being bought varied between 20 kg and 100 kg per transaction, but about 50 kg were regularly transported.

The trustworthy business relationship between the source of supply and actors of the cannabis network was further strengthened by improving the clients' loyalty. Thus, when the quality of hashish happened to be low, it was exchanged immediately by the source of supply.

> "D: Just once I had to return it. All the other times it was of good quality. I: What do you mean by sending it back? The product? D: Yes, the product. The goods were exchanged in such a case. That isn't possible with everyone. You have to know each other for some time and trust each other well. Someone else would let you fall into the trap. You couldn't do it this way; you would have to check the quality of the whole shipment. When you start checking 50 kg that takes some time." (I-D 2.3, §83)

The relevance of trust also shows when it comes to the exchange of currencies. For paying the supplier, Austrian Schilling had to be exchanged into Dutch Guilder or Spanish Peseta. One actor of the network entertained a friendship with a bank employee who helped to exchange currencies. Due to this solid relationship based on trust, the amounts of money were not recounted, which would have been a time consuming task.

> "VCX told LKJ that 100.000 Dutch Guilder were in the envelope and told him 'we don't need to recount it, it was always correct'." (G-UR 1.12, §618)

Additionally, organising the transport from Austria to the Netherlands or Spain was handled differently during the course of the period analysed. When the network started its operations, the interviewed drug dealer was driving the van to the source of supply himself. After some time, couriers were hired step-by-step to do the smuggling. At the beginning, the couriers did not know which goods or amounts they were transporting nor did they carry any money.

> "P: You did not know how much you were smuggling? Z: No, not in the beginning. Over time, they started trusting me. Then they told me. " (G-HV 1.7, §128)

Thus, other actors from the network took a plane to get to the source of supply, tested the quality beforehand and payed for the drugs. Later on, after the couriers had proven themselves by returning the laden vehicle to the destination a couple of times, they got more responsibilities. They were introduced to the source of supply and were allowed to perform a complete tour independently and without having to contact other actors of the network in the meantime, e.g. by directly carrying and handing over the money to the source of supply. The couriers were also provided with higher compensation for their commitment.

A further indicator for increasing trust over time was access to the storage places. Before the illicit drugs were resold in Austria, they were stored for days or sometimes even weeks. Over the course of time, actors of the network rented five apartments, several open-air storage places and one garage. Some of the vans were additionally used to store the shipments. Certain players had unlimited access to the storage locations, e.g. couriers who performed a tour independently or a person who was involved in reselling hashish in the area of greater Vienna.

> "(...) she got access to the drugs and was allowed to take as much as she wanted to. H: Yes, this was based on trust. Then she told us how much she had taken." (G-HV 1.4, §110)

Moreover, the social relations between the actors of the network were mostly shaped by secrecy and trust. Although these are different social mechanisms, they were coded in the same category. However, secrecy is a social resource to conceal information, which is necessary to minimise risks and to avoid detection (Zaitch 2005). Secrecy was substantial for the collaboration of the actors, as the following quotes illustrate:

> "P: You told us that in your 'organisation' nobody knew what the others were doing exactly; is this correct? W: Yes, this is true." (G-HV 1.9, §185)

> "V: Did you trust him in that matter? W: I did not have any other choice." (G-HV 1.11, §1676)

According to the self-assessment of the interviewed drug trafficker, he was a reliable and credible business partner.

> "I: Was the term 'stability' applicable for your business relations? D: Yes, sure, how should I put it? What is stable? What can be regarded as stable these days? With such a thing [doing illicit activities], there is always something that can go wrong. However, from my point of view, I did everything possible to have the goods in stock. That's why customers came to buy from me. The others were doing that [reselling drugs at a wholesale level] for a longer period, they knew them better. For me, 'stability' means being reliable. When you are reliable, you can do business. Oh well, it's always the same, no matter what you do. When someone comes to you and you do a good job then he will come to you again. Even if he doesn't like you, it doesn't matter, as long as he knows he will get what you agreed upon. He will come again. It was the same with me." (I-D 2.2, §341)

Regarding his self-perceived business approach and the relationship to his business partners, the interviewee presented himself as being reliable and underlined the importance of always having goods in stock for doing business successfully, while being aware of the fact that this is a difficult terrain.

As indicated earlier, trust can be boosted when working with friends or family members. Desroches (2003) notes that business partners on higher levels of drug distribution usually have known each other for years and that family ties and friendships strengthen the trust base. Numerous actors of the network were friends and some actors were in a love relationship with each other – exactly three couples were counted. The drug dealer interviewed described who his friends were:

> "…the guy working at the bank and the car dealer. These were the people I went for a beer with from time to time; these were my friends." (I-D 2.1, §94)

3.2.2 Distrust, betrayal and fraud

The social relations of the actors were not exclusively characterized by trust, reliability and secrecy, though. Betrayal and distrust occurred in their relationships and sometimes business relationships were even terminated due to unresolved disputes.

In the following passage, the interviewee got to the heart of the ambivalence of the internal social relations.

> "And I tell you, all these guys with previous convictions, I never experienced anyone, ok, maybe one or two, but with most of them it doesn't make a difference if you have known them for years, if you have been friends for years, they will talk [to the police] when it matters." (I-D 2.2, §49)

The drug dealer noticed that he could rely on his friends and colleagues until the police interrogated them.

> "It doesn't matter if they [the police] are threatening you with a high sentence or with force. Most of them [his colleagues] feel intimidated. Everyone blames the other for having betrayed him, but at the end, they all talk. There are very few people that keep their mouth shut." (I-D 2.3, §126)

The interviewed drug trafficker regretted that he had shared his strategies how to launder and invest money with some of the actors involved as this information was used against him in court.

> "Well, it was my own fault, because I told them that 'I'll take care of it – I'll ask for a loan'. That is why they knew about buying a house on loan." (I-D 2.2, §293)

> "If they had not known about it, they also would not have been able to talk about it [to the police]. Then they [the police] would not have followed up on the loan." (I-D 2.3, §162)

In addition, some actors terminated their business relationships in conflict situations. E.g., one business relationship broke up because the business partner wanted to sell hashish for a higher price and did not pass on the money to his colleague.

Another business relation was terminated because an actor sold more on commission than had been agreed upon beforehand.

> "T: Why did your relationship to WCD fall apart? E: He didn't appreciate the way I did business. I sold too much on commission. I don't know what he did with the goods that were still with him. I didn't have any contact with him ever since." (G-HV 1.3, §306)

The material analysed illustrates that internal social relations were ambivalent to a certain degree. Information and knowledge shared with colleagues and friends while doing illicit activities, for example, were sometimes used against this actor when being questioned by the court or by police.

4 Conclusion

In the light of the research question, the role of violence and trust in upper-level drug dealing, an empirical analysis on a network of higher-level drug dealers in Austria was conducted. Drug dealers operate in an environment of constant threat of prosecution and arrest by law enforcement agencies (Paoli 2013; Reuter 2009). Additionally, conflicts and disputes among drug trafficking networks – internally and in relation to competing networks – shape the field that was analysed in the study. The use of violence or the threat to do so as well as building trust are social mechanisms that actors may apply within this risky environment.

When summarising the findings of the analysis, two approaches of what drives the actors of the network could be identified. On the one hand, some actors dealt with drugs for making profit and therefore for their personal enrichment. Almost all actors made a living by contributing to illicit activities in the network. According to Dorn et al. (2005), they correspond with a type called 'business criminals', in contrast to 'politico-military' traffickers and 'adventurers'. Striving for personal enrichment is also opposed to the concept of social supply as discussed in various chapters of this anthology for a large part of retail drugs distribution (however, it is assumed that also among socially inconspicuous small-scale dealers, a significant minority starts selling drugs in order to make profit; see Werse & Müller in this volume). Although the roles of the actors changed over time, there was a core group of about four to eight individuals, which lasted over years. This core group hired other actors according to their specific needs. At the beginning, it was merely a loose connection between the actors of the core group. Over the course of time, the network became more professionally organised.

The use of physical violence played a minor role. We suggest two possible interpretations for this finding. First, violence attracts the attention of police and/or mass media, which is per se detrimental for illicit activities and impacts negatively on customer relations (Desroches 2003; Zaitch 2002; Pearson & Hobbs 2001; Reuter & Haaga 1989; Reuter 1983). Second, the extent of violence may depend on intact rule-of-law structures, as suggested by Paoli (2013). Hence, violence used by illicit networks may be lower in Western countries, which enforce their national government's monopoly on power, compared to weak state authorities. Furthermore, trustworthy relationships to suppliers, colleagues and customers were successfully established over time. Long-lasting business relationships turned out to be mutually beneficial.

On the other hand, the network did not apply the rational approach described above consistently. Firstly, the network was not organised in a hierarchical way with clear chains of command. Secondly, not each actor of the whole network consisting 55 people had the same mind-set. E.g., some actors were mainly motivated by the need to repay their debts, while others were dealing for profit. Thirdly, although the use of physical violence was not very widespread in this network, it was once used by an actor whose character was described by an interviewee as principally unrestrained and probably not following a rational approach. Finally, trust was built successfully as a social strategy necessary to minimise risks, but it was by no means limitless. Trustworthy relationships established beforehand could not be relied upon later, especially when the actors were questioned by the police. In addition, it was mentioned that in some cases, there was no other option than to trust a colleague, even if the person was not considered to be fully reliable.

To conclude, a core group of dealers did pursue a 'business for profit' strategy. However, as there were inconsistencies and ambivalences, the activities and social interactions did not consequently follow this approach.

We would like to address some limitations of the study presented in this chapter. The findings from a single in-depth and explorative case study cannot be generalised (Yin 2009). In addition, it is not intended to produce quantifiable data of any kind. The network was mainly involved in the distribution of hashish, and within the chapter, it is not intended of to draw conclusions on dealing with other types of illicit drugs. The research presented in this chapter is part of a larger study on organisational dynamics of an upper-level drug-dealing network in Austria, which were not addressed in detail in this chapter.

Future research activities should be undertaken that relate to multi-perspective, theoretically elaborated definitions of various levels of drug markets. There seems to be a considerable potential for more differentiated considerations of higher levels of drug markets. For example, regional and political specifics should be included in these definitions. It seems to be arbitrary to define upper-level drug distribution merely at a global level. Additionally, the scientific community could benefit from further research on supply-focused approaches of drug markets (in Europe) that is of empirical nature and does not solely analyse data generated by or for law enforcement agencies or intergovernmental organization/agencies. In-depth knowledge may contribute to a better understanding of different stages of illicit drug supply and inform a more comprehensive public and policy debate.

References

Adler, P. (1993): Wheeling & Dealing: An Ethnography of an Upper-Level Drug Dealing and Smuggling Community. (2nd. ed.). New York: Columbia University Press.

Arlacchi, P. (1986): Mafia business: The Mafia Ethic and the Spirit of Capitalism. London: Verso.

Besozzi, C. (2001): Illegal, legal – egal? Zu Entstehung, Struktur und Auswirkungen illegaler Märkte. Bern: Verlag Paul Haupt.

Coomber, R., & Moyle, L. (2013): Beyond drug dealing: Developing and extending the concept of 'social supply' of illicit drugs to 'minimally commercial supply'. Drugs: Education, Prevention, and Policy, 21(2): 157-164.

Desroches, F. (2003): Drug Trafficking and Organized Crime in Canada: A Study of High-Level Drug Networks. M. E. Beare (ed.), Critical Reflections on Transnational Organized Crime, Money Laundering, and Corruption (pp 237-255). Toronto: University of Toronto Press.

Desroches, F. (2007): Research on Upper Level Drug Trafficking: A Review. Journal of Drug Issues, 37 (4): 827-844.

Dorn, N., Levy, M. & King, L. (2005): Literature Review on Upper Level Drug Trafficking. Home Office Online Report 22/5. London: Home Office.

Dorn, N., Murji, K. & South, N. (1992): Traffickers: drug markets and law enforcement. London: Routledge.

Gambetta, D. (ed.) (1990): Trust. Making and Breaking Cooperative Relations. Oxford: Basil Blackwell.

Gambetta, D. (1996): The Sicilian Mafia: The Business of Private Protection. Cambridge, MA: Harvard University Press.

Gambetta, D. (2009): Codes of the Underworld: How Criminals Communicate. Princeton, NJ: Princeton University Press.

Goldstein, P. (1985): The drug/violence nexus: A tripartite conceptual framework. Journal of Drug Issues, 39: 143-174.

Kenney, M. (2007): The Architecture of Drug Trafficking: Network Forms of Organisation in the Colombian Cocaine Trade. Global Crime, 8 (3): 233-259.

Krauthausen, C. (1997): Moderne Gewalten. Organisierte Kriminalität in Kolumbien und Italien. Frankfurt/Main: Campus Verlag.

Marez, C. (2004): Drug Wars: The Political Economy of Narcotics. Minneapolis: University of Minnesota Press.

Mayring, P. (2008): Qualitative Inhaltsanalyse. Grundlage und Techniken. (10th ed.). Weinheim/ Basel: Beltz Verlag.

Matrix Knowledge Group (2007): The illicit drug trade in the United Kingdom. Home Office Online Report 20/07. London: Home Office.
Natarajan, M. (2000): Understanding the Structure of a Drug Trafficking Organization: A Conversational Analysis. M. Natarajan & M. Hough (eds.), Illegal Drug Markets: From Research to Policy (pp 273-298). Monsey, NY: Criminal Justice Press.
Paoli, L. (2000): Drug Markets in Frankfurt and Milan. Freiburg: Max Planck Institute.
Paoli L. (2003): Mafia Brotherhoods: Organized Crime, Italian style. New York: Oxford University Press.
Paoli, L. (2013): The Determinants of Organized Crime: Some Initial Reflections. Behemoth - A Journal on Civilisation, 6 (1): 10-26.
Patton, M. Q. (1990): Qualitative Evaluation and Research Methods. (2nd. ed.). Beverly Hills: Sage Publications.
Pearson, G., & Hobbs, R. (2001): Middle market drug distribution. Home office research study 227. London: Home Office.
Reuter, P. (1983): Disorganized Crime: The Economics of the Visible Hand. Cambridge: MIT Press.
Reuter, P. (2009): Systemic Violence in Drug Markets. Crime, Law and Social Change: An Interdisciplinary Journal, 52 (3): 275-284.
Reuter, P. (2014): Drug Markets and Organized Crime. L. Paoli (ed.), The Oxford Handbook on Organized Crime (pp 359-380). Oxford: Oxford University Press.
Reuter, P. & Haaga, J. (1989): The Organization of High-Level Drug Markets: An Exploratory Study. Santa Monica: Rand.
Reuter, P. & Trautmann, F. (eds.) (2009): Report on Global Illicit Drug Markets 1998-2007. Full Report. Brussels: European Commission.
Ritter, A. (2006): Studying illicit drug markets: Disciplinary contributions. International Journal of Drug Policy, 17 (6): 453-463.
Schreier, M. (2012): Qualitative Content Analysis in Practice. London: Sage.
Thoumi, F. E. (2003): Illegal drugs, economy and society in the Andes. Baltimore: Johns Hopkins University Press.
Tzanetakis, M. (2013): A case study of upper-level dealing. J. Fountain, M. Wouters, & D. J. Korf (eds.), Snapshots of Social Drug Research in Europe (pp 16-18). Lengerich: Pabst Science Publishers.
Verbi GmbH (2011): MAXQDA 10 [computer software]. Berlin.
von Lampe, K. & Johansen, P. O. (2004): Organized Crime and Trust: On the conceptualization and empirical relevance of trust in the context of criminal networks. Global Crime, 6 (2): 159-184.
Wehinger, F. (2011): Illegale Märkte: Stand der sozialwissenschaftlichen Forschung. MPIfG Working Paper, 11/6. Köln: Max-Planck-Institut für Gesellschaftsforschung.
Wilson, L. & Stevens, A. (2008): Understanding Drug Markets and how to Influence Them. Oxford: The Beckley Foundation.
Yin, R. K. (2009): Case Study Research: Design and Methods. (4th ed.). Thousand Oaks, CA: Sage.
Zaitch, D. (2002): Trafficking cocaine. Colombian drug entrepreneurs in the Netherlands. The Hague: Kluwer Law International.

Zaitch, D. (2005): The Ambiguity of Violence, Secrecy, and Trust among Colombian Drug Entrepreneurs. Journal of Drug Issues, 35 (1): 201-228.

About the contributors

Monica Barratt's (PhD) research concerns the social and public health implications of digital technologies for people who use illicit and new psychoactive drugs, and the impacts of legislative responses to drug use and drug problems. She is a research fellow at the Drug Policy Modelling Program at Australia's National Drug and Alcohol Research Centre, UNSW, a visiting fellow at the Burnet Institute and an Adjunct Fellow at the National Drug Research Institute, Curtin University, Australia.

Vendula Belackova is an economist and addictologist. Her work consists of interdisciplinary research in cannabis and in new psychoactive substances. She focuses on economic perspectives of drug issues, including social costs and effectiveness of drug policies. She has worked as assistant professor at the Department of Addictology, Charles University in Prague, Czech Republic. She was a Fulbright visiting scholar at the College of Social Sciences, Florida State University, U. S. (2008 / 2009), and Endeavour visiting scholar at the Drug Policy Modelling Program, UNSW, Australia (2014).

Christiane Bernard, PhD, works at the State Coordination Office "Women and Addiction" of North Rhine-Westphalia. Prior to that, she was a research associate at the Centre for Drug Research, Goethe University Frankfurt, and a visiting scholar and adjunct professor at the City University of New York. Her research interests lie in the areas of women's use of drugs, drug use in pregnancy and parenthood. Her PhD thesis focused on women in street drug scenes in Frankfurt and New York City.

Ross Coomber, PhD, is Professor and Director of the Griffith Criminology Institute, Griffith University, Australia. Until recently he was Professor of Sociology and Director of the Drug and Alcohol Research Unit at Plymouth University (UK). He has been involved in researching a wide range of issues relating to drug use, drug supply and formal and informal interventions in many societies around the world for over twenty-five years. He has published extensively within the drug field and is the author of Pusher Myths: Re-Situating the Drug Dealer (2006) and co-editor (with N. South) of Drug Use and Cultural Contexts 'Beyond the West' (2004), among others. His latest book is Key Concepts in Crime and Society (2015; co-authored with J. Donnermeyer, K. McElrath and J. Scott).

Jodie Grigg is a Research Associate at the National Drug Research Institute (NDRI) at Curtin University in Perth, Western Australia. Since 2010, she has conducted over 300 research interviews across a range of illicit drug projects. In 2014, she commenced a PhD at NDRI with a thesis investigating drug use at outdoor music festivals, with a focus on illicit drug use, drug policy and harm reduction.

Pekka Hakkarainen, PhD, Adjunct Professor in Sociology at the University of Turku, is working as the Research Professor in the Alcohol and Drugs Unit at the National Institute for Health and Welfare (THL) in Helsinki, Finland. He has published several studies on the epidemiology of illicit drugs, drug culture, drug policy, treatment issues and social problems.

Simon Lenton is Professor and Deputy Director at the National Drug Research Institute, at Curtin University in Perth Western Australia and works part time as a Clinical Psychologist in private practice. He has published more than 90 refereed articles and book chapters on drug policy. His research interests include bridging the gap between drug policy research and drug policy practice, illicit drug use and harm reduction and naloxone for peer administration. He is a co-author of Cannabis Policy: Moving beyond stalemate published by OUP in 2010.

Leah Moyle is a Lecturer in the School of Law at Royal Holloway, University of London, UK. Leah has a research interest in drug markets and non-commercial drug supply. She has published a number of drug market related research articles and reports and is currently working on a range of projects around 'new psychoactive substances' 'user-dealing' and 'social supply'.

Daniela Müller, M.A. in sociology, research assistant at the Centre for Drug Research (Goethe University, Frankfurt, Germany) since 2015, currently working on two research projects: The first project explores the use of e-cigarettes among adolescents in Germany. The second is a transnational European study on the use of new psychoactive substances (NPS).

Jussi Perälä, PhD, Postdoctoral researcher at the University of Helsinki, Finland. He has done his ethnographic PhD study of drug market in Helsinki in 2011. His research interests have been focused in groups classified as criminal. He has also interviewed cannabis cultivators and users for national and international studies. Currently he is doing ethnography among an international outlaw motorcycle club.

Gary R. Potter is Senior Lecturer in Criminology at Lancaster University Law School. His primary research interests are cannabis cultivation and retail level drug markets – his most recent book in this area is 'Change and Continuity: Researching evolving drug landscapes in Europe', co-edited with J. Fountain and M. Wouters. He also writes about green criminology and is co-editor, with A. Nurse and M. Hall, of 'The Geography of Environmental Crime: Conservation, wildlife crime and environmental activism'.

John Scott is a Professor in the School of Justice, Queensland University of Technology, Australia. He has published over seventy papers and book chapters on diverse topics, including sex work, rural crime and gendered violence. Recent publications include Crime and Society (with Coomber, Donnermeyer and McElrath, 2014) and Male Sex Work and Society (Co-ed. with Mincichello, 2014).

Nigel South is a Professor in the Department of Sociology and a member of the Centre for Criminology at the University of Essex, England. He is a visiting Adjunct Professor in the School of Justice at Queensland University of Technology, Brisbane and in 2013 received a Lifetime Achievement Award from the American Society of Criminology, Division on Critical Criminology. He has published widely on drug use, markets, health and crime. He currently serves as the European Editor for Critical Criminology and on the Editorial Boards of Deviant Behavior and the International Journal for Crime, Justice and Social Democracy.

Meropi Tzanetakis, PhD, is Senior Researcher at the Vienna Centre for Societal Security. She holds a degree in political science from the University of Vienna. Her doctoral thesis is one of the few qualitative studies in the field of upper-level drug dealing for German-speaking countries. Meropi is currently working on a research project exploring relations between virtual and traditional drug markets. Recent publications include: The transparency paradox. Building trust, resolving disputes and optimising logistics on conventional and online drugs markets (with G. Kamphausen, B. Werse & R. v. Laufenberg, IJDP, 2015).

Marieke Vlaemynck obtained a Master degree in Criminology at the Catholic University of Leuven. As a research fellow she is affiliated with the Institute for Social Drug Research (University of Ghent, Belgium). Her PhD project explores (social) supply patterns within personal networks of cannabis users. She is also actively involved in a practice oriented research, and is currently conducting a drug monitor study at the city level.

Bernd Werse, PhD, senior researcher at the Centre for Drug Research at the Goethe University, Frankfurt, Germany. Since 2002, he is the responsible person for various social scientific research projects on drug use, e.g. the annual Frankfurt local drug monitoring system "MoSyD", two projects on small-scale drug dealing, and various studies on new psychoactive substances (NPS). He edited a German language anthology on small-scale dealing ("Drogenmärkte", 2008) and published papers, chapters and reports on various subjects in the field of social drug research.

Tomas Zabransky is a drug epidemiologist. His work consists of research into risk behaviour related to substance abuse (blood-borne diseases, drug-related mortality) and in evaluation of drug policies. He has been involved in implementation of drug monitoring programs in Central Asia. At current, he is a scientific reader at the Department of Addictology, Charles University in Prague, and advisor to the Ministry of Health of the Czech Republic. In 2004, he underwent Hubert H. Humphrey / NIDA Fellowship at the Bloomberg School of Public Health, Johns Hopkins University, Baltimore, USA.

The Global Cannabis Cultivation Research Consortium (GCCRC) is an affiliation of researchers from around the world who share a common interest in the sociology, economics and politics of cannabis cultivation – particularly within economically advanced 'western' nations more usually seen as drug importing rather than drug producing countries. To date (2015), online surveys which were based on this questionnaire have been carried out in 13 countries of the world. The paper reproduced here, ('Global patterns of domestic cannabis cultivation') reports the main findings of their ground-breaking international collaborative research. To find out more about their past, current and future projects, see the group's website worldwideweed.nl.

Apart from the authors mentioned above, the following consortium members have contributed to the respective book chapter:

Aili Malm, Ph.D., Associate Professor of Criminology and Criminal Justice, School of Criminology, Criminal Justice, and Emergency Management, California State University, Long Beach, USA.

Martin Bouchard, Associate Professor at the Simon Fraser University in the School of Criminology, Burnaby, B.C, Canada.

Thomas Blok, former intern at the Bonger Institute of Criminology, University of Amsterdam, the Netherlands.

Anne-Sofie Christensen, former employee, Centre for Alcohol and Drug Research, Aarhus University, Denmark.

Tom Decorte, Professor, Institute for Social Drug Research, Department of Penal Law and Criminology, University of Gent, Belgium.

Vibeke Asmussen Frank, Professor, Director of the Centre for Alcohol and Drug Research, Aarhus University, Denmark.

Axel Klein, Team Leader for the European Commission funded Cocaine Route Monitoring and Support Project, Royal United Services Institute, London, UK.

Marije Wouters, Ph.D., Bonger Institute of Criminology, University of Amsterdam, the Netherlands.

MIX
Papier aus verantwortungsvollen Quellen
Paper from responsible sources
FSC® C105338

FSC
www.fsc.org

If you have any concerns about our products,
you can contact us on
ProductSafety@springernature.com

In case Publisher is established outside the EU,
the EU authorized representative is:
Springer Nature Customer Service Center GmbH
Europaplatz 3, 69115 Heidelberg, Germany

Printed by Libri Plureos GmbH
in Hamburg, Germany